Tolley's
Sickness and Maternity Pay

A comprehensive guide to payroll practice and procedure

by
Paul Tew
and Mike Nicholas

LexisNexis™ UK

Members of the LexisNexis Group worldwide

United Kingdom	LexisNexis UK, a Division of Reed Elsevier (UK) Ltd, 2 Addiscombe Road, CROYDON CR9 5AF
Argentina	LexisNexis Argentina, BUENOS AIRES
Australia	LexisNexis Butterworths, CHATSWOOD, New South Wales
Austria	LexisNexis Verlag ARD Orac GmbH & Co KG, VIENNA
Canada	LexisNexis Butterworths, MARKHAM, Ontario
Chile	LexisNexis Chile Ltda, SANTIAGO DE CHILE
Czech Republic	Nakladatelství Orac sro, PRAGUE
France	Editions du Juris-Classeur SA, PARIS
Germany	LexisNexis Deutschland GmbH, FRANKFURT and MUNSTER
Hong Kong	LexisNexis Butterworths, HONG KONG
Hungary	HVG-Orac, BUDAPEST
India	LexisNexis Butterworths, NEW DELHI
Ireland	LexisNexis, DUBLIN
Italy	Giuffrè Editore, MILAN
Malaysia	Malayan Law Journal Sdn Bhd, KUALA LUMPUR
New Zealand	LexisNexis Butterworths, WELLINGTON
Poland	Wydawnictwo Prawnicze LexisNexis, WARSAW
Singapore	LexisNexis Butterworths, SINGAPORE
South Africa	LexisNexis Butterworths, Durban
Switzerland	Stämpfli Verlag AG, BERNE
USA	LexisNexis, DAYTON, Ohio

First published in 2002

Published by LexisNexis UK

A CIP Catalogue record for this book is available from the British Library.

ISBN 0 75452 4590

Typeset by Letterpart Ltd, Reigate, Surrey

Printed and bound in Great Britain by Hobbs the Printers Ltd, Totton, Hampshire

Visit LexisNexis UK at www.lexisnexis.co.uk

Preface

The *Sickness and Maternity Pay Handbook* is specifically written for payroll managers and for those overseeing the payroll function. Its primary aim is to provide practical guidance to the often-overworked practitioner with responsibilities for operating the Statutory Sick Pay (SSP) and Statutory Maternity Pay (SMP) schemes.

Increasingly, SSP and SMP have ceased to be social security benefits and have become minimum levels of employee benefits, payable by the employer, according to statute and in defined circumstances. With SSP now being financed almost exclusively by the employer, except in the cases of the very smallest of businesses, effective absence and sickness monitoring is even more vital for employers.

The modern prevalence of women in the workplace has forced employers into recognising their particular needs, both from a pay and employment perspective and when considering maternity provisions. The introduction of Statutory Adoption and Paternity Pay and leave in 2003 again brought the work–life balance sharply into focus. Now more so than ever, maternity and sickness are areas that employers choose to ignore at their peril.

Within this work, the main body of text provides a summary of the essential procedures to be followed by employers, with checklists, sample forms and 'in practice' points to ensure the user complies with the relevant SSP and SMP legislation.

In addition, there are separate and unique areas detailing the relevant rates of payments and a list of the questions at the end of each chapter that you, as the employer, are asking. These questions look at topical issues both from the point of view of the experienced manager and the relative newcomer, with comprehensive answers and problem-solving hints to help the employer achieve a high level of compliance. Each area of analysis is self-contained but the work is fully cross-referenced throughout.

Warning messages are interspersed throughout to highlight areas of special concern, for example where the legislation is subject to change or the point under discussion is a common problem area for employers. The practical and accessible nature of the book is further emphasised by the frequent use of worked examples, flowcharts and case studies giving the user step-by-step guidance on how to make timely and accurate payments.

Sickness and maternity are complicated topics and they are unlikely to become less so. This handbook cuts through the theory of the legislation and offers the reader a clear and concise commentary together with touches of humour to lighten what are very serious subjects for payroll professionals.

The author would like to thank Ruth Thomas-McCann for her assistance and input into the preparation of this work, and Mike Nicholas for updating the text for this edition.

Paul Tew

Glossary of Key Terms

Additional Adoption Leave (AAL) — This is a period of 26 weeks which follows on immediately from the end of the 26 weeks of ordinary adoption leave. Only employees who meet the service requirements are entitled to take AAL.

Additional Maternity Leave (AML) — This is a period of 26 weeks, which follows on immediately from the end of the 26 weeks of ordinary maternity leave. Only employees who meet the service requirements are entitled to take AML.

Associated employers — Two employers are 'associated employers' if one is a company, which the other directly or indirectly controls, or both are companies, which are controlled by a third person.

Average weekly earnings — Calculated over the relevant period, these determine whether an employee earns below the Lower Earnings Limit and is therefore excluded from being able to receive SSP, SMP, SAP or SPP.

Benefits Agency (BA) — An executive office of the Department of Social Security responsible for establishing benefit entitlement for employees who are sick or pregnant but have no entitlement to SSP or SMP.

Childbirth or confinement — Any labour, resulting in the issue of a living child, or labour after 24 weeks of pregnancy (i e the 16th week before the expected week of confinement) resulting in the issue of a child, whether alive or dead.

Change-over form — Statutory Form SSP1, to be completed by an employer when an employee is excluded or becomes excluded, from payment of SSP.

Compulsory maternity leave — This is a period of either two (or four) weeks taken around the woman's confinement. The employer must not allow the employee to work during this period.

Doctor's Statement — The medical statement or 'sick note' completed on a prescribed form by an employee's GP or other medical practitioner.

Employee — For the purposes of SSP, SMP, SAP and SPP an employee is defined as someone over age 16, gainfully employed in Great Britain either under a contract of service or in an office (including elective office) with general earnings chargeable to income tax. A person may also be treated as an employee for these purposes by virtue of regulations.

Employer — Whoever is liable to pay the employer's share of Class 1 NICs is the employer for the operation of SSP, SMP, SAP and SPP.

Expected Week of Confinement (EWC) — The week, beginning with midnight Saturday, which in the opinion of the medical practitioner examining the woman, is the week that the baby will be born.

Incapacity for work — This is where the employee cannot do the work reasonably expected under the contract of employment as a result of some specific disease or bodily or mental disablement or for precautionary reasons.

Leaver's Statement — Statutory Form SSP1(L), which must be completed by the employer when requested to do so by their employee. The employee can only make such a request where he or she is leaving the employment.

Linking periods — Two or more periods of incapacity for work, which are separated by a gap of 56 calendar days or less are treated as linked for SSP purposes.

Linking letter — Notification from the Department for Work and Pensions that an employee has recently claimed either Incapacity Benefit or Severe Disablement Allowance.

Lower Earnings Limit (LEL) — The point at which Class 1 NICs become payable, and which the employee's average weekly earnings must reach in order to be eligible for SSP, SMP, SAP and SPP.

MATB1 — The certificate issued by a doctor or midwife giving the date on which the baby is due. It cannot be issued prior to the 20th week before the employee's EWC.

Matching Certificate — This is the certificate given by the approved adoption agency to the person adopting the child when notified of having been matched with a child.

Matching week — The matching week is the week in which the person adopting the child is notified that he or she has been matched with a child.

Maternity Allowance period — The period of up to 18 weeks (to be extended to 26 weeks in 2003) during which Maternity Allowance is payable by the Benefits Agency where the pregnant woman is not eligible for SMP and satisfies certain employment and earnings tests.

Maternity pay period (**MPP**) — The period of up to 26 weeks in which SMP is payable. This period coincides with the period of ordinary maternity leave.

Medical Services — An organisation which provides the Department for Work and Pensions and Inland Revenue with advice on the medical aspects of claims to State Benefits.

National Insurance contributions (**NICs**) — The deductions taken from an employee's pay in an earnings period and for which pay count as earnings for the purpose of establishing eligibility for either SSP, SMP, SAP or SPP.

National Insurance compensation — A percentage of the total SMP paid, to compensate for the employer's Class 1 NICs paid on SMP by employers eligible to claim employer's relief.

Notification week — The 15th week before the EWC in which the pregnant employee is required to notify her employer that she is pregnant, her EWC and her intended start date for taking maternity leave.

Occupational Maternity Pay (**OMP**) — A voluntary payment scheme, which may be offered by employers, providing contractual maternity pay at or above the minimum levels of SMP, afforded under the State scheme.

Occupational Sick Pay (**OSP**) — A voluntary payment scheme, which may be offered by employers, providing contractual sick pay at or above the minimum levels of SSP, afforded under the State scheme.

Ordinary Maternity Leave (**OML**) — This is a period of 26 weeks. All pregnant employees are entitled to OML.

PAYE Settlement Agreement (**PSA**) — A PAYE Settlement Agreement is an agreement reached by an employer and the Inland Revenue under which the employer agrees to pay tax on certain items on behalf of his employees for a particular tax year. Some of these items would normally be liable to Class 1 NICs, but are excluded from such liability because they are included in the PSA. This may mean, in some cases, that the employee's average weekly earnings in the relevant period do not reach the Class 1 NICs LEL so the employee is not eligible for SSP, SMP, SAP or SPP.

Percentage Threshold Scheme (PTS) — The scheme under which all employers, if satisfying certain conditions, can reclaim some or all of the SSP paid to their employees, in a particular tax month, from the State.

Period of incapacity for work (PIW) — A period of incapacity for work for purposes of SSP must last at least four consecutive calendar days (including Sundays, public and annual holidays).

Permanent Health Insurance (PHI) — A scheme by which employers can continue to provide an employee with a level of income whilst they are incapacitated and unable to work due to long-term sickness or disability.

Placement — Placement is when a child actually starts living with their new family in adoption cases.

Qualifying day (QD) — A day of the week, usually as agreed by the employer and employee, for which SSP will be payable, provided all other conditions are satisfied. Usually these days are the employee's normal working days.

Qualifying week (QW) — The 15th week before the beginning of the week in which the baby is due.

Qualifying tax year — The qualifying tax year for the purpose of establishing eligibility for small employer's relief is the last complete tax year before each pregnant employee's qualifying week (ie the 15th week before the woman's EWC).

Relevant period — The period used to establish the employee's average weekly earnings. The relevant period is typically eight weeks but can be longer (or shorter) in certain circumstances. The beginning and end of the relevant period depends on various issues.

Self-certification — Self-certification applies for the purposes of SSP and SPP. Self-certification is usual where the employee is absent because of incapacity for work. Self-certification is also required where the employee wishes to take paternity leave and claim SPP.

Small employer's relief — Certain small employers are able to claim 100% of SMP paid to their employees, where they have paid, or were liable to pay, gross Class 1 NICs, of a set amount or less in the qualifying tax year.

Test period — The period used to see if a person is eligible to receive Maternity Allowance, where they fail to qualify for SMP. The person must have earned on average at least £30 a week in a 13-week period within the 'test period', which comprises 66 weeks up to and including the week before the employee's EWC.

Waiting days — SSP is not payable for the first three qualifying days in a PIW and these three days are called 'waiting days'. A waiting day must be a qualifying day.

Contents

Table of Statutes

Table of Statutory Instruments

Table of Cases

Abbreviations and References

ACAS	=	Advisory, Conciliation and Arbitration Service
AML	=	Additional Maternity Leave
BA	=	Benefits Agency
CA	=	Court of Appeal
DPTC	=	Disabled Person's Tax Credit
DSS	=	Department of Social Security
DWP	=	Department for Work and Pensions
EAT	=	Employment Appeal Tribunal
ECJ	=	European Court of Justices
EEA	=	European Economic Area
ERA	=	Employment Rights Act
EWC	=	Expected week of confinement (or childbirth)
GB	=	Great Britain
GP	=	General Practitioner
IB	=	Incapacity Benefit
IRLR	=	Industrial Relations Law Reports
LEL	=	Lower Earnings Limit
NI	=	National Insurance
NICs	=	National Insurance contributions
MA	=	Maternity Allowance
MW	=	Matching Week
NICO	=	National Insurance Contributions Office
OML	=	Occupational Maternity Leave
OMP	=	Occupational Maternity Pay
OSP	=	Occupational Sick Pay
PAYE	=	Pay As You Earn
PHI	=	Permanent Health Insurance
PIW	=	Period of incapacity for work
PSA	=	PAYE Settlement Agreement
PTS	=	Percentage Threshold Scheme
QD	=	Qualifying Day
QW	=	Qualifying Week
SDA	=	Severe Disablement Allowance
SI	=	Statutory Instrument

SAP	=	Statutory Adoption Pay
SMP	=	Statutory Maternity Pay
SSP	=	Statutory Sick Pay
SPA	=	State Pension Age
SPP	=	Statutory Paternity Pay
UK	=	United Kingdom
WD	=	Waiting Day

1. Introduction to Statutory Sick Pay

Introduction [1.1]

Statutory Sick Pay (SSP) is a very dry subject. This is unless you are an employee who is off work sick and requiring information on pay entitlement, or you are an employer charged with responsibility for potentially administering and making payments to employees using the various SSP scheme rules governing eligibility and entitlement.

This does not make SSP any more interesting, but an employer's understanding of SSP legislation is paramount, particularly as the compliance costs of getting it wrong are high both in terms of harming employee–employer relations and the financial penalties that can be imposed by the Inland Revenue.

SSP was first introduced on 6 April 1983 under the provisions of the *Social Security and Housing Benefits Act 1982* (*SSHBA 1982*). Since then it has been payable by employers to those employees who qualify and provides a minimum level of sick pay on behalf of the State. For most employees it replaced entitlement to sickness benefit, which had been payable by the Department of Social Security (DSS).

Before 6 April 1991 SSP was a social security benefit paid for in total by the State but administered by employers on behalf of the DSS. However, on that date the rules were changed and employers were no longer able to recover all their SSP costs. After 6 April 1994 SSP ceased to be a social security benefit paid for in general by the State. From then, with certain exceptions, the funding of SSP was wholly transferred to the employer.

A consultation document entitled *Statutory Sick Pay – Cutting Red Tape* was issued in March 1995 and, as a direct result, the previous Government introduced radical changes to the SSP scheme from 6 April 1997. Employers are not permitted to opt out of the SSP scheme if they pay at least the equivalent to SSP by way of Occupational Sick Pay (OSP). However, in an attempt to ease the burden of administration, the Government introduced from 6 April 1997 an exemption from the need to operate the detailed SSP rules where employers pay contractual remuneration at or above the SSP rate for a day of incapacity for work (see **1.3**).

The responsibility for administering SSP transferred from the Contributions Agency, an executive agency of the DSS, to the Inland Revenue National Insurance Contributions Office (NICO) in April 1999. As a consequence, the DSS (from 7 June 2001, the Department for Work and Pensions (DWP)) is responsible for policy and the Inland Revenue is the first of the authorities who resolve queries on entitlement to SSP.

Terms of Reference [1.2]

There are four key terms and abbreviations commonly used in considering payment of SSP:

(a) day of incapacity for work;

(b) period of incapacity for work (PIW);

(c) qualifying day (QD); and

(d) waiting day (WD).

Day of incapacity for work [1.3]

A day on which an employee is sick and unable to work is called a 'day of incapacity for work'. Under the SSP legislation, it is broadly defined as a day when he or she cannot do the work reasonably expected under the contract of employment as a result of some specific disease or bodily or mental disablement. This can also include days when he or she is excluded from work by a medical certificate for precautionary reasons.

Checklist: Deemed Incapacity

An employee will be deemed to be incapable of work:

(a) if he or she is a carrier of, or has been in contact with, an infectious disease and the Medical Officer for Environmental Health issues a statement advising them not to go to work; or

(b) for precautionary reasons, such as if there was an outbreak of German measles (rubella) at the employee's workplace, which could place the health of the unborn child at risk; or

(c) for convalescent reasons, where the registered medical practitioners states he or she should refrain from work eg after major surgery.

Bereavement is a potentially tricky issue when considering SSP entitlement. Although the bereavement itself does not constitute entitlement to be absent from work, the results of the bereavement may lead to a physical or mental condition that incapacitates the employee from continuing to be able to work normally, such as depression, shock or a stress-related illness. The employer must decide whether the absence constitutes a period of incapacity for work, based on the relevant facts of each case.

Only complete days of incapacity can count for SSP. If an employee does some work on a particular day and then falls sick, that day is not counted as a day of incapacity for work. However, a day will count as a day of incapacity for work if the employee falls sick part way through that day provided the employee has not, and does not, carry out any work on that day under his or her contract of employment. It does not have to be a day on which the employee was due to work, eg it can be a rest day.

> ***Example***
>
> Rachel slips and falls over on a jagged paving stone, breaking a leg on the way to begin a new job. There is no entitlement to SSP since, at that point, no work has been carried out under the employment contract. However, if having started work, Rachel had slipped on the stairs carpet and fallen down the stairs, breaking a leg in the process, then there would be a potential entitlement to SSP.

Period of Incapacity for Work [1.4]

SSP can only become payable in respect of any particular day of incapacity for work if that day forms part of a 'period of incapacity for work (PIW)'. In the SSP legislation a PIW is defined as: 'any period of four or more consecutive days, each of which is a day of incapacity for work in relation to the contract of service [ie contract of employment] in question'.

If an employee is sick for less than four consecutive days (including holidays and weekends), there is no PIW and no SSP is payable. SSP rules are triggered by the sickness, not the absence. This is important for employees contracted to work from Monday to Friday but who are sick during a weekend.

> ***Example***
>
> Andy is employed under a contract of service, which requires him to work Monday to Friday inclusive. Andy falls sick on a Saturday and remains incapable of work until the following Wednesday. Even though Andy was not due to work on Saturday or Sunday, the period ➡

of incapacity comprises of four consecutive days (Saturday to Tuesday) and therefore counts as a PIW for SSP purposes.

If Andy had recovered by Tuesday and returned to work, there would be only three consecutive days of incapacity for work, so there would not have been a PIW.

Checklist: PIW and SSP

(a) The employer must establish if a PIW is formed.

(b) Calculate how many qualifying days (QDs) (see **1.6**) are in the PIW.

(c) From this total deduct the three waiting days (see **1.7**).

(d) The remaining days constitute the employer's SSP liability and SSP is payable if all other qualifying conditions are satisfied.

Linked Period of Incapacity for Work [1.5]

However, this relatively straightforward situation is further complicated as the SSP legislation stipulates that: 'any two periods of incapacity for work which are separated by a period of not more than eight weeks [56 calendar days] shall be treated as a single period of incapacity for work.'

Therefore, any two PIWs that are separated by eight weeks or less are said to be linked PIWs and so count as one PIW. To be linked, the period of time between the last day of the first PIW and the first day of the second PIW must be 56 days or less.

Example

Alison is sick from 22 April to 28 April inclusive and again from 24 June to 22 July inclusive. The two PIWs are linked because the period of time in between 29 April and 23 June is exactly 56 days. There may be a string of PIWs and, provided that between any PIW and the subsequent PIW there is a period of eight weeks (56 days) or less, all these PIWs will be linked and treated as a single PIW.

The Inland Revenue produces tables to help employers establish if two PIWs link.

Checklist: Using SSP Linking Tables

(a) Look for the month in which the employee first became sick and a PIW was established.

(b) For that month, find from the first column the first calendar (not necessarily working) day of sickness.

(c) Move across to the second column noting the date stated.

(d) Check if there was a previous PIW and establish the period this represents and note the last day.

(e) Compare the two dates noted in (c) and (d).

(f) If the date in (d) is on or after the date in (c), the PIWs link.

The SSP linking tables are reproduced from page 6 onwards.

Qualifying Day [1.6]

SSP is only payable for qualifying days that fall in a PIW. Each week must have at least one qualifying day (QD). The number of QDs in a week can affect the daily rate of SSP and, therefore, the amount of SSP payable.

A QD is defined in the SSP legislation as those days of the week on which an employee is required to be available for work for the employer under the contract of employment, or which are chosen to reflect the terms of the contract of employment. Hence, it is necessary for the employer and employee to agree the QDs in advance of any period of sickness. The arrangement of having to specify QDs is to ensure that liability for payment of SSP arises in relation to specific days of the week. Bank Holidays do not usually interrupt the normal pattern of QDs (see **6.7**). However, there must be at least one QD in every week, Sunday to Saturday inclusive, even during holiday periods, and the QDs cannot be defined by reference to an employee's sickness pattern.

Tables for linking periods of incapacity for work

2004/05

APRIL 2004

First day of PIW	*Previous PIW links if on or after*
6	07/02/04
7	08/02/04
8	09/02/04
9	10/02/04
10	11/02/04
11	12/02/04
12	13/02/04
13	14/02/04
14	15/02/04
15	16/02/04
16	17/02/04
17	18/02/04
18	19/02/04
19	20/02/04
20	21/02/04
21	22/02/04
22	23/02/04
23	24/02/04
24	25/02/04
25	26/02/04
26	27/02/04
27	28/02/04
28	29/02/04
29	01/02/04
30	02/02/04

MAY 2004

First day of PIW	*Previous PIW links if on or after*
1	03/03/04
2	04/03/04
3	05/03/04
4	06/03/04
5	07/03/04
6	08/03/04
7	09/03/04
8	10/03/04
9	11/03/04
10	12/03/04
11	13/03/04
12	14/03/04
13	15/03/04
14	16/03/04
15	17/03/04
16	18/03/04
17	19/03/04
18	20/03/04
19	21/03/04
20	22/03/04
21	23/03/04
22	24/03/04
23	25/03/04
24	26/03/04
25	27/03/04
26	28/03/04
27	29/03/04
28	30/03/04
29	31/03/04
30	01/04/04
31	02/04/04

JUNE 2004		JULY 2004	
First day of PIW	*Previous PIW links if on or after*	*First day of PIW*	*Previous PIW links if on or after*
1	03/04/04	1	03/05/04
2	04/04/04	2	04/05/04
3	05/04/04	3	05/05/04
4	06/04/04	4	06/05/04
5	07/04/04	5	07/05/04
6	08/04/04	6	08/05/04
7	09/04/04	7	09/05/04
8	10/04/04	8	10/05/04
9	11/04/04	9	11/05/04
10	12/04/04	10	12/05/04
11	13/04/04	11	13/05/04
12	14/04/04	12	14/05/04
13	15/04/04	13	15/05/04
14	16/04/04	14	16/05/04
15	17/04/04	15	17/05/04
16	18/04/04	16	18/05/04
17	19/04/04	17	19/05/04
18	20/04/04	18	20/05/04
19	21/04/04	19	21/05/04
20	22/04/04	20	22/05/04
21	23/04/04	21	23/05/04
22	24/04/04	22	24/05/04
23	25/04/04	23	25/05/04
24	26/04/04	24	26/05/04
25	27/04/04	25	27/05/04
26	28/04/04	26	28/05/04
27	29/04/04	27	29/05/04
28	30/04/04	28	30/05/04
29	01/05/04	29	31/05/04
30	02/05/04	30	01/06/04
		31	02/06/04

AUGUST 2004		SEPTEMBER 2004	
First day of PIW	*Previous PIW links if on or after*	*First day of PIW*	*Previous PIW links if on or after*
1	03/06/04	1	04/07/04
2	04/06/04	2	05/07/04
3	05/06/04	3	06/07/04
4	06/06/04	4	07/07/04
5	07/06/04	5	08/07/04
6	08/06/04	6	09/07/04
7	09/06/04	7	10/07/04
8	10/06/04	8	11/07/04
9	11/06/04	9	12/07/04
10	12/06/04	10	13/07/04
11	13/06/04	11	14/07/04
12	14/06/04	12	15/07/04
13	15/06/04	13	16/07/04
14	16/06/04	14	17/07/04
15	17/06/04	15	18/07/04
16	18/06/04	16	19/07/04
17	19/06/04	17	20/07/04
18	20/06/04	18	21/07/04
19	21/06/04	19	22/07/04
20	22/06/04	20	23/07/04
21	23/06/04	21	24/07/04
22	24/06/04	22	25/07/04
23	25/06/04	23	26/07/04
24	26/06/04	24	27/07/04
25	27/06/04	25	28/07/04
26	28/06/04	26	29/07/04
27	29/06/04	27	30/07/04
28	30/06/04	28	31/07/04
29	01/07/04	29	01/08/04
30	02/07/04	30	02/08/04
31	03/07/04		

OCTOBER 2004

First day of PIW	*Previous PIW links if on or after*
1	03/08/04
2	04/08/04
3	05/08/04
4	06/08/04
5	07/08/04
6	08/08/04
7	09/08/04
8	10/08/04
9	11/08/04
10	12/08/04
11	13/08/04
12	14/08/04
13	15/08/04
14	16/08/04
15	17/08/04
16	18/08/04
17	19/08/04
18	20/08/04
19	21/08/04
20	22/08/04
21	23/08/04
22	24/08/04
23	25/08/04
24	26/08/04
25	27/08/04
26	28/08/04
27	29/08/04
28	30/08/04
29	31/08/04
30	01/09/04
31	02/09/04

NOVEMBER 2004

First day of PIW	*Previous PIW links if on or after*
1	03/09/04
2	04/09/04
3	05/09/04
4	06/09/04
5	07/09/04
6	08/09/04
7	09/09/04
8	10/09/04
9	11/09/04
10	12/09/04
11	13/09/04
12	14/09/04
13	15/09/04
14	16/09/04
15	17/09/04
16	18/09/04
17	19/09/04
18	20/09/04
19	21/09/04
20	22/09/04
21	23/09/04
22	24/09/04
23	25/09/04
24	26/09/04
25	27/09/04
26	28/09/04
27	29/09/04
28	30/09/04
29	01/10/04
30	02/10/04

DECEMBER 2004		JANUARY 2005	
First day of PIW	*Previous PIW links if on or after*	*First day of PIW*	*Previous PIW links if on or after*
1	03/10/04	1	03/11/04
2	04/10/04	2	04/11/04
3	05/10/04	3	05/11/04
4	06/10/04	4	06/11/04
5	07/10/04	5	07/11/04
6	08/10/04	6	08/11/04
7	09/10/04	7	09/11/04
8	10/10/04	8	10/11/04
9	11/10/04	9	11/11/04
10	12/10/04	10	12/11/04
11	13/10/04	11	13/11/04
12	14/10/04	12	14/11/04
13	15/10/04	13	15/11/04
14	16/10/04	14	16/11/04
15	17/10/04	15	17/11/04
16	18/10/04	16	18/11/04
17	19/10/04	17	19/11/04
18	20/10/04	18	20/11/04
19	21/10/04	19	21/11/04
20	22/10/04	20	22/11/04
21	23/10/04	21	23/11/04
22	24/10/04	22	24/11/04
23	25/10/04	23	25/11/04
24	26/10/04	24	26/11/04
25	27/10/04	25	27/11/04
26	28/10/04	26	28/11/04
27	29/10/04	27	29/11/04
28	30/10/04	28	30/11/04
29	31/10/04	29	01/12/04
30	01/11/04	30	02/12/04
31	02/11/04	31	03/12/04

FEBRUARY 2005

First day of PIW	*Previous PIW links if on or after*
1	04/12/04
2	05/12/04
3	06/12/04
4	07/12/04
5	08/12/04
6	09/12/04
7	10/12/04
8	11/12/04
9	12/12/04
10	13/12/04
11	14/12/04
12	15/12/04
13	16/12/04
14	17/12/04
15	18/12/04
16	19/12/04
17	20/12/04
18	21/12/04
19	22/12/04
20	23/12/04
21	24/12/04
22	25/12/04
23	26/12/04
24	27/12/04
25	28/12/04
26	29/12/04
27	30/12/04
28	31/12/04

MARCH 2005

First day of PIW	*Previous PIW links if on or after*
1	01/01/05
2	02/01/05
3	03/01/05
4	04/01/05
5	05/01/05
6	06/01/05
7	07/01/05
8	08/01/05
9	09/01/05
10	10/01/05
11	11/01/05
12	12/01/05
13	13/01/05
14	14/01/05
15	15/01/05
16	16/01/05
17	17/01/05
18	18/01/05
19	19/01/05
20	20/01/05
21	21/01/05
22	22/01/05
23	23/01/05
24	24/01/05
25	25/01/05
26	26/01/05
27	27/01/05
28	28/01/05
29	29/01/05
30	30/01/05
31	31/01/05

APRIL 2005

First day of PIW	*Previous PIW links if on or after*
1	01/02/05
2	02/02/05
3	03/02/05
4	04/02/05
5	05/02/05

2003/04

APRIL 2003

First day of PIW	*Previous PIW links if on or after*
6	08/02/03
7	09/02/03
8	10/02/03
9	11/02/03
10	12/02/03
11	13/02/03
12	14/02/03
13	15/02/03
14	16/02/03
15	17/02/03
16	18/02/03
17	19/02/03
18	20/02/03
19	21/02/03
20	22/02/03
21	23/02/03
22	24/02/03
23	25/02/03
24	26/02/03
25	27/02/03
26	28/02/03
27	01/03/03
28	02/03/03
29	03/03/03
30	04/03/03

MAY 2003

First day of PIW	*Previous PIW links if on or after*
1	05/03/03
2	06/03/03
3	07/03/03
4	08/03/03
5	09/03/03
6	10/03/03
7	11/03/03
8	12/03/03
9	13/03/03
10	14/03/03
11	15/03/03
12	16/03/03
13	17/03/03
14	18/03/03
15	19/03/03
16	20/03/03
17	21/03/03
18	22/03/03
19	23/03/03
20	24/03/03
21	25/03/03
22	26/03/03
23	27/03/03
24	28/03/03
25	29/03/03
26	30/03/03
27	31/03/03
28	01/04/03
29	02/04/03
30	03/04/03
31	04/04/03

JUNE 2003		JULY 2003	
First day of PIW	*Previous PIW links if on or after*	*First day of PIW*	*Previous PIW links if on or after*
1	05/04/03	1	05/05/03
2	06/04/03	2	06/05/03
3	07/04/03	3	07/05/03
4	08/04/03	4	08/05/03
5	09/04/03	5	09/05/03
6	10/04/03	6	10/05/03
7	11/04/03	7	11/05/03
8	12/04/03	8	12/05/03
9	13/04/03	9	13/05/03
10	14/04/03	10	14/05/03
11	15/04/03	11	15/05/03
12	16/04/03	12	16/05/03
13	17/04/03	13	17/05/03
14	18/04/03	14	18/05/03
15	19/04/03	15	19/05/03
16	20/04/03	16	20/05/03
17	21/04/03	17	21/05/03
18	22/04/03	18	22/05/03
19	23/04/03	19	23/05/03
20	24/04/03	20	24/05/03
21	25/04/03	21	25/05/03
22	26/04/03	22	26/05/03
23	27/04/03	23	27/05/03
24	28/04/03	24	28/05/03
25	29/04/03	25	29/05/03
26	30/04/03	26	30/05/03
27	01/05/03	27	31/05/03
28	02/05/03	28	01/06/03
29	03/05/03	29	02/06/03
30	04/05/03	30	03/06/03
		31	04/06/03

AUGUST 2003		SEPTEMBER 2003	
First day of PIW	*Previous PIW links if on or after*	*First day of PIW*	*Previous PIW links if on or after*
1	05/06/03	1	06/07/03
2	06/06/03	2	07/07/03
3	07/06/03	3	08/07/03
4	08/06/03	4	09/07/03
5	09/06/03	5	10/07/03
6	10/06/03	6	11/07/03
7	11/06/03	7	12/07/03
8	12/06/03	8	13/07/03
9	13/06/03	9	14/07/03
10	14/06/03	10	15/07/03
11	15/06/03	11	16/07/03
12	16/06/03	12	17/07/03
13	17/06/03	13	18/07/03
14	18/06/03	14	19/07/03
15	19/06/03	15	20/07/03
16	20/06/03	16	21/07/03
17	21/06/03	17	22/07/03
18	22/06/03	18	23/07/03
19	23/06/03	19	24/07/03
20	24/06/03	20	25/07/03
21	25/06/03	21	26/07/03
22	26/06/03	22	27/07/03
23	27/06/03	23	28/07/03
24	28/06/03	24	29/07/03
25	29/06/03	25	30/07/03
26	30/06/03	26	31/07/03
27	01/07/03	27	01/08/03
28	02/07/03	28	02/08/03
29	03/07/03	29	03/08/03
30	04/07/03	30	04/08/03
31	05/07/03		

OCTOBER 2003		NOVEMBER 2003	
First day of PIW	*Previous PIW links if on or after*	*First day of PIW*	*Previous PIW links if on or after*
1	05/08/03	1	05/09/03
2	06/08/03	2	06/09/03
3	07/08/03	3	07/09/03
4	08/08/03	4	08/09/03
5	09/08/03	5	09/09/03
6	10/08/03	6	10/09/03
7	11/08/03	7	11/09/03
8	12/08/03	8	12/09/03
9	13/08/03	9	13/09/03
10	14/08/03	10	14/09/03
11	15/08/03	11	15/09/03
12	16/08/03	12	16/09/03
13	17/08/03	13	17/09/03
14	18/08/03	14	18/09/03
15	19/08/03	15	19/09/03
16	20/08/03	16	20/09/03
17	21/08/03	17	21/09/03
18	22/08/03	18	22/09/03
19	23/08/03	19	23/09/03
20	24/08/03	20	24/09/03
21	25/08/03	21	25/09/03
22	26/08/03	22	26/09/03
23	27/08/03	23	27/09/03
24	28/08/03	24	28/09/03
25	29/08/03	25	29/09/03
26	30/08/03	26	30/09/03
27	31/08/03	27	01/10/03
28	01/09/03	28	02/10/03
29	02/09/03	29	03/10/03
30	03/09/03	30	04/10/03
31	04/09/03		

DECEMBER 2003		JANUARY 2004	
First day of PIW	*Previous PIW links if on or after*	*First day of PIW*	*Previous PIW links if on or after*
1	05/10/03	1	05/11/03
2	06/10/03	2	06/11/03
3	07/10/03	3	07/11/03
4	08/10/03	4	08/11/03
5	09/10/03	5	09/11/03
6	10/10/03	6	10/11/03
7	11/10/03	7	11/11/03
8	12/10/03	8	12/11/03
9	13/10/03	9	13/11/03
10	14/10/03	10	14/11/03
11	15/10/03	11	15/11/03
12	16/10/03	12	16/11/03
13	17/10/03	13	17/11/03
14	18/10/03	14	18/11/03
15	19/10/03	15	19/11/03
16	20/10/03	16	20/11/03
17	21/10/03	17	21/11/03
18	22/10/03	18	22/11/03
19	23/10/03	19	23/11/03
20	24/10/03	20	24/11/03
21	25/10/03	21	25/11/03
22	26/10/03	22	26/11/03
23	27/10/03	23	27/11/03
24	28/10/03	24	28/11/03
25	29/10/03	25	29/11/03
26	30/10/03	26	30/11/03
27	31/10/03	27	01/12/03
28	01/11/03	28	02/12/03
29	02/11/03	29	03/12/03
30	03/11/03	30	04/12/03
31	04/11/03	31	05/12/03

FEBRUARY 2004

First day of PIW	*Previous PIW links if on or after*
1	06/12/03
2	07/12/03
3	08/12/03
4	09/12/03
5	10/12/03
6	11/12/03
7	12/12/03
8	13/12/03
9	14/12/03
10	15/12/03
11	16/12/03
12	17/12/03
13	18/12/03
14	19/12/03
15	20/12/03
16	21/12/03
17	22/12/03
18	23/12/03
19	24/12/03
20	25/12/03
21	26/12/03
22	27/12/03
23	28/12/03
24	29/12/03
25	30/12/03
26	31/12/03
27	01/01/04
28	02/01/04
29	03/01/04

MARCH 2004

First day of PIW	*Previous PIW links if on or after*
1	04/01/04
2	05/01/04
3	06/01/04
4	07/01/04
5	08/01/04
6	09/01/04
7	10/01/04
8	11/01/04
9	12/01/04
10	13/01/04
11	14/01/04
12	15/01/04
13	16/01/04
14	17/01/04
15	18/01/04
16	19/01/04
17	20/01/04
18	21/01/04
19	22/01/04
20	23/01/04
21	24/01/04
22	25/01/04
23	26/01/04
24	27/01/04
25	28/01/04
26	29/01/04
27	30/01/04
28	31/01/04
29	01/02/04
30	02/02/04
31	03/02/04

APRIL 2004

First day of PIW	*Previous PIW links if on or after*
1	02/02/04
2	03/02/04
3	04/02/04
4	05/02/04
5	06/02/04

2002/03

APRIL 2002

First day of PIW	*Previous PIW links if on or after*
6	08/02/02
7	09/02/02
8	10/02/02
9	11/02/02
10	12/02/02
11	13/02/02
12	14/02/02
13	15/02/02
14	16/02/02
15	17/02/02
16	18/02/02
17	19/02/02
18	20/02/02
19	21/02/02
20	22/02/02
21	23/02/02
22	24/02/02
23	25/02/02
24	26/02/02
25	27/02/02
26	28/02/02
27	01/03/02
28	02/03/02
29	03/03/02
30	04/03/02

MAY 2002

First day of PIW	*Previous PIW links if on or after*
1	05/03/02
2	06/03/02
3	07/03/02
4	08/03/02
5	09/03/02
6	10/03/02
7	11/03/02
8	12/03/02
9	13/03/02
10	14/03/02
11	15/03/02
12	16/03/02
13	17/03/02
14	18/03/02
15	19/03/02
16	20/03/02
17	21/03/02
18	22/03/02
19	23/03/02
20	24/03/02
21	25/03/02
22	26/03/02
23	27/03/02
24	28/03/02
25	29/03/02
26	30/03/02
27	31/03/02
28	01/04/02
29	02/04/02
30	03/04/02
31	04/04/02

JUNE 2002

First day of PIW	*Previous PIW links if on or after*
1	05/04/02
2	06/04/02
3	07/04/02
4	08/04/02
5	09/04/02
6	10/04/02
7	11/04/02
8	12/04/02
9	13/04/02
10	14/04/02
11	15/04/02
12	16/04/02
13	17/04/02
14	18/04/02
15	19/04/02
16	20/04/02
17	21/04/02
18	22/04/02
19	23/04/02
20	24/04/02
21	25/04/02
22	26/04/02
23	27/04/02
24	28/04/02
25	29/04/02
26	30/04/02
27	01/05/02
28	02/05/02
29	03/05/02
30	04/05/02

JULY 2002

First day of PIW	*Previous PIW links if on or after*
1	05/05/02
2	06/05/02
3	07/05/02
4	08/05/02
5	09/05/02
6	10/05/02
7	11/05/02
8	12/05/02
9	13/05/02
10	14/05/02
11	15/05/02
12	16/05/02
13	17/05/02
14	18/05/02
15	19/05/02
16	20/05/02
17	21/05/02
18	22/05/02
19	23/05/02
20	24/05/02
21	25/05/02
22	26/05/02
23	27/05/02
24	28/05/02
25	29/05/02
26	30/05/02
27	31/05/02
28	01/06/02
29	02/06/02
30	03/06/02
31	04/06/02

AUGUST 2002		SEPTEMBER 2002	
First day of PIW	*Previous PIW links if on or after*	*First day of PIW*	*Previous PIW links if on or after*
1	05/06/02	1	06/07/02
2	06/06/02	2	07/07/02
3	07/06/02	3	08/07/02
4	08/06/02	4	09/07/02
5	09/06/02	5	10/07/02
6	10/06/02	6	11/07/02
7	11/06/02	7	12/07/02
8	12/06/02	8	13/07/02
9	13/06/02	9	14/07/02
10	14/06/02	10	15/07/02
11	15/06/02	11	16/07/02
12	16/06/02	12	17/07/02
13	17/06/02	13	18/07/02
14	18/06/02	14	19/07/02
15	19/06/02	15	20/07/02
16	20/06/02	16	21/07/02
17	21/06/02	17	22/07/02
18	22/06/02	18	23/07/02
19	23/06/02	19	24/07/02
20	24/06/02	20	25/07/02
21	25/06/02	21	26/07/02
22	26/06/02	22	27/07/02
23	27/06/02	23	28/07/02
24	28/06/02	24	29/07/02
25	29/06/02	25	30/07/02
26	30/06/02	26	31/07/02
27	01/07/02	27	01/08/02
28	02/07/02	28	02/08/02
29	03/07/02	29	03/08/02
30	04/07/02	30	04/08/02
31	05/07/02		

OCTOBER 2002		NOVEMBER 2002	
First day of PIW	*Previous PIW links if on or after*	*First day of PIW*	*Previous PIW links if on or after*
1	05/08/02	1	05/09/02
2	06/08/02	2	06/09/02
3	07/08/02	3	07/09/02
4	08/08/02	4	08/09/02
5	09/08/02	5	09/09/02
6	10/08/02	6	10/09/02
7	11/08/02	7	11/09/02
8	12/08/02	8	12/09/02
9	13/08/02	9	13/09/02
10	14/08/02	10	14/09/02
11	15/08/02	11	15/09/02
12	16/08/02	12	16/09/02
13	17/08/02	13	17/09/02
14	18/08/02	14	18/09/02
15	19/08/02	15	19/09/02
16	20/08/02	16	20/09/02
17	21/08/02	17	21/09/02
18	22/08/02	18	22/09/02
19	23/08/02	19	23/09/02
20	24/08/02	20	24/09/02
21	25/08/02	21	25/09/02
22	26/08/02	22	26/09/02
23	27/08/02	23	27/09/02
24	28/08/02	24	28/09/02
25	29/08/02	25	29/09/02
26	30/08/02	26	30/09/02
27	31/08/02	27	01/10/02
28	01/09/02	28	02/10/02
29	02/09/02	29	03/10/02
30	03/09/02	30	04/10/02
31	04/09/02		

DECEMBER 2002		JANUARY 2003	
First day of PIW	*Previous PIW links if on or after*	*First day of PIW*	*Previous PIW links if on or after*
1	05/10/02	1	05/11/02
2	06/10/02	2	06/11/02
3	07/10/02	3	07/11/02
4	08/10/02	4	08/11/02
5	09/10/02	5	09/11/02
6	10/10/02	6	10/11/02
7	11/10/02	7	11/11/02
8	12/10/02	8	12/11/02
9	13/10/02	9	13/11/02
10	14/10/02	10	14/11/02
11	15/10/02	11	15/11/02
12	16/10/02	12	16/11/02
13	17/10/02	13	17/11/02
14	18/10/02	14	18/11/02
15	19/10/02	15	19/11/02
16	20/10/02	16	20/11/02
17	21/10/02	17	21/11/02
18	22/10/02	18	22/11/02
19	23/10/02	19	23/11/02
20	24/10/02	20	24/11/02
21	25/10/02	21	25/11/02
22	26/10/02	22	26/11/02
23	27/10/02	23	27/11/02
24	28/10/02	24	28/11/02
25	29/10/02	25	29/11/02
26	30/10/02	26	30/11/02
27	31/10/02	27	01/12/02
28	01/11/02	28	02/12/02
29	02/11/02	29	03/12/02
30	03/11/02	30	04/12/02
31	04/11/02	31	05/12/02

FEBRUARY 2003

First day of PIW	*Previous PIW links if on or after*
1	06/12/02
2	07/12/02
3	08/12/02
4	09/12/02
5	10/12/02
6	11/12/02
7	12/12/02
8	13/12/02
9	14/12/02
10	15/12/02
11	16/12/02
12	17/12/02
13	18/12/02
14	19/12/02
15	20/12/02
16	21/12/02
17	22/12/02
18	23/12/02
19	24/12/02
20	25/12/02
21	26/12/02
22	27/12/02
23	28/12/02
24	29/12/02
25	30/12/02
26	31/12/02
27	01/01/03
28	02/01/03

MARCH 2003

First day of PIW	*Previous PIW links if on or after*
1	03/01/03
2	04/01/03
3	05/01/03
4	06/01/03
5	07/01/03
6	08/01/03
7	09/01/03
8	10/01/03
9	11/01/03
10	12/01/03
11	13/01/03
12	14/01/03
13	15/01/03
14	16/01/03
15	17/01/03
16	18/01/03
17	19/01/03
18	20/01/03
19	21/01/03
20	22/01/03
21	23/01/03
22	24/01/03
23	25/01/03
24	26/01/03
25	27/01/03
26	28/01/03
27	29/01/03
28	30/01/03
29	31/01/03
30	01/02/03
31	02/02/03

APRIL 2003

First day of PIW	*Previous PIW links if on or after*
1	03/02/03
2	04/02/03
3	05/02/03
4	06/02/03
5	07/02/03

Checklist: Definition of Qualifying Day

A qualifying day can be a day of the week:

(a) on which the employee is required to be available for work under the terms of the contract of employment; or

(b) if the employee and employer agree that there were no such contractual days, the Wednesday will be the default qualifying day; or

(c) if there is no agreement as to which days the employee would have been required to work, all the days of the week will be QDs except the days of the week which it is agreed were rest days for all employees in that particular organisation or business. This is known as the overriding rule.

An employer may well decide that it would be better to agree specific QDs with employees rather than use the normal contractual working days.

Example

An employer may operate a rotation system or shift pattern and, on the grounds of simplicity, will want to agree with employees that the same days in every week are QDs. Therefore, where Brian is required to work Monday to Wednesday every other week, agreement could be made that Monday, Tuesday, Wednesday are the QDs, regardless of the days worked. Alternatively, Monday to Friday could be the QDs, even though they are not always work days.

It is advisable to agree QDs at the start of employment and include details of these days in the statement of employment particulars, which the employer must provide to every employee within two months of the start date of the employment. If the QDs are agreed collectively with a trade union or staff association, that agreement should form part of the employee's contract of employment.

A sample clause could state: 'the qualifying days for SSP purposes are the same days that you [the employee] are required to work. These days, until otherwise varied, are Monday to Friday inclusive'.

However, if the employee and employer agree that QDs are the same days as they are required to work under the contract, then a mixed pattern of QDs can emerge

Example

Diane is a part-time secretary who works five days every fortnight. She works Mondays and Tuesdays in one week and Wednesdays, Thursdays and Fridays in the next week. It is agreed that her QDs will be her working days. Thus, she has two QDs in 26 weeks of the year and three QDs in the remaining 26 weeks of the year.

Different QDs can be agreed for individual employees or groups of employees.

Case study: determining qualifying days

Jerome works shifts for a local engineering company, which has no Occupational Sick Pay (OSP) scheme. He works Monday through to Thursday in week 1, does not work at all in week 2, and works Friday through Sunday in week 3. The pattern then is repeated. Jerome and his employer have agreed, in writing, that these are designated working days, all other days are rest days. There is no formal agreement about which days are SSP QDs. By default, the QDs will be:

- *Week 1:* Monday, Tuesday, Wednesday and Thursday;
- *Week 2:* Wednesday; and
- *Week 3:* Friday, Saturday and Sunday.

Jerome falls sick after returning home on Sunday evening at the end of week 3. He has not previously been absent from work due to sickness. He notifies his employer by telephone early on Monday morning of week 1. He also subsequently supplies a medical certificate and does not return to work until the Friday of working week 3. The current applicable weekly rate of SSP is £64.35 (see **6.2**).

Monday, Tuesday, and Wednesday of working week 1 serve as the first three waiting days (see **1.7**) since there is no linking PIW. SSP is payable on the Thursday of working week 1. Since Jerome has four QDs in working week 1, the SSP rate paid for the Thursday is £16.09 (see **6.3**).

In working week 2, Jerome has the Wednesday as the default QD. He is still absent from work on this day. Since Jerome has one QD in working week 2, the SSP rate for the Wednesday is £64.35.

In working week 3, Jerome returns to work on the Friday and so SSP ceases to be payable.

There are no proportions of a day's SSP.

> ***Example***
>
> A local shop may have half-day closing on Wednesday afternoons, but Wednesdays count as QDs for its employees who, where appropriate, would receive a full day's SSP.

Waiting Days [1.7]

SSP is not payable for the first three QDs in a PIW. These three days are called 'waiting days'. A waiting day must also be a QD. If the PIW is linked with an earlier PIW (see **1.5**), then the three waiting days may have been served in full or in part in the earlier PIW.

> ***Example***
>
> Fred's QDs are Mondays to Fridays inclusive. He is absent sick from the Friday of one week and returns to work on the following Tuesday. Three weeks later he is absent sick from the Monday of one week, returning to work on the Wednesday of the following week. Both absences are PIWs and are linked. The waiting days in the first PIW are Friday and Monday, as these are the only days designated as QDs. Therefore, the Monday of the second PIW counts as the third waiting day in the linked PIW. SSP can be considered for the remaining QDs in the second period of sickness.

Once the three waiting days have been served, SSP becomes payable on any subsequent QD within the PIW or linked PIW.

> ### Questions and Answers [1.8]
>
> *Question*
>
> When must an employer first consider paying SSP?
>
> *Answer*
>
> The first consideration is whether the employee has been sick for four or more days in a row including weekends, holidays and other days when the employee would not normally be expected to work. ➡

Question

Why is it necessary to have all these different qualifying day patterns to choose from, as it makes the administration of SSP very complex?

Answer

The Government recognises that all employers are different; as such the legislator has put together a set of rules to try to cater for all possible employment patterns and work schedules. Employers and employees are therefore left to decide which qualifying day pattern best suits their requirements. The simplest way to administer the scheme is to choose the days the employee works where there is a regular pattern, or to decide that all calendar days are qualifying days where there is an irregular work pattern.

Question

Qualifying days, waiting days, periods of incapacity for work – isn't this all a lot of mumbo jumbo? What does it all mean?

Answer

SSP can be complex, so there has to be a set of rules to which labels can be attached. Whether the terms used are the best is open to conjecture. However, to summarise, for SSP to be payable to an employee for any particular day, that day must be a day of incapacity for work which falls within a period of incapacity for work (PIW). For SSP to be payable, the particular day must also be a qualifying day (QD) in respect of that employee. SSP, however, will not be payable if the particular day is a waiting day. Nevertheless, there are circumstances when SSP is not payable even when the necessary conditions outlined above have been met. Further eligibility and entitlement conditions exist and these are explained in **Chapter 5 – The Employment Contract**.

Question

One of our employees is off work visiting a sick relative in hospital. Does this count as a day of incapacity?

Answer

If an employee is away from work on a day for any other reason than his or her own sickness, then that day is not treated as a day of incapacity for work and SSP is not payable on that day. This can include cases of looking after a sick child or making funeral arrangements, or where there has been a death in the immediate family. Many employers are likely to grant the employee compassionate leave of absence in such circumstances, which may be paid at the discretion of the employer.

Question

One of our full-time employees has been absent with a respiratory condition. She now feels able to return and we are happy that she does so. However, in order to ease herself back into the job, she is initially only coming back on a two-day basis to see how things go. Do these days counts as days of incapacity for work as she has not really resumed normal duties?

Answer

Sometimes both parties can agree to a return to work on a therapeutic basis. Some employees will return to work part-time for therapeutic reasons when recovering from a major illness. The days that they work, even if for only part of the day, do not form part of a PIW.

Question

We employ night-shift workers and their work pattern spans more than one day. How can we possibility define qualifying days?

Answer

There is a special rule to deal with night-shift workers. The normal rule is that to count as a day of incapacity the employee must not have done any work on that day – not even for just one minute. In the case of a night-shift worker, work done in any shift that extends over midnight is treated as done entirely on the first of the two days. Thus, if the employee is incapable of work after a night shift, the second day is treated as a day of incapacity even though he or she worked part of it.

2. Statutory Sick Pay

Introduction [2.1]

All employers, subject to certain exceptions (see **2.4**), resident in the UK must currently participate and operate the Statutory Sick Pay (SSP) scheme. There is no general exemption (even for small employers) from the requirement to ensure that an employee receives, as a minimum, his or her SSP entitlement. Neither the employer nor the employee can choose not to be a party to the SSP scheme.

In particular:

(a) any contract of employment which purports to exclude, limit or modify the statutory provision of SSP will be held to be void; and

(b) no employer is permitted to require an employee to contribute, directly or indirectly, to the cost of providing SSP.

An employer will remain liable to pay an employee SSP if the employer ends the employee's contract of employment solely, or mainly, for the purpose of avoiding paying the employee SSP.

> ***Example***
>
> Andrea is dismissed by her employer and it is subsequently established that the dismissal was solely or mainly for the purpose of avoiding paying her SSP. Andrea's employer is therefore liable to pay her SSP beyond the termination date of the employment. This means that SSP payments must continue until her PIW ceases or she reaches the maximum entitlement (see **7.3**) or, if earlier, the date when the contract of employment would ordinarily have come to an end.

Freedom from Operating the SSP Scheme [2.2]

There is, however, the freedom not to record separately payments of SSP where, and for as long as, the employer pays contractual remuneration to the employee at or above the SSP daily rate for a day of incapacity to work (see **1.3**). This relaxation of the SSP rules came into effect from 6 April 1997.

Checklist: SSP Easement Arrangements

This means that:

(a) all employers are free to choose between paying SSP and operating the rules of the scheme or paying contractual remuneration at or above the SSP rate to employees who are sick;

(b) employers with Occupational Sick Pay (OSP) schemes (see **12.5**) which meet or exceed the SSP rate no longer have to keep two sets of records for SSP and OSP schemes; and

(c) employees' rights are protected by the retention of their employer's liability to pay the relevant daily rate of SSP in respect of days of incapacity for work.

The easement on record keeping for employers operating an adequate OSP scheme is purely voluntary. The guidance from the Inland Revenue points out that there is no need to make any formal application if an employer wishes to adopt these arrangements. There is, therefore, no kind of initial formal inspection, for example, to see that the employer does indeed provide contractual remuneration to an employee at or above the SSP rate, and also for every day of incapacity for work when SSP is payable.

However, employers must remain aware that the employee already has a statutory right to SSP where he or she satisfies the qualifying conditions for any day of incapacity where contractual pay is:

- not paid for that day; or
- paid at less than the SSP rate for that day.

The employee also has a right of appeal (see **10.5**) to the Inland Revenue if SSP is not paid when it is due. If the employer does adopt the arrangements, the employer remains free to apply the arrangements to some employees and not to others.

> *i* In practice, the main potential advantage in this deregulation move is that employers with adequate OSP schemes can reduce their administration costs by not having to operate the SSP scheme in addition to their own in-house arrangements. For many employers, the effort of administering SSP for the majority of sick absences has been eliminated.

> ! To be excused from operating SSP, the employer must pay company pay at or above the SSP rate for the total (not just part of) the SSP payment period, a maximum of 28 weeks. Form SSP1 (see **7.10**) must still be issued when the employee has been sick for 28 weeks in a single PIW or linked PIW.

Mandatory SSP Record Keeping [2.3]

Employers opting out of the SSP scheme must still keep a number of records. These are broadly as follows.

Checklist: SSP Record Retention

(a) basic details of sickness absence lasting at least four calendar days in a row and amounts of SSP paid during a PIW;

(b) information to enable completion of Form SSP1 (Change-over Form) (see **7.10**), which will allow employees to transfer to State Incapacity Benefit if necessary;

(c) information to enable completion of Form SSP1 (L) (Leaver's Statement) (see **7.6**), if requested by the employee;

(d) the dates on which SSP liability starts and ends (these may not be the same as the first and last days of sickness);

(e) the number of weeks and days of SSP entitlement; and

(f) the number of QDs (see **1.6**).

Excluded Employers [2.4]

Certain employers are specifically excluded from the scope of the SSP scheme.

(a) HM Forces – In respect of persons serving as members of HM Forces, including the Reserve Forces.

(b) Mariners – Employers of foreign-going mariners, for whom a special rate of secondary (employer) Class 1 National Insurance contributions (NICs) is payable, are outside the scheme. The scheme does apply, however, to mariners employed on a British ship or where the owner of the vessel has a place of business in Great Britain and is paying the mariner under a contract entered into in the UK.

(c) Foreign organisations – Certain foreign or international organisations which, as employers, do not meet the conditions of residence or presence in Great Britain, are not required to pay SSP. Basically these are employers who do not have a liability to pay secondary Class 1 NICs.

Mariners are not covered by SSP if they are employed:

(a) on board a foreign-going ship and their earnings are paid exclusively for that employment;

(b) partly on a foreign-going ship and partly elsewhere and the earnings for the employment on the foreign-going ship are paid during that employment; or

(c) have been employed on a foreign-going ship within the last 13 weeks and:

- remain employed by the same employer; and
- are not employed by anyone on terms which would stop them returning to their employment on the foreign-going ship within 13 weeks of leaving it.

Questions and Answers [2.5]

Question

Why, if we as an employer are not operating the SSP scheme, do we need to keep records?

Answer

SSP is just one small part of the State Social Security system. Therefore, records need to be maintained in order to ensure that the employee can be transferred onto State Incapacity Benefit (see **13.2**), for example, where the employee has received maximum entitlement or were not entitled to receive SSP after they had exhausted their OSP (see **12.5**).

Question

Can the employer still recover amounts of SSP from the State, even if they do not operate the SSP scheme?

Answer

The Percentage Threshold Scheme (see **8.2**) will continue to apply, even if the employer is not operating the SSP scheme but relying instead on a more generous in-house scheme. To do so, the employer's payroll will still have to know what the SSP liability was in any tax month and whether it exceeded 13% of the employer's and employee's gross Class 1 NI liability for the same tax month.

3. Who is Eligible?

Introduction [3.1]

Employees (including apprentices) who are entitled to receive SSP are those working under a contract of employment or in an office where their earnings attract a liability for employers Class 1 National Insurance contributions (NICs). This is provided that they are not specifically excluded from the scheme and they fulfil the relevant qualifying conditions (see **Chapter 5**). There does not have to be a written contract of employment, as long as the employee has performed some work under the contract.

Married women and widows who retain the right to pay Class 1 NICs at the reduced rate qualify for SSP if they satisfy the qualifying conditions. Likewise, part-time, temporary and casual employees may be entitled to SSP if they satisfy the qualifying conditions.

> *i* In practice, an employee working only part-time hours may be excluded from SSP, as in some cases the reduced hours may result in the employee's level of earnings disqualifying them from SSP.

Mariners are covered by SSP if either:

- they are employed on a home-trade ship or vessel belonging to Her Majesty or whose port of registry is a port in Great Britain; or
- their contract was entered into in the United Kingdom and the person paying the mariner's earnings or the owner of the ship or vessel (or the managing owner if there is more than one owner) has a place of business in Great Britain.

Aircrew and employees working on the continental shelf are covered by the SSP scheme.

More Than One Employment [3.2]

An employee may work under two or more separate contracts of employment for the same employer. In such a case, SSP liability may arise separately under each contract of employment provided the employer's Class 1 NICs are paid separately for each contract. If, however, the employee's gross wages are aggregated for National Insurance purposes, there is only one SSP liability. In which case the employee must be incapable for work under all contracts before they are entitled to SSP.

The general rule is that where the employee has more than one job with the same employer or employers 'trading in association' then the gross wages are aggregated together unless it is not reasonably practicable to do so. The decision whether two or more employers should be treated as one for SSP may be resolved by an Inland Revenue formal decision (see **10.4**).

> *i* In practice, provided that the employee is entitled to SSP from at least one employer, he or she is not entitled to Incapacity Benefit from the Benefits Agency.

Where an employee works under separate contracts for different employers, each employer must consider only its own SSP liability and take no account of the other contract or contracts. If an employee has more than one employment, he or she may be able to continue working in one or more employment(s) whilst being incapable of working in the others. This depends on the nature of the work in each job and what physical functions the worker is required to perform.

> ***Example***
>
> David is employed as a bingo caller during the daytime. He is diagnosed as suffering from laryngitis and therefore cannot perform this job. However, he has another part-time job in the evenings as a male stripper, which he is still able to perform, despite his condition. Therefore, he may be entitled to SSP under his daytime contract only.

Where the individual is both employed and self-employed, the occupation which is classified as employment has to consider SSP entitlement. However, a self-employed individual's earnings will never attract employer's Class 1 NICs, because there is no employer and therefore the individual only has a liability to pay Class 2 and Class 4 NICs. Self-employed individuals can claim Incapacity Benefit (see **13.2**), where they meet the contributory-related qualifying conditions.

National Health Service Trusts [3.3]

Two separate and distinct sets of regulations apply to National Health Service Trust employees. These provide that employees whose contracts of employment have been divided into two or more contracts with different employing bodies as a consequence of the creation of National Health Service Trusts may elect to have those contracts treated as one contract for the purposes of entitlement to SSP.

The special rules only apply to employees that were employed by a Health Authority at the time the contract was split between the Health Authority and Trust(s), or between Trusts. Employees who start working for the Trust(s) after the split:

(a) are not entitled to make this election; and

(b) will only qualify for SSP from their employers if the conditions are satisfied.

This does not affect the rules where an employee has more than one contract with the same employer (see **3.2**).

An election should be made at the same time as their employers are advised of their sickness. The election lasts until the end of the PIW or linked PIWs. Employees can make a separate election, if they wish, for each PIW.

Case study: hospital trust worker — split contracts

Coral was working for a Health Authority at three different hospitals, 'A', 'B' and 'C'. In June 1991, after she commenced employment, Hospital 'A' became a National Health Service Trust.

Coral is sick from 11 September 2003 to 6 November 2003. The Lower Earnings Limit (LEL) on the first day of incapacity (tax year 2003/04) is £77.00.

Her average weekly earnings (see **5.7**) from the Trust (Hospital 'A') are calculated as £70.15 and from the Health Authority (aggregating her earnings from Hospitals 'B' and 'C') they are £71.84. Under the normal rules Coral would not qualify for SSP from the Trust or the Health Authority. However, because the Health Authority employed her at the time the contracts were split, she can elect to have her SSP entitlement calculated as though the split had not taken place.

If Coral makes an election she will qualify for SSP. If Coral does not make an election, Hospital 'A' and the Health Authority will each issue Form SSP1 (see **7.10**) and she will need to claim Incapacity Benefit (see **13.2**) from the Department for Work and Pensions. Coral would only be entitled to make one claim for Incapacity Benefit, regardless of how many employers she had.

At any time after 1 April 1999, two Trusts, or a Health Authority and a Trust, may merge to become one employer. If the *Transfer of Undertakings Protection of Employment* (*TUPE*) *Regulations* (*SI 1981 No 1794*) apply, an employee working for more than one employer prior to the merger, with an SSP entitlement with each merging employer, spanning the merger date, will keep their multiple entitlement to SSP until they return to work. This multiple entitlement will last only until the end of the current spell of sickness that spans the merger date. During any future linked or unlinked PIWs for that employee, entitlement to only one payment of SSP will arise.

Questions and Answers [3.4]

Question

What does an employer have to do about odd days of sickness?

Answer

For the purposes of SSP not a lot. Employees that are sick for three calendar days in a row or less, are not covered by the SSP scheme. The employer may pay OSP at their discretion.

Question

How does an employer know when earnings are to be aggregated for Class 1 NIC purposes?

Answer

Two sets of aggregation rules operate for Class 1 NIC purposes: those where the employments are with the same employer, and those under different employers, carrying on business in association. The onus is on the employer to show that aggregation is not reasonably practicable. In making a judgement, the employer needs to take into account the costs, resources, and the effects on running the business. Cost is a material pointer but not necessarily a decisive factor. Costs to the employer are not just financial. Time, effort and the effect on the business have to be considered because the weight of the cost of compliance should not be disproportionate to the loss of NICs and benefit entitlement eg SSP.

Employers, their advisers and Inland Revenue staff need to consider the costs and the risks to future benefits based on all the facts of the individual cases.

4. Notification and Evidence Requirements

Introduction [4.1]

Employees must notify their employer if they are incapable of work due to sickness. However, notification does not of itself establish that any absence from work was due in fact to sickness and evidence may be needed to satisfy the employer. The issues of notification and evidence need to be considered separately.

The employer should consider the following points in order to ensure that all the eligibility criteria have been met before paying SSP to the employee:

- Was the employee incapacitated (see **1.4**)?
- Has notification of sickness been received (see **4.2**)?
- Has medical evidence of sickness been received (see **4.7**)?

Notification of Sickness [4.2]

Employers are free to impose their own notification requirements but if SSP is to be withheld for failing to meet these in-house requirements the employer is subject to the following rules and limitations:

Checklist: SSP Notification Rules

(a) The employer may set a time limit for notification but cannot require notification earlier than the first qualifying day (QD) (and not by any special time on the first QD) in a period of incapacity for work (PIW). This is so even if the employee knows in advance that he or she will be absent due to sickness, eg because he or she is due to go into hospital for an operation.

(b) If a time limit or a particular manner for giving notification is set, the employer must have taken all reasonable steps to advise employees of that time limit, eg by specifying this in the company sickness rules, issued at the start of the employment.

(c) An employee may give notification later than the time limit set by the employer and still preserve entitlement to SSP provided he or she can show 'good cause' (see **4.3**) for giving the notification late.

(d) If the employer has not set any time limit for notification, a default limit is set for SSP purposes. An employee should inform his or her employer by the seventh calendar day following the first QD. Again, this is subject to an easement if the employee can show good cause for giving later notification.

(e) Provided the employer accepts that the employee can show good cause for the delay, the employer must accept that notification is given correctly if it is given within one calendar month of the specified time, or of the seven-day period after the relevant day of incapacity. As a protection for the seriously ill, this period is extended to 91 days as an absolute limit. The employer must accept that notification is given correctly if it is up to 91 days after the relevant day of incapacity provided the employer is satisfied that it was not reasonably practicable for the employee to have given notification earlier.

(f) If an employee posts his or her notification in a properly addressed and prepaid letter, notification must be taken as given on the day on which the letter was posted ie the postmark.

(g) An employer may not require an employee to give notification more than once in every seven days during the same period of entitlement.

(h) Unless otherwise agreed between the parties, the notification should be in writing.

The rules for notification must be given to the employee in advance of any period of sickness.

An employer may not require that:

- notification is given personally by the sick employee (notification should be accepted if given by a relative or close friend);
- the employee should produce a medical certificate as a means of notification of absence; or
- the employee should use any particular document for the purpose of giving notification (eg an employer cannot insist that the employee use an in-house form).

> **i** In practice, the limitations, as stated in the above checklist, only apply for SSP purposes. Employers often make more stringent requirements for entitlement to their own OSP schemes (see **12.5**) and can also use their own in-house disciplinary rules to enforce these requirements.

Defining Good Cause [4.3]

'Good cause' is not defined precisely in the SSP legislation. The employer will have to examine the circumstances of each case of late notification and make a judgement as to whether there was a justifiable reason.

Generally recognised examples of where an employer might accept there is a good cause for delay is where the employee:

- lives alone, has no telephone and is unable to go out; or
- is the victim of a serious road accident; or
- suffers a heart attack or stroke.

Withholding SSP [4.4]

If the employee fails to observe the notification procedures, then subject to the statutory rules given above, eg good cause for late notification, the employer may withhold SSP for each QD for which the notification is late. However, the employer may, if he chooses, pay SSP for those days.

If SSP for one or more QDs is withheld because of late notification, the day(s) do not count towards the maximum entitlement. However, such days will count for the purpose of linking with any previous or subsequent PIW. QDs that are withheld because of late notification are not counted as waiting days.

> ***Example***
>
> Neil, whose QDs are Monday to Friday inclusive, commences a PIW on Monday. His contract of employment requires that notification for OSP purposes is made by midday on the first working day of absence, but there are no such specific rules for SSP notification. Hence, Neil first informs his employer on the following Friday of his incapacity for work. Neil's employer decides not to pay contractual pay for the first four days in the absence. However, the employer is still obliged to pay SSP from the Thursday of that week, ie after the serving of three ➡

waiting days (see **1.7**), as Neil has satisfied the statutory fall-back rule of notifying sickness absence within seven days of the first day of incapacity (see **4.2**).

i In practice, compliance with the contractual notification rules will usually suffice to meet notification requirements for SSP purposes. However, an employee's failure to comply with contractual requirements will not of itself mean that he or she will not qualify for SSP.

Each notification must cover at least seven calendar days from the day it is given. An employer's notification rules may require an employee to continue to provide notification throughout the PIW, subject to each notification covering this minimum period. If any renewed notification is late, SSP can also be withheld for every QD for which notification is late.

Example

Neil's (from example above) sickness continues into a second week. If renewal notification is not given until the Monday of the third week of absence and there was no good cause for the delay, then SSP can be withheld for the whole of the second week of absence. The first notification of his incapacity only covered the first seven calendar days of absence.

If necessary, QDs for which SSP is to be withheld can be carried forward into any subsequent linked PIW (but not into a subsequent unlinked PIW).

Employee Rights [4.5]

If the employer withholds SSP from an employee because he does not accept that there was good cause for late notification (see **4.3**), and the employee does not accept the employer's reasons, the employee has the right:

- to ask his or her employer for a written statement (see **10.3**) which explains why SSP is not being paid for the day(s) in question; and
- if the employee does not agree with the decision, he or she can ask the Inland Revenue to give a formal decision (see **10.4**).

Disciplinary Offence [4.6]

Where late notification is treated as a disciplinary offence as well as a potential disqualification from SSP for the period in question, care must be taken not to act inconsistently. Paying SSP and treating the matter as a serious disciplinary offence could be regarded as contradictory and may create problems if the employer gets to the stage of trying to show that the employee's ultimate dismissal for persistent late notification was fair.

At any 'informal' warning stage, or perhaps, at a formal stage which represents the employee's first (formal) warning about unjustified late notification, the employer may reasonably be prepared to pay SSP to the employee. However, payment of SSP is tantamount to accepting that the employee was incapable of work due to sickness.

> *i* In practice, it is perfectly feasible that late notification for SSP purposes may be different from late notification for the purposes of an occupational sickness scheme.

Evidence of Sickness [4.7]

The onus is on the employer to decide whether to accept that an employee is genuinely incapable of working because of sickness. The SSP legislation does not specify what an employer may require from an employee as adequate proof of sickness. However, the employee is obliged to give the employer such evidence as may be reasonably required to enable the employer to determine whether or not SSP is due.

> *i* In practice, it is important for the employer to differentiate between evidence and notification of incapacity for work.

Notification provides for a system whereby the employee, either in accordance with the employer's own rules or the statutory rules, notifies his or her employer that he or she is absent because of incapacity (see **4.2**). Evidence concerns the information that may be received and considered in establishing that the employee is or is not genuinely incapable of work.

The employer has to exercise judgement in deciding whether the evidence is acceptable for the purposes of SSP. (Such evidence will often be required in any case for occupational pay purposes.) If the employer decides that the evidence does not confirm that the employee is genuinely incapable of work then he or she can refuse to pay SSP.

Case study: supplying medical evidence

John drinks eight pints of real ale on a Sunday night, as the thought of going into work on Monday is not appealing. He awakes on Monday with a thick head, dry mouth and a general fuzziness. He decides to pull the covers back over his head, reaches for his mobile phone and telephones his employer and advises him that he will not be in today, as he is feeling 'under the weather'.

Mid-afternoon, John opens his curtains to find a glorious sunny day. He decides that this is too good an opportunity to miss and arranges a game of golf for Tuesday, a spot of fishing on Wednesday and a pub lunch on Thursday and Friday. Unfortunately, Friday's lunch disagrees with him and on attending evening surgery, the doctor diagnoses 'a severe bout of food poisoning' and signs him off for the following week. On Saturday John logs on to his company's Intranet at home and completes online the employer's own self-certification form for the previous week's absence.

He faxes the doctor's standard medical certificate across to his employer's payroll office to cover him for the following week's absence, and puts the original certificate in the post. Having completed and supplied the relevant medical evidence for SSP purposes, he sits back in his chair to watch the racing from Ascot for the rest of the second week of absence.

Self-Certification [4.8]

Employers are free to require employees to complete a self-certification form in cases of sickness. Since medical evidence (doctor's statement) cannot be required for the first seven days of a PIW, self-certification will in practice be the only evidence that the employer can obtain for short periods of sickness absence (see **12.3**).

Checklist: Acceptable Self-certification

Employers can use a self-certification form:

(a) of their own design;

(b) one produced by an employer's organisation;

(c) a letter or note; or

(d) the Inland Revenue self-certification Form SC2 (see below). Supplies can be ordered from local Benefits Agency offices or by going to www.inlandrevenue.gov.uk/employers/emp-form-170603.htm

Sample Form: Self-certification

Name: ....

Employee number: ....

I was absent from work because of sickness from:

First calendar day of illness (not necessarily the first working day) .... to .... (enter the date you returned to work)

Reason for absence. ....

When did you first notify the company of your absence? ....

Is a doctor's certificate attached? NB This is only required for absence of eight or more days calendar days. YES/NO

Signed .... Dated .... [Employee]

Employer use

Is the employee eligible for discretionary company sick pay? YES/NO

Signed .... Dated .... [Employer]

i In practice, the majority of employers require a self-certificate from their employees for all absences due to incapacity for work, even those which are less than four days in duration.

Medical Certificates [4.9]

The employer may require medical evidence for an employee's sickness and, if so, this must be provided in the form prescribed by the *SSP (Medical Evidence) Regulations 1985 (SI 1985 No 1604)*. However, employers must remain aware, that an employee cannot be required to supply medical evidence covering the first seven calendar days of illness.

Normally there are just two variants in the prescribed form of the doctor's statement (see **13.3**), a standard and a special statement:

(a) The doctor examining the employee issuing the standard statement. This must be given within one day of the examination.

Form SC2

Inland Revenue

Statutory Sick Pay

Employee's statement of sickness

1 About this form

Statutory Sick Pay (SSP) is money paid by employers to employees who are away from work because they are sick.

2 What to do now

Please:

- fill in part 6 of this form, **Your statement**, when you have been sick for 4 days or more in a row
- tear off **Your statement**, and give it to your employer, it will help them decide if you can get SSP
- keep this page for your own information.

3 What happens next

If you can get SSP, your employer will pay you in the same way they usually pay you your wages.

If you cannot get SSP, your employer will give you form **SSP1** to tell you why. You can use form **SSP1** to claim Incapacity Benefit.

If you disagree with your employer you can ask the inland Revenue for a decision about your entitlement.

4 If you have changed jobs

If you have:

- changed jobs within the last 8 weeks, and
- received at least one weeks SSP from your old employer in the 8 weeks *(52 weeks if you are a Welfare to Work Beneficiary)* before this current spell of sickness (odd days of SSP may count) the SSP from your old employer can be counted towards your 28 weeks maximum SSP payment. This means you may be able to transfer to a higher rate of Incapacity Benefit earlier.

▶ *Please turn over*

SC2 August 2001 1

Form SC2

4 If you have changed jobs (continued)

Ask your old employer to fill in form **SSP1(L)** *Leaver's statement of SSP*. Give form **SSP1(L)** to your new employer, it will help them to make sure that you get the right amount of SSP, and that you transfer to Incapacity Benefit at the right time.

5 Other help while you are sick

You can get more information about other help while you are sick in leaflet **SD1** *Sick and disabled?*

If you do not have much money coming in while you are sick, you may be able to get Income Support. Income Support is a Social Security benefit for people who do not have enough money to live on. You can find about more about Income Support from your nearest Social Security office, now part of the Department for Work and Pensions.

You can get leaflet **SD1** from:

- any Department for Work and Pensions
- most advice centres like the Citizens Advice Bureau, or
- any Post Office, (except in Northern Ireland).

If you want to know more about benefit entitlement while you are sick, ring the Benefit Enquiry Line for people with disabilities.
The phone call is free. The number is 0800 882 200, or in Northern Ireland 0800 220 674.

If you have any problems with hearing or speaking and use a textphone, ring 0800 243 355 or in Northern Ireland 0800 243 787. The phone call is free.
If you do not have your own textphone system, they are available from the Citizens Advice Bureau and main libraries.

Disabled Persons Tax Credit (DPTC) helps people with an illness or disability to return to, or take up work by topping up earnings. It is a tax credit for people on low to middle incomes, who are working 16 hours or more a week and who have an illness or disability which puts them at a disadvantage in getting a job.

There is a route to DPTC called DPTC Fast-Track, which has been specifically designed to help people who become long-term sick or disabled while they are in work.

For more information about the qualifying conditions for DPTC Fast-Track, ring the Disabled Persons Tax Credit Helpline on 0845 605 5858 or textphone 0845 608 8844. In Northern Ireland, the Helpline number is 0845 609 7000 or textphone 0845 607 6078.

If you want to know more about SSP, contact your nearest Inland Revenue office. You can find the telephone number in The Phone Book under Inland Revenue.

▶ *Please see opposite page*

2

Form SC2

6 Your statement - *tear-off*

About you

Surname

Other names

Title Mr/Mrs/Miss/Ms

National Insurance number

Date of birth / /

Clock or payroll number

About your sickness

Please give brief details of your sickness

What date did your sickness begin? / /

What date did your sickness end? / /
If you do not know when your sickness will end, leave this box blank.

- The dates you put in these 2 boxes may be days you do not normally work.
- If you are sick for more than 7 days, your employer may ask you for a medical certificate from your doctor. Medical certificates are also called sick notes or Doctor's statements.

Was you sickness caused by an accident at work or an industrial disease? Yes ☐ No ☐

If you answered 'Yes', you may be able to get Industrial Injuries Disablement Benefit. If you want information about claiming this benefit, ask at your nearest Department for Work and Pensions.

Your signature

Signature

Date / /

Tear off this page and give it to your employer.

3

(b) A special statement is given when the doctor is making use of another medical report carried out by another registered medical practitioner or is making the statement more than one day after the examination.

Every doctor's statement must be signed by the doctor and contain the following particulars.

Checklist: Detail in Doctor's Statement

(a) the patient's name;

(b) the date of the examination on which the doctor's statement is based;

(c) the diagnosis of the patient's disorder for which the doctor is advising the patient to refrain from work, or which has already caused the patient's absence from work;

(d) the date on which the doctor's statement is given; and

(e) the name and address of the doctor.

The doctor must specify his or her diagnosis 'as precisely as the doctor's knowledge of the patient's condition at the time of the examination permits'. However, the diagnosis may be specified less precisely where, in the doctor's opinion, 'a disclosure of the precise disorder would be prejudicial to the patient's well-being, or to the patient's position with his employer'.

Where the doctor anticipates that the employee will be well enough to resume work within two weeks of the examination date, the date that the employee is considered to be ready to return to work should be specified on the statement. Otherwise, the doctor should state the minimum period for which the employee should remain off work. This period should not exceed six months, unless the patient has already been absent from work, on the advice of a doctor, for a period of at least six months prior to the date of the present examination. In such a case, if the doctor considers that the patient should not work for the foreseeable future it should be stated that the employee should refrain from work 'until further notice'.

Where the special statement is used on the basis of a written report of another doctor, the statement must be issued within one month of the date of the written report. In such a case, the doctor may not specify a recommended period away from work of more than one month.

Once a doctor has issued a statement, no further doctor's statement based on the same examination may be given other than a replacement statement for an original which has been lost or mislaid. Any such replacement statement must be clearly marked 'duplicate'.

> *i* In practice, employers usually require their employees to provide a doctor's statement after the first seven calendar days of absence (if only because of contractual terms under an OSP scheme). It is not imposed by the SSP legislation and other forms of evidence can be considered.

Non-registered Practitioners [4.10]

It would be wrong to reject evidence solely because it is supplied by a non-registered practitioner: the test is whether the employee was genuinely sick or not. As with evidence supplied by a registered medical practitioner, the onus is still with the employer to decide whether or not to accept the evidence.

Certificates supplied by non-registered medical practitioners often support claims for Incapacity Benefit (see **13.2**) from the DWP and most are successful.

Non-registered practitioners can include the following.

Checklist: Non-registered Practitioners

(a) osteopaths;

(b) christian scientists;

(c) chiropractors;

(d) herbalists;

(e) acupuncturists; and

(f) dentists.

This list is not exhaustive.

Strength of Evidence [4.11]

Although a doctor's statement is strong evidence that an employee is genuinely ill and should usually be accepted as conclusive, there may be circumstances where other evidence needs to be considered which could prove more persuasive.

> ***Example***
>
> John (see the case study at **4.7** above) who claims that he is incapable of work because of being 'under the weather' is seen on the golf course by one of the line managers at his workplace. Such information, if passed on by the line manager, may convince the employer that the evidence of incapacity for work (self-certification) is unacceptable.

There are, however, circumstances where the employer is required by law to accept a medical certificate as evidence. These are known as cases of 'deemed incapacity' (see **1.3**).

Disputed Incapacity [4.12]

The employer must decide if the employee is incapable of work. If the employer wants to seek medical advice about the incapacity, they may do so in certain circumstances (see **12.3**). Any such decision made by the employer should be included within an appropriate grievance procedure in order to resolve the dispute, without recourse to the adjudicating authority (Board of Inland Revenue).

SSP legislation provides that if the employee disagrees with the employer's decision, they have the right to ask the employer for:

- a written statement (see **10.3**); and
- an Inland Revenue decision on the matter (see **10.4**).

Inland Revenue decisions are based on the facts and the law.

> ## Questions and Answers [4.13]
>
> *Question*
>
> I think one of my employees is lying about their sickness absence and could return to work but simply doesn't want to. What can I do about it?

Answer

If the employer has good reason to believe their incapacity is not genuine, he or she can refuse to pay SSP. A vague suspicion or general mistrust on the part of the employer must be substantiated if it is to be taken into account in deciding an incapacity question. For example, if an employee was said to be incapable of work because of an ankle injury, but was seen playing football.

Question

Why does an employer have to have different rules for occupational and statutory sick pay? It just confuses matters.

Answer

The answer is you don't, it is just that the employer has the option to apply a different set of rules, which may better suit the culture and ethics of the company's attitude towards staff sickness. For example, SSP is not payable for the first three QDs (waiting days) in an unlinked PIW, therefore the employer may consider it reasonable to follow the same pattern with OSP on the premise that loss of pay would discourage short-term absences. However, it could be argued that it may have the reverse effect, in that the employee may deliberately prolong their absence to qualify for payment, in cases where the employee might otherwise only have been absent for an odd day or two.

Question

What evidence of sickness is required?

Answer

Reasonable evidence of incapacity is required. For spells of sickness lasting between four and seven days a self-certificate should be completed by the relevant employee, thereafter a doctor's statement will usually need to be obtained. However, there is no restriction on employers accepting self-certificates as evidence for absences that are longer than seven days.

Question

Do we have to pay SSP, if the illness is self-inflicted, for example, an infection caused by a body piercing?

Answer

The employer's obligation to pay SSP is dictated by statute rather than personal discretion, so whilst an employer may not pay OSP, in these circumstances, SSP must be considered according to the normal rules. Whilst this form of self-expression has become increasingly popular amongst young people in recent years, the scenario is not a new one. Employees have been breaking bones on skiing holidays for years. If the employee satisfies the qualifying conditions for SSP then payment must be made.

Question

We have had an employee who has been off sick for more than two weeks. He self-certified for the first seven days and as we had no further sickness notification we discontinued paying SSP. When the employee received no pay for the second week, he telephoned to ask why not and subsequently produced a backdated doctor's certificate. Do we have to pay SSP for the back dated period?

Answer

As the certificate was late, in theory the employer could withhold SSP for the number of qualifying days the notification was late if they do not accept there was a good cause for the lateness.

However, should the employer decide to do this the employee has the right to ask the employer for a written statement of reasons for withholding SSP and the Inland Revenue for a formal decision on the matter (see **10.4**).

5. Who is Excluded?

Introduction [5.1]

As long as certain conditions are met, all employees with a contract of service (ie employment) and apprentices whose earnings are liable to Class 1 NICs, or would be if they were high enough, are eligible for SSP. Such employees may include part-time, temporary and casual workers. However, certain categories of employees are excluded from the SSP scheme, and no period of entitlement arises, even if they are on the employer's payroll (see **2.4**). If an employee is excluded from SSP, then his or her employer should issue Form SSP1 (often referred to as the Change-over Form) which transfers liability to the Benefits Agency (see **7.10**).

Checklist: Basic Conditions for SSP Entitlement

(a) The employee must have performed some work under the contract of service.

(b) The employee must have been incapable of working for their employer for a period of four or more consecutive calendar days, which can include non-working days. This is known as a PIW (see **1.4**).

(c) The employee must have average weekly earnings in the relevant period (see **6.17**) of at least the LEL – £77 for tax year 2003/04.

(d) The employee must be over 16 years of age but under 65, for either sex at the start of their PIW, or the original PIW if the later one links to a previous PIW (see **1.5**).

(e) The employee must have complied with the sickness notification requirements of their employer and provided evidence (see **4.7**) of their incapacity to work.

Age Restrictions [5.2]

An employee is excluded from receiving SSP if on the first day of the PIW he or she is over the age of 65. However, an employee over the age of 65 is not excluded from SSP when he or she is receiving SSP at the moment he or she reaches 65. The age at the start of the PIW determines SSP entitlement. In such a case entitlement lasts until the end of the illness (linked PIWs included and subject to the three-year rule) (see **7.5**) or until he or she retires from employment, whichever is earlier.

> ***Examples***
>
> 1. Harry reaches his 65th birthday on 6 May 2003. On 8 May 2003, he commences a PIW which is not linked to an earlier PIW. There is no entitlement to SSP for the PIW. However, if Harry had a PIW spanning from 1 May 2003 to 25 May 2003, than as the PIW started before his birthday, SSP is payable until the end of the PIW.
>
> A linked PIW is treated as one. Therefore, if the PIW links to an earlier PIW, which started on or before the attainment of the age 65, entitlement to SSP continues.
>
> 2. Raj is 65 on 20 September 2003. He is sick from 4 August to 18 August 2003 and then again from 30 September to 15 October 2003. The PIWs are separated by less than 56 days and link. SSP is therefore payable for the second PIW, even though it starts after his 65th birthday.

If the employer thinks that an employee might be 65 or over but cannot find out for certain, they should contact the employee's nearest Benefit Agency office (address in telephone book) or the employer's nearest Inland Revenue office to ask if the employee is entitled to SSP. The *Data Protection Act 1998* prevents Benefits Agency and Inland Revenue offices from informing an employer of their employee's age. They can, however, advise an employer whether or not their employee is excluded from the SSP scheme.

The definition of 'employee' used for National Insurance purposes has the result of excluding from the SSP scheme any person who is under the age of 16 at the start of a PIW.

Short-term Contract Workers [5.3]

Prior to 1 October 2002, short-term and fixed-term contract workers were excluded from receiving SSP if on the first day of the PIW (or linked PIW) they were contracted to work for less than three months. Entitlement to SSP would arise, however, where the employee continued to work beyond three months. The *Employment Act 2002* provided for regulations to be made for the purpose of:

- securing that employees in fixed-term employment are treated no less favourably than employees in permanent employment; and

- preventing abuse arising from the use of successive periods of fixed-term employment.

The *Fixed Term Employees (Prevention of Less Favourable Treatment) Regulations 2002* (*SI 2002 No 2034*) came into force on 1 October 2002 and removed the exclusion within the *Social Security Contributions and Benefits Act 1992* that had imposed the requirement that an employee had to be contracted to work for three months in order to be eligible for SSP. From this date, all employees, including those with contracts of three months or less, are eligible for SSP if they satisfy the remaining qualifying conditions.

Recent Claim for Social Security Benefit [5.4]

The employee is excluded from receiving SSP if, at any time in the previous 57 days ending immediately before the first day of the PIW, the employee had at least one day on which he or she was entitled to one of the following social security benefits:

- Incapacity Benefit (or would have been entitled if he or she had satisfied the contribution conditions); or
- Severe Disablement Allowance (see **13.4**).

When the initial entitlement to State benefit ends the employee will receive a 'linking letter' from the Benefits Agency giving notification of the period of exclusion from the SSP scheme with instructions to hand the document over to the employer. Each linking letter (Forms BF220 and, in Northern Ireland, BF219) specifies the date 57 clear days after the social security benefit ceased being paid and before which SSP is not payable.

Since 5 October 1998, the *Social Security (Welfare to Work) Regulations 1998* (*SI 1998 No 2231*) have made provisions for certain people to have their entitlement to Incapacity Benefit or Severe Disablement Allowance protected, by giving them a 52-week linking period with their recent benefit claim. These are individuals:

- receiving Incapacity Benefit or Severe Disablement Allowance; and
- starting, or returning to, work within seven days of the last day of benefit entitlement and notifying the Benefits Agency within one month that he or she has done so.

The employer is not liable to pay SSP for any PIW commencing before the 52-week link date shown on the form.

From 5 October 1998, the following new linking letters have been introduced:

Checklist: Linking Letters

(a) Form BF220A is an eight-week linking letter but indicates that the employee may be entitled to a 52-week linking period.

(b) Form BF220B is a 52-week linking letter for those formerly on Incapacity Benefit or Severe Disablement Allowance qualifying as a 'Welfare to Work' beneficiary.

(c) Form BF220C is an eight-week linking letter for those not entitled to Incapacity Benefit or Severe Disablement Allowance.

The employer may wish to consider issuing the following letter to all new employees.

Sample Form: Linking Letter

> The following information is required for SSP purposes.
>
> Have you recently (within the last 52 weeks) been in receipt of any of the following state benefits?
>
> Incapacity Benefit YES/NO (delete as appropriate)
>
> Severe Disablement Allowance YES/NO (delete as appropriate)
>
> If yes, my benefit claim was stopped on .... and I enclose a DWP 'linking letter'.
>
> Signature of employee .... Date ....

Employers not in receipt of a linking letter from the employee may wish to check with their local Benefits Agency office to see if there is a link with a social security benefit in cases where a PIW arises within the first 52 weeks of a new employee starting work. This will reduce of the risk of an employer wrongly paying SSP to an employee.

Any payment of SSP made to a 'Welfare to Work' beneficiary who has continued entitlement to Incapacity Benefit will have been wrongly paid (see **9.6**). If the employer makes such a payment he or she may recover the amount paid from the employee concerned and then make good any erroneous recovery made under the Percentage Threshold Scheme (see **8.2**), in the same way as he or she would correct any other incorrect payment of SSP.

If an employee leaves his or her employment and the employer holds a linking letter which is still current in respect of that employee, the employer must return the linking letter to the departing employee so that it can be presented to any new employer.

Stoppage of Work [5.5]

An employee is excluded from receiving SSP if on the first day of the PIW (or linked PIW) there is a stoppage of work at the employee's place of employment due to a trade dispute. This is unless the employee can prove that at no time did he or she have a direct interest in or participate in the dispute in question up to and including the first day of the PIW. If the employee was absent due to sickness before the dispute began, he or she is not excluded from receiving SSP. Trade dispute means a strike, walkout, lockout or any other dispute about work. If there is a disagreement about whether or not an employee has participated in, or had a direct interest in, a stoppage, the employee can ask an Officer of the Board of Inland Revenue to decide the matter (see **10.4**).

> *i* In practice, linked PIWs count as one. It is the situation at the start of the first PIW with the employer that counts when deciding if SSP is payable or not.

If the trade disputes ends but the employee is still unable to work, the employer cannot pay SSP because it is the beginning of the PIW, that is the first point of consideration in determining SSP liability.

If the employer is forced to 'lay-off' an employee because of an industrial dispute elsewhere but their contract of service continues, SSP will be payable if they satisfy the other qualifying conditions, unless they have a direct interest in the trade dispute.

Pregnancy [5.6]

Generally, there is no entitlement to SSP for a PIW during the disqualifying period. Where the woman is entitled to SMP (or the State Maternity Allowance (MA)) the disqualifying period correlates to her maternity pay (or MA) period of 26 weeks. Where, however, the woman is not entitled to SMP (or MA) she is not entitled to SSP for a period of 18 weeks.

In the case of an employee who is or has been pregnant and is entitled to either SMP or MA, entitlement to SSP ceases on the day immediately preceding the beginning of the disqualifying period. However, this does not apply to an employee if her pregnancy terminated before the beginning of the disqualifying period otherwise than by confinement.

A woman's maternity pay (or MA) period will begin on the day following the day on which she is absent from work wholly or partly because of pregnancy or confinement, which falls on or after the beginning of the fourth week before the EWC, but not later than the week immediately following the week in which she is confined. (Typically a week for SMP or MA purposes begins on a Sunday, but in exceptional circumstances the maternity pay period or MA period can begin on any day of the week. Where such circumstances apply, a week means a period of seven consecutive days, which may or may not begin on a Sunday.) If the absence is not related to pregnancy or confinement the woman's maternity pay (or MA) period does not automatically start.

Examples

1. Naishel has been absent from work because of a pregnancy-related illness since 14 January 2004. Her EWC is the week beginning Sunday, 2 May 2004. Because she is incapable of work on Sunday, 4 April, which is the first day of the fourth week before the EWC, her entitlement to SSP ceases on 3 April and her maternity pay period begins on 4 April. A period of entitlement to SSP cannot arise for 26 weeks, ie not until 3 October 2004.

2. Myleene is first incapable of work for a pregnancy-related reason on Wednesday, 9 June 2004. Her EWC is the week commencing Sunday, 27 June 2004. Myleene's maternity pay period begins on Thursday 10 June 2004. There is no entitlement to SSP for the absence on 9 June 2004.

The position is somewhat different for a woman who is not entitled to SMP or MA. If she is incapable of work wholly or partly because of pregnancy or confinement on any day which falls on or after the beginning of the fourth week before her EWC, entitlement to SSP does not arise in respect of a PIW where the first day in that period falls within 18 weeks of the beginning of:

- the fourth week before the EWC; or
- if earlier, the week in which the woman was confined.

> ***Example***
>
> Gaynor is not entitled to SMP or MA. She is expecting her baby in the week commencing, Sunday 4 April 2004. She stops work on Thursday, 1 April 2004, as she is incapable of work because of her pregnancy. She will not be entitled to SSP from Sunday 28 March to Saturday 31 July.

Where the woman had begun a period of incapacity for work, which entitles (or would entitle) her to SSP, and is:

- pregnant or has been confined; and
- incapable of work wholly or partly because of pregnancy or confinement on any day which falls on or after the beginning of the fourth week before the expected week of confinement; and
- not entitled to SMP or MA;

the period of entitlement ends on that day or, if earlier, on the day she was confined.

> *i* In practice, an employee who is pregnant and is incapable of work can receive SSP unless she is absent from work due to an illness which is connected to her pregnancy within the four weeks before her EWC.

> ***Example***
>
> Mary is not entitled to SMP or MA. She has been sick with an illness unrelated to her pregnancy from 3 May 2004. Mary gives birth on 21 May. If the qualifying conditions are met, the employer should pay Mary SSP up to and including 21 May and give her Form SSP1 from 22 May.

Where a PIW starts during or continues into the disqualifying period, SSP is not payable for any subsequent linked PIW (see **11.9** for further information about linking).

Low Average Earnings [5.7]

As part of the procedures for establishing entitlement to SSP it is necessary to calculate the employee's average weekly earnings in at least an eight-week period immediately before the first day of the PIW (see **6.17**). If the average weekly earnings are below the National Insurance LEL, which applied on the first day of the PIW, then the employee is excluded.

> ***Example***
>
> Lawrence works on a part-time basis. On 1 April 2003, he starts a PIW. His average weekly earnings for this PIW are £76.00. Although the PIW continues into the 2003/04 tax year when the LEL is increased to £77.00, he is entitled to SSP as his average earnings reached the LEL, which applied at the first day of the PIW (£75 tax year 2002/03). A tax year runs from 6 April to next 5 April.

Where there are linked PIWs it is the period prior to the first PIW which is used for calculating average earnings. If an employee has average weekly earnings below the LEL at the start of the PIW and is therefore not eligible for SSP they remain ineligible for the rest of the PIW and any subsequent linked PIW, even if their earnings fluctuate subsequently.

> ***Example***
>
> Paul was sick from 6 May to 16 May 2003 and received SSP. Paul reduced his hours in June and as a consequence his earnings are now below the LEL for NICs. Paul is sick again from 9 July to 18 July. Here, the PIWs are separated by less than 56 days, they link and so Paul is entitled to SSP even though his earnings in the eight weeks before 9 July 2003 are below the LEL.

Legal Custody [5.8]

An employee is excluded from receiving SSP during any period in which he or she is detained in legal custody or sentenced to a term of imprisonment (but not including cases where the sentence is suspended).

Legal custody means detained, kept in custody or in prison; not voluntarily helping police with their enquiries. Entitlement will stop for an employee if he or she is taken into legal custody and cannot resume in that PIW or any linked PIW even after he or she is later released on bail.

New Employees [5.9]

An employee who has done no work under a contract of service when the PIW begins cannot receive SSP. As soon as an employee has done some work, even a few minutes' work, they can qualify for SSP. However, if the employee reports sick instead of turning up on their first day, SSP is not due.

If an employee has a contract of service, which begins 56 days, that is eight weeks, or less after the end of their previous contract with the same employer, the two contracts will link and count as one. If the employee had worked under the first contract, but had done no work under the second linking contract when the PIW began, they would be entitled to SSP if the other qualifying conditions were met.

Outside the United Kingdom [5.10]

Until 6 April 1996 an employee was excluded from receiving SSP if at any time on the first day of the PIW (or a linked PIW) he or she was outside the territory of the European Economic Area (EEA). The EEA comprises of the following countries.

Checklist: EEA Countries

Austria, Belgium, Denmark, Finland, France, Germany, Gibraltar, Greece, Iceland, Eire, Italy, Liechtenstein, Luxembourg, Netherlands, Norway, Portugal, Spain, Sweden and the United Kingdom.

Similarly, any PIW came to an end (and so SSP ceased to be payable) as soon as an employee left the territory of the EEA. However, from 6 April 1996, employees who fall sick outside the EEA or who go outside the EEA during a period of sickness are entitled to SSP provided that they satisfy the qualifying conditions. This extension of SSP entitlement applies to these employees who are on holiday and those who are sent temporarily to work outside the EEA by their UK employer.

Employers are not, however, liable to pay SSP to those employees who work outside the UK on a long-term basis if the employer has no liability to pay Class 1 NICs on behalf of those employees. If an employee's PIW or linked PIW continues but the liability of the employer to pay Class 1 NICs ceases, the employee continues to be entitled to SSP until his or her entitlement stops for another reason (eg the employee has received the maximum 28 weeks' entitlement) (see **7.4**).

Case study: overseas secondment

Roy is sent to work in Japan on Wednesday 2 January 2003 by his UK employer. Japan and the United Kingdom have signed a Double

Contributions Convention to cover NIC liability for the first 52 contribution weeks of a detached duty.

Roy falls ill on 14 July 2003 to 24 July 2003, but he qualifies for SSP, as his UK employer is still liable to pay Class 1 NICs for the first 52 weeks of the seconded duty.

Roy becomes sick again from 31 December 2003 to 9 February 2004. Although the employer's liability for Class 1 NICs ceases from week beginning Sunday 4 January 2004 as he will have worked abroad for 52 contribution weeks, he can qualify for SSP for the whole of that PIW.

If Roy is sick on or before 7 April 2004 the PIWs will link (56 days or less since end of last PIW on 9 February 2004), the employer will need to continue paying SSP. If Roy is sick on or after 8 April 2004 the PIWs will not link and he cannot qualify for SSP, if he is still outside the United Kingdom, and the employer is not liable to pay Class 1 NICs.

If Roy returns to the UK to resume his normal UK duties, then entitlement to SSP can be considered afresh, applying the normal SSP eligibility rules (including linking PIWs), as the employer will recommence liability to pay Class 1 NICs.

Questions and Answers [5.11]

Question

How do I know if one of my employees is over 65 years of age?

Answer

The employer may hold a certificate of age exception, Form CA4140 or CF384, for male employees, where they have reached 65 years of age. Otherwise, the employer should see sight of some other definite proof that the employee has reached aged 65, for example, a birth certificate. The employer is responsible for any overpayment of SSP. The certificate of age exception gives a 'valid from' date and this is the date the employee has reached State Pension Age (currently 65 for a male).

Question

Linking letters seem very important when considering SSP, but we as an employer have never seen one – are we missing something?

Answer

Probably not. There are a number of different linking letters that can be issued, but in practice they are issued relatively rarely in relation to the number of SSP cases that arise in the UK. However, it is important that employers check with the employee, if they are sick for four or more calendar days in a row, within 52 weeks of starting work, to see if they have a linking letter, in order to avoid overpaying SSP.

Question

Why does there have to be an earning qualification for SSP?

Answer

An employee whose average weekly earnings are below the LEL for NIC purposes are not entitled to SSP. This primarily affects those employees that are working part-time of which by far the majority are women. So it could be argued that an earnings threshold amounts to indirect sex discrimination. It is understood that the Government is reviewing the imposition of the average earnings qualification rule.

Question

How do we know if an employee is taken into legal custody?

Answer

It is the responsibility of the employee to advise their employer if they are taken into legal custody. This means being kept in custody by the police or detained in prison. Legal custody does not include helping the police voluntarily with their enquiries.

6. How to Calculate Payments

Introduction [6.1]

The *Social Security and Housing Benefits Act 1982* first introduced SSP and it was originally payable at one of three rates depending on the employee's average earnings (see **6.15**).

The three rates were subsequently reduced to just two rates. The lower rate was payable to all employees whose average earnings were on or above the current LEL but less than a specified earnings threshold. The standard (or higher) rate was payable to all employees whose average earnings were not less than the earnings threshold.

The earnings band was determined by reference to the average weekly earnings before the PIW began (or the first PIW in a linked PIW began). Therefore, a change in earnings during a PIW did not affect SSP payments.

From April 1990 the standard rate remained unchanged although the lower rate was reviewed normally to coincide with the start of the tax year. The *Statutory Sick Pay Act 1991* extended the coverage of the lower rate SSP across the whole range of earnings bands on which employers paid lower rates of NICs. As a result the higher rate of SSP, which was payable to those with weekly earnings of £125 or more during 1990/91, became payable to those earning £185 or more a week in 1991/92.

The SSP payment rates from 6 April 1990 to 5 April 1995 were as follows.

Year	Lower rate SSP (weekly rate)	Standard rate SSP (weekly rate)	Average weekly earnings
	£	£	£
1990/91	39.25	52.50	125.00
1991/92	43.50	52.50	185.00
1992/93	45.30	52.50	190.00
1993/94	46.95	52.50	195.00
1994/95	47.80	52.50	200.00

Single Weekly Rate of Payment [6.2]

The *Social Security (Incapacity for Work) Act 1994* abolished, with effect from 6 April 1995, the lower rate of SSP payment. Since the 1995/96 tax year, SSP has been payable at one unified weekly rate irrespective of the employee's average weekly earnings provided that they are not less than the LEL applying at the start of the employee's PIW. The Inland Revenue updates the new unitary weekly rate of SSP by issuing a Statutory Instrument and this is usually laid before Parliament, shortly after the rate has been announced in the Chancellor's Pre-Budget Report. The Pre-Budget statement is normally made in November and published on the Inland Revenue web pages at www.inlandrevenue.gov.uk

The SSP payment rates from 6 April 1995 to 5 April 2003 were as follows.

Year	Rate of SSP (weekly rate)
	£
1995/96	52.50
1996/97	54.55
1997/98	55.70
1998/99	57.70
1999/00	59.55
2000/01	60.20
2001/02	62.20
2002/03	63.25
2003/04	64.35

SSP Daily Rate [6.3]

Although stated in the SSP legislation as a weekly rate, SSP is payable to all eligible employees at a daily rate. The daily rate is found by dividing the weekly rate applicable on the day that SSP is due to be paid by the number of QDs which fall in that same week (beginning with Sunday).

The following table gives the daily rates (for 2003/04) of SSP payable at £64.35 a week depending on the number of QDs in the week in which SSP is payable. The rates given are unrounded and are values used by computer software payroll systems for calculating SSP payments.

Number of qualifying days in week in which SSP payable	Unrounded daily rate
	£
7	9.1929
6	10.7250
5	12.8700
4	16.0875
3	21.4500
2	32.1750
1	64.3500

SSP Rounding Rules [6.4]

SSP legislation requires that the total amount of SSP payable to an employee, which includes any fraction of a penny to be rounded up the next whole number of pence.

Example

Ann is sick during tax year 2003/04, the weekly rate of SSP is £64.35 a week. If one day of SSP is payable to Ann and her QDs are Monday to Saturday in that week, Ann should be paid £10.73 rather than £10.72, using the six QD daily rate value.

The following table gives the rounded rates of SSP payable depending on the number of QDs in the week in which SSP is payable and the number of days in that week for which SSP is actually due to be paid. That is the number of QDs on which the employee is sick, which are not treated as waiting days.

The table uses a unified weekly SSP rate of £64.35 (2003/04 rate).

No of QDs	Number of days for which SSP is paid						
	1	2	3	4	5	6	7
	£	£	£	£	£	£	£
7	9.20	18.39	27.58	36.78	45.97	55.16	64.35
6	10.73	21.45	32.18	42.90	53.63	64.35	
5	12.87	25.74	38.61	51.48	64.35		
4	16.09	32.18	48.27	64.35			
3	21.45	42.90	64.35				
2	32.18	64.35					
1	64.35						

See Appendix 1 for a list of the SSP rounded daily rates in the tax years preceding 2003/04.

Example

Ali works a five-day week Monday to Friday. Each day of the week is a QD. Ali is sick from Monday to Friday and is entitled to SSP at the weekly rate of £64.35 and no waiting days have yet been served in this unlinked PIW.

(a) Monday, Tuesday and Wednesday are the three waiting days and so SSP is not payable for these days. SSP is, however, payable for Thursday and Friday as these are QDs in the PIW.

(b) Since there are five QDs in the week, identify the row in which '5' appears in the 'No of QDs' column.

(c) Since SSP is payable for two days, move across to the column headed by '2'.

(d) This gives the rate of SSP payable to Ali for that week – ie £25.74

Changes in the SSP Daily Rate [6.5]

Using the above rounding rules, the calculation of the daily rate of SSP is relatively straightforward. However, complications can arise in the following circumstances:

- if the number of QDs for an employee varies between the weeks in the PIW (eg the employee works a shift pattern, so that in some weeks he or she has anything between four and seven QDs depending on the number of days he or she is scheduled to work), the daily rate of SSP in the PIW will also vary; and
- if the weekly rate of SSP changes, at the start of a new tax year, ie 6 April, the weekly rate of SSP in the PIW may vary, thereby affecting the daily rate of SSP in that week in the PIW.

This means that it is necessary to determine the number of QDs in that week for each week in which SSP is payable and determine the weekly rate of SSP applicable for each day.

i In practice, for SSP purposes, a week begins on a Sunday. Each week commencing Sunday is treated as a separate pay period for SSP purposes.

Examples

1. Christine's QDs are the days that she is scheduled to work according to a shift rota. During the week commencing Sunday, 7 March 2004 she is scheduled to work each day including Sunday and Saturday. In the following week she is scheduled to work Sunday, Monday and Tuesday only.

Christine commences a PIW on Tuesday, 9 March 2004, returning to work on Tuesday, 16 March. In the first of the two weeks she is absent on five QDs, and in the second on two QDs. As the first three QDs in the PIW are waiting days, Christine is entitled to SSP for four days (12 March to 15 March). For both the 12 and 13 March she is entitled to one-seventh of the weekly rate of SSP, and for both the 14 and 15 March she is entitled to one-third of the weekly rate of SSP.

Using the weekly rate of SSP applicable in 2003/04, Christine would be entitled to:

£18.39 in the first week (£64.35 ÷ 7 = £9.1929 × 2); and

£42.90 in the second week (£64.35 ÷ 3 = £21.4500 × 2)

This makes a total of £61.29 SSP being due to her for the PIW 9–16 March 2004.

2. William has a PIW that starts on 20 March 2003 and ends on 14 April 2003. His QDs are Sundays to Saturdays, i e seven days each week. As the SSP rate increased on 6 April 2003, from £63.25 to £64.35 per week, the daily rounded rate of SSP payable for the period to 5 April 2003 was £9.04 (£63.25 ÷ 7) and the daily rounded rate for 6 April 2003 and beyond is £9.20 (£64.35 ÷ 7).

Thus, the SSP payable for week commencing Sunday 30 March to Saturday 5 April 2003 is £63.42 (£54.22 + £9.20), comprising six days at the 'old' rate of SSP using the unrounded rules (see **6.3**) and one day at the new rate of SSP.

Offsetting SSP [6.6]

If the employer provides OSP (see **12.5**) to employees, the amount of contractual sick pay paid to a sick employee counts towards the amount of SSP that is due. Similarly, if there is a contractual undertaking to pay OSP to an employee, the payment of SSP goes towards satisfying the contractual obligation. This mutual discharge of SSP and contractual remuneration to prevent double payment is referred to as 'offsetting'.

i In practice, if a payment of SSP and a contractual payment are due for different days, they cannot be offset against each other. This rarely happens.

Any entitlement to SSP does not affect any right of an employee to contractual remuneration. However, the level of contractual remuneration does affect the amount of SSP payable. Only remuneration that is earnings for Class 1 NIC purposes can count for offsetting, for example, wages or salary.

Example

Gayle is due contractual pay for a day on which she is entitled to SSP. The amount of contractual pay is £25.00, and the daily rate of SSP is £12.87 (64.35 ÷ 5) for tax year 2003/04. As the contractual pay exceeds the SSP, the employer's liability to pay SSP for that day has been met.

The daily amount of SSP calculated is the minimum due for a day of incapacity to work. If the contractual pay for a day is less than the SSP due for that day, then the minimum amount due for that day is the amount of SSP.

> ***Example***
>
> Harvey works part-time and is on half pay as per his OSP scheme rules. Harvey is therefore only due contractual pay of £12.00 for a day on which SSP is payable in tax year 2003/04. As the daily rate of SSP is £16.09 (64.35 ÷ 4) (ie he has four QDs in a week), the minimum amount of pay for the day is £16.09.

If an employee receives SSP for a day and subsequently it is discovered that he or she is entitled to contractual pay for that day, then the SSP counts towards the contractual pay. If there is contractual pay, eg commission or a bonus, which is not in respect of, or identifiable with, a particular day for which SSP is to be paid, then offsetting between these amounts cannot occur.

> ***Example***
>
> Jerome is a salesperson, paid on a commission-only basis, with no basic wage or salary. In the pay period in which he receives SSP for a PIW, he receives commission which relates to a period prior to the start of the PIW. This payment cannot be used to offset the SSP liability for any day in the PIW.

> **!** It is important to recognise that even though an employee may be due contractual pay and SSP in the same pay period, the pay must relate to the same day of incapacity for work for offsetting to apply.

SSP Relationship with Holiday Pay [6.7]

Contractual pay for a holiday, including a bank, public or annual holiday (whether or not the employee was due to attend work), counts towards any SSP payable for that day. In other words, the holiday pay is treated no differently to any other contractual pay, such as OSP, payable for a QD in a PIW. This is provided the holiday pay counts as earnings for Class 1 NICs.

However, if a holiday does not count as a QD then there may be no SSP for a particular day to offset with contractual pay for that day.

Example

Katrina starts her summer holiday on 11 August 2003, with the intention of returning to work on 28 August 2003, as per her completed holiday form. Her contract of service states that she has five QDs in each week (Monday to Friday) but bank and public holidays do not count as QDs.

While on holiday she falls sick on Tuesday 19 August 2003, only recovering on 28 August. Her waiting days are the 19–21 August. SSP is payable for 22, 26 and 27 August. This is because the 23–24 are not QDs and Monday 25 August is not a QD as it is a Bank Holiday in England and Wales.

The daily rate of SSP for 22 August would be based on five QDs and the daily rate of SSP for 26 and 27 August would be based on four QDs.

When a period of illness occurs during the employee's holiday, the contract of employment should be examined to ascertain whether OSP is payable and, if so, what arrangements (if any) exist for days on holiday to count as QDs for SSP purposes.

Case study: sickness during holiday

Liz works part-time in a factory as a toolmaker and receives payment for her holiday period in advance as per the workplace collective agreement. For each day of the ten working day period she receives £20.00, equivalent to her normal daily rate of pay.

Liz finishes work at lunchtime on Friday 16 May 2003 and flies out for a fortnight in Ibiza for a sun, sea and something else holiday. She arrives and duly downs several cocktails, which makes her somewhat light-headed and she trips and passes out, only to awake in the local hospital with a sprained ankle.

Now Liz is a fastidious woman and whilst packing her suitcase, she also remembers to put in a copy of her contract of employment. On returning to her hotel, she notes that she has sick pay entitlement, equivalent to five days at full pay and five days at half pay, which, under the OSP scheme, replaces her holiday pay. Her QDs are Monday to Friday inclusive as per her normal work pattern.

Heartened by this news, she takes out her pocket calculator and calculates her OSP as follows:

(£20.00 × 5 = £100.00) + (£20.00 × 0.5 × 5 = £50.00) = £150

However, SSP is payable for seven of the ten days (after taking into account the three waiting days), at a daily rate of £12.87: £12.87 × 7 = £90.09.

As the contractual sick pay for five of the days for which SSP is payable is only at half pay, ie £10.00, the minimum payable for these days is £12.87.

Partial offsetting on these five days occurs, but full offsetting occurs for the other two days for which SSP is payable. Thus, the total amount of contractual sick pay and SSP payable for the period of sickness is:

(£20.00 × 5 = £100.00) + (£12.87 × 5 = £64.35) = £164.35.

Under her contract of employment Liz is required to repay the net difference of her total holiday pay of £200, less the amount due of £164.35. She has a gross deficit of £35.65, therefore not making too big a dent in her holiday spending budget.

Furthermore, the contract provides that she will be able to take another holiday later in the year, if the relevant self-certification procedure is followed upon her return. She puts her glad rags on and goes out to celebrate with another night on the town (albeit on crutches).

Holiday or Sick Pay Schemes [6.8]

If an employee contributes to an employer-provided holiday pay or a sick pay scheme, whether directly or indirectly, any payment which he or she receives from this scheme cannot count as remuneration for offsetting purposes, even if the employer distributes it.

However, if the employee and the employer jointly fund the scheme, and payments count as earnings for Class 1 NIC purposes, then a proportion of any payment from the scheme can be used for offsetting against SSP where appropriate.

> ### *Example*
>
> Marlene contributes £3.00 a week to a sickness benefit scheme arranged with an insurance provider, which is matched by an identical contribution by her employer. The scheme pays Marlene £30.00 for each day of sickness. For offsetting purposes the employer can offset £15.00, ie 50%, against any payment of SSP for a day on which Marlene receives a payment from the scheme.

Timing of SSP Payment [6.9]

SSP legislation does not specify a time by which an employer must pay SSP due to an employee. Normally it would be convenient for SSP to be paid on the next pay date with any OSP, which may also be due. If SSP is paid in this way it is less likely that there will be any financial hardship for the employee.

> *i* In practice, employers cannot obtain compensation under the Percentage Threshold Scheme (see **8.2**) by deliberately delaying payment of SSP.

To establish the number of full weeks of SSP to pay, count the number of Saturdays in each earnings period. A full week of SSP commences Sunday to the following Saturday.

There may be weeks when no normal payment of earnings will be made, such as Christmas or summer holidays if the business closes down, or employees may have periods of unpaid leave. In some cases, payment of earnings for the period of closure may have been made early. However, SSP must be paid for all periods of entitlement regardless of whether or not earnings would normally be due for the same period.

Special rules govern the situation where an Inland Revenue officer gives a formal decision (see **10.4**) that the employee is entitled to SSP. The employer must then either appeal that decision within 30 days or pay the SSP to the employee no later than the first normal pay date after the time allowed for appeal expires. If the employer's method of accounting for and paying wages and sick pay prevent payment being made on the first normal pay date, payment must be made no later than the following pay date.

> ### *Example*
>
> An employer operates a computerised monthly payroll. The payroll run is 23 June 2003 for payment due on 30 June 2003. A written decision ➡

that SSP is payable is issued by the Inland Revenue on the 25 June and the employer declines to exercise their right to appeal. The Inland Revenue accepts the employer cannot reasonably pay the SSP on the 30 June but the employer must pay it on 31 July.

Method of Payment [6.10]

SSP may be paid through any usual method of payment (such as cash, cheque or BACS) but may not be paid:

- in kind; nor
- in the form of board and lodging; nor
- by the provision of services.

SSP may lawfully be paid through an agent (eg a payroll bureau or outsourcing service) but it remains the employer's responsibility to ensure that payments are made on time and correctly.

Deductions from SSP [6.11]

SSP is subject to PAYE income tax and Class 1 National Insurance. Deductions which may legally be made from an employee's pay may also be made from SSP; eg employee contributions to an occupational pension scheme. Any other deductions which the employer makes from pay such as trade union subscriptions, student loans and attachment of earnings can also lawfully be made from SSP.

If an employee is paid on a weekly or monthly basis, the amount of SSP will be below the threshold at which Class 1 NICs are payable – this is the Earnings Threshold. For a director, who in strictness has an annual earnings period, any SSP paid must be included as part of the total pay for the tax year. This applies even when the individual payment is below the weekly or monthly LEL.

Pay Statements [6.12]

There is no statutory requirement to show on the employee's pay statement the values of SSP either paid in the current pay period or paid to date within the tax year. However, many employers produce pay statements that itemise all payments. Where this occurs, and there has been offsetting, attention must be given to deciding how the SSP and contractual pay are to be shown. In some cases, just the contractual pay may be shown, but in others both SSP and contractual pay, adjusted as appropriate to reflect offsetting, will be detailed.

> ***Example***
>
> Sam is paid a monthly salary of £1,000, and in the month of July 2003, he receives seven days' SSP, payable at a daily rate of £12.87. His pay statement for this month shows basic pay equivalent to £909.91 and SSP equivalent to £90.09, giving a total gross pay equal to his normal monthly salary.

Recovering SSP Overpayments [6.13]

The timing of receipt of notification of sickness absence by the payroll department frequently means that employees are paid their normal basic pay in a particular pay period even though they have been absent from work due to sickness. If an employer provides no immediate entitlement to OSP, an overpayment of wages or salary will have been made.

The employees' contracts of employment may clearly state that any recovery of an overpayment may be made in the following pay period. Sometimes all that is available for payment to the employee in the next period will be the employee's entitlement to SSP. It is not uncommon company practice, therefore, to recover the overpaid basic pay from the SSP.

Overpayments of earnings can be recovered from SSP. SSP legislation provides for the following:

> 'For the avoidance of doubt, any agreement between an employer and an employee authorising any deductions from SSP, which the employer is liable to pay to the employee in respect of any period shall *not be void* … if the employer:
>
> (a) is authorised by that or another agreement to make the same deductions from any contractual remuneration which he is liable to pay in respect of the same period; or
>
> (b) would be so authorised if he were liable to pay contractual remuneration in respect of that period.'

Therefore, provided the contract of employment gives the employer the right to deduct any overpayment of earnings from later earnings, the deduction can be made from the employee's SSP, even if that is the only earnings receivable by the employee for that later period. A sample clause may read as follows:

> 'Deductions can be made from my wages or salary in respect of any previous overpayment of earnings including SSP.'

> *i* In practice, there is no statutory bar preventing an employer from enforcing a term of a contract of employment whereby an overpayment of earnings is in effect recovered from SSP.

People Unable to Act for Themselves [6.14]

It may be that an employee is so unwell that they cannot act for themselves. If so, and it is not obvious to whom the SSP should be paid, the Inland Revenue office will be able to appoint someone to handle the employee's SSP.

If the Board of the Inland Revenue appoints someone, he or she will take over all the employee's SSP rights and obligations.

He or she will be able to ask for:

- information from the employer;
- formal Inland Revenue decisions; and
- lodge appeals and receive any SSP due.

The employer will be able to ask the appointed representative to supply information about the employee's SSP. The employer can expect the appointed representative to notify incapacity and supply doctor's statements, when appropriate.

The Board of the Inland Revenue appointment will end if the employer is notified that:

- in England and Wales, the Court of Protection has appointed a receiver with power to deal with the employee's SSP;
- in Scotland, the employee's affairs are being handled by a tutor, curator bonis or other guardian acting or appointed in terms of law;
- in Northern Ireland, the Office of Care and Protection has appointed a committee with power to deal with the employee's SSP.

Calculating Average Earnings [6.15]

The calculation of an employee's average earnings is important to establish whether an employee's earnings are deemed to be at or above the LEL used for Class 1 National Insurance purposes. The calculation is therefore most likely to be critical in cases of part-time employees.

Calculating average earnings is often straightforward, and even unnecessary, as in many cases it is obvious from just a glance that an employee's earnings in the relevant period comfortably reach the weekly LEL.

It is important to be clear what counts as a normal pay date.

A normal pay date is defined in SSP legislation as:

- the pay day specified in the contract; or
- the day on which it is the practice in the employee's employment for them to be paid if they have no contract; or
- the day on which it is the practice in the employee's employment for them to be paidif their contract does not specify when they should be paid.

The intention of the legislation is to arrive at a representative level of average earnings; however it is by no means an exact science.

In order to calculate the average weekly earnings it is necessary to identify:

- the relevant period (see **6.17**);
- the earnings in the relevant period that must be used in the average earnings calculation; and
- the National Insurance weekly LEL applicable on the first day of the PIW, although from 6 April 2001 an employee does not start paying Class 1 NICs until his or her earnings exceed the Employees' Earnings Threshold.

Definition of Earnings [6.16]

All payments on which Class 1 NICs are due count towards the calculation (and so this will include any SSP payments themselves). The gross figure before any deductions must be used.

Gross pay for Class 1 NIC purposes includes the following:

Checklist: Class 1 NIC Earnings

(a) Wages or salary.

(b) Overtime.

(c) Holiday pay.

(d) SMP.

(e) Commission, including any unusual payments, such as an annual bonus.

(f) Round sum allowances.

(g) Gains from unapproved share options where certain conditions are met etc.

This list is not exhaustive. 'Earnings' also includes, amongst other things, the profit element of other payments liable to Class 1 NIC, such as payment of an employee's private telephone bill or excess mileage allowances paid for use of his or her own private vehicle on business travel.

It does not include:

- the taxable benefit of a company car and car fuel, which attracts an employer-only Class 1A liability;
- items that attract Class 1B National Insurance as included in an employer's PAYE Settlement Agreement;
- money drawn by directors in anticipation of voting; and
- the Working Tax Credit (previously Working Families and Disabled Persons Tax Credits).

Relevant Period [6.17]

The general rule is that earnings are added together over the eight weeks up to and including the last normal pay date i e before the start of the PIW, or in the case of a subsequent linked PIW, the start of the first PIW.

i In practice, the Inland Revenue refers to this period between (a) the last normal pay date before the start of the PIW and (b) the last normal pay date falling at least eight weeks before (a) as the relevant period.

The use of the term 'normal pay date' can sometimes complicate the calculation (see **6.15**).

> ***Example***
>
> Winifred is paid monthly. She starts a PIW on 14 November 2003. Her last normal pay date before this is 29 October 2003. The last normal pay date at least eight weeks before that is 29 August 2003. The relevant period is therefore 30 August 2003 to 29 October 2003.

Weekly Paid **[6.18]**

Average weekly earnings for weekly paid employees are normally calculated by averaging the employee's gross earnings on the last eight pay dates before the start of the employee's PIW or linked PIW. In most cases, the employer adds together these eight payments and divides the sum by eight. However, all payments in the relevant period must be taken into account.

Example

Lawrence is away from work, sick from the 1 April to 8 April and he is paid each Tuesday. The relevant period is determined as being the 29 January to 25 March 2003. During this period he received the following payments:

Pay date	£	Pay date	£
4 February 2003	60.00	4 March 2003	50.00
11 February 2003	40.00	7 March 2003	70.00
14 February 2003	10.00	11 March 2003	50.00
18 February 2003	50.00	18 March 2003	50.00
21 February 2003	50.00	25 March 2003	40.00
25 February 2003	50.00	Total	520.00

The additional payments on 14 and 21 February and 7 March 2003 are for late submissions of overtime and a quarterly bonus. The number of weeks in the relevant period is eight, which gives average gross weekly earnings of £65 per week. Therefore, average earnings have not reached the LEL, so SSP cannot be considered.

Lawrence's pay day on 28 January 2003 is not included as the relevant period starts on the day *after* the normal pay day that is at least eight ➡

weeks before the last normal pay day before the start of the PIW on 1 April. The last normal pay date, in Lawrence's case, is 25 March 2003.

Employees can also be paid in multiples of weeks (eg fortnightly, three-weekly, four-weekly, five-weekly). All the earnings in the relevant period (see **6.17**) should be added together and divided by the number of weeks in the relevant period. In many cases it will simply be sufficient to divide the total earnings in the relevant period by eight.

However, if say, a part-time employee is paid every month (see **6.20**), but in multiples of weeks on a four/five-weekly basis and his total earnings in the relevant period before the start of his PIW are £585, the average weekly earnings are £65, calculated as £585 ÷ 9 = £65.

Mistimed Payments [6.19]

Normal regular payments of earnings are sometimes made early or late. For instance, a pay date may be brought forward at Christmas, due to normal pay date falling on or near a public holiday. Where the relevant period contains more or less than eight weeks' pay or is it is not an exact number of weeks, the total earnings should be divided by the number of weeks covered by the payments rather than by the number of weeks in the relevant period.

Example

Xavier is paid weekly. He starts a PIW on 13 October 2003. His last normal pay day before this was 9 October 2003 . The last normal pay day at least eight weeks before this was 14 August 2003. However, Xavier received no pay on either 21 or 28 August as he was on holiday. He received two weeks' holiday pay in advance on 14 August. There are, therefore, only six weeks' earnings in the relevant period and the divisor of six rather than eight should be used in determining average earnings in the relevant period.

i In practice, this interpretation of the SSP legislation, which has been in force since 1998, applies only to regular payments of earnings. Any other payments made during the relevant period such as irregular payments (see **6.21**) of bonus or commission must still be included in the normal way.

Monthly Paid [6.20]

The calculation of average earnings for monthly paid employees uses the same principle as for those employees paid weekly or in multiples of a week.

Checklist: Average Earnings Calculation – Monthly Payees

(a) Establish the relevant period, ie the period between the last normal pay date before the start of the PIW and that falling at least eight weeks before the pay date.

(b) Aggregate together the gross earnings (pay that incurs a Class 1 NIC liability) in the relevant period.

(c) Divide by the total number of months in the relevant period to give the average weekly earnings (if it is not a whole number of months, round to the nearest whole number).

(d) Multiply by 12.

(e) Divide by 52.

Example

Geeta is sick from 18 December to 26 December 2003. Her contract does not specify when she is paid. It is her employer's practice to pay employees their December salary early but, apart from that, employees are paid on the last working day of each month.

The last normal pay date before the start of her PIW is 16 December 2003. The last pay day at least eight weeks before that is 30 September 2003. The period over which to average the employee's earnings is 1 October 2003 to 16 December 2003. In that period, the employer paid Geeta £647 on 31 October, £535 on 28 November and £645 on 16 December.

Total earnings in the period = £1,827.

The payment covers three months (two months and 16 days is rounded up).

£1,827 ÷ 3 = £609

£609 × 12 = £7,308

£7,308 ÷ 52 = £140.53846 average weekly earnings

If there is not a whole number of calendar months in the relevant period, then where the month contains 30 or 31 days, 15 days or less is rounded down and 16 days or more is rounded up. Where the employee has both weekly and monthly pay date(s) within the relevant period eg their pay frequency changes, each is calculated separately to establish the average weekly earnings.

Case study: average earnings calculation for part-time employee

Throughout 2003, Trudy, a young mum, worked part-time as a kitchen help for a large oil company in its corporate headquarters restaurant. She worked Monday to Friday from 1.00 pm to 2.30 pm and was paid weekly at the rate of £8.00 per hour. Occasionally, if a special function was organised, Trudy was offered extra hours' work at the same rate of pay.

The company operated a discretionary bonus scheme, which that year provided Trudy with a £200 bonus. However, as one door opened with the money generated from the bonus, another one slammed shut, quite literally in fact, causing her arm to be fractured in two places.

This happened on the Monday following payment of her bonus in November 2003. Her husband phoned her employer the same day to explain that she had broken her arm and could not come into work and that the injury was expected to keep her off work for four weeks. She provided the necessary medical evidence, after completing a self-certificate for the first seven calendar days. On the eight previous pay dates before the PIW began, her earnings were as follows:

Week 1	£60
Week 2	£70
Week 3	£60
Week 4	£60
Week 5	£60
Week 6	£80
Week 7	£60
Week 8	£60 + £200

Mr Know-all, the Payroll Manager, quickly looking at her basic wage, telephones Trudy to advise that as her earnings were below the

National Insurance LEL (£77.00 a week for 2003/04), she was ineligible to be considered for SSP. He said he would issue a Change-over Form SSP1 (see **7.10**), which she should use to try and claim State benefit from the Department of Work and Pensions. Trudy was upset and rang her husband at his accountancy practice. Surprisingly for an accountant, he knew something about the mechanics of payroll and remembering the annual bonus his wife had received, did his own average earnings calculation.

He established that if Trudy had not been paid the bonus, her average weekly earnings would have been £63.75 (ie £510 ÷ 8) and this was below the National Insurance LEL. However, all gross earnings over the previous eight weeks must be included in the calculation. Therefore, counting the £200 bonus payment, Trudy's average weekly earnings were £88.75 (£710 ÷ 8). This was greater than the weekly LEL and so she was entitled to SSP at the rate of £64.35 for each of the four weeks she was absent, subject to the normal eligibility and entitlement rules. He telephoned Mr Know-all, who reluctantly agreed with the calculation, mumbled a vague apology, blamed the computer, tore up the SSP1 Form and put through the SSP payment in time for the next payroll run.

Irregular or Other Pay Intervals [6.21]

When employees are paid at other intervals, the average weekly earnings are calculated using the following procedure.

Checklist: Irregular Payments Calculation

(a) Establish the relevant period: this is the period between the last normal pay date before the start of the PIW and that falling at least eight weeks before the pay date.

(b) Aggregate together the gross earnings (pay that incurs a Class 1 NIC liability) in the relevant period.

(c) Divide by the total number of days in the relevant period.

(d) Multiply by seven.

Example

Ron is paid on a commission basis at irregular intervals. He is sick from 21 November 2003 to 1 December 2003. The last pay date ➡

before the start of the PIW is 15 August 2003. The last pay date at least eight weeks before that is 30 May 2003. Therefore, the relevant period is 31 May 2003 to 15 August 2003.

His earnings in that period were:

11 June 2003	£1200.54
2 July 2003	£1649.16
15 August 2003	£6494.46
Total	£9344.16

Number of days in the relevant period = 77

Average weekly earnings = £9344.16 ÷ 77 × 7 = £849.46904

New Employees [6.22]

In the case of new employees, average weekly earnings are calculated as follows where the employee has not worked long enough for the earnings rules to apply.

Employees in receipt of at least one payment, but which does not cover eight weeks at the start of the PIW, should have average weekly earnings 'calculated as if the period for which all the earnings under his contract of service received … were the relevant period'. So, if the employee has only received three days' pay, the relevant period is three days.

For an employee who has not been paid at all before the start of the PIW, his or her contractual remuneration per week is taken as the gross weekly earnings. The average weekly earnings will be:

- normal contractual earnings for a week's work;
- normal contractual earnings for a month's work, multiplied by 12 and divided by 52; or
- annual salary divided by 52.

Examples

1. Anthea is sick from 18 July 2003 to 25 July 2003. It is the practice of the employer to pay all employees on the last working day of each month. Employment commenced on 19 May 2003, 13 days before the end of the month. The last normal pay date before the start of PIW is

27 June 2003. The last normal pay date at least eight weeks before that is 30 April 2003 but this does not apply to the new employee. Therefore, the relevant period is 19 May 2003 to 27 June 2003, that is the period of employment to the last normal pay date before the PIW started.

Their earnings in that period were:

30 May 2003	£500.54
27 June 2003	£1340.76

Total £1841.30

Number of months in the relevant period = 1 (1 month and 14 days rounded down).

Average weekly earnings = £1841.30 ÷ 1 × 12 ÷ 52 = £424.91538

2. Brian starts work on 3 November 2003 at an annual salary of £15,000 paid monthly in equal amounts. He receives no other remuneration. He starts a PIW on 17 November, one day before his first normal pay date. As he has received no payments in the period before his PIW, his average weekly earnings are calculated as follows: £15,000 ÷ 52 = £288.46153.

If a new employee has worked for the same employer before but under a previous contract, the previous earnings do not count towards the calculation of average earnings in the current contract. The earnings of an employee in a previous employment are not taken into account for the purpose of calculating average weekly earnings. However, if the contract is legally treated as continuous under the *Transfer of Undertakings (Protection of Employment) Regulations 1981 (SI 1981 No 1794)*, the new employer must count the earlier earnings.

If the employee has more than one consecutive contract of service with the same employer and the period between the contracts is less than eight weeks, the length of the contracts should be treated as one linked contract. The average earnings calculation will include earnings over a period of at least eight weeks, excluding the periods between contracts, but pay dates in a previous contract can be taken into account if there are not enough pay dates in a second or further contract to establish the relevant period.

An employee who has done no work for the employer under his or her contract of employment has no entitlement to SSP.

Directors [6.23]

The calculation of the average weekly earnings for SSP purposes of any director of a limited company that is paid contractually on a weekly or monthly basis should be carried out in exactly the same way as for employees in general (see **6.18**).

> **!** A director may not have reached the annual Earnings Threshold for Class 1 NIC purposes but the income for any week or month may have exceeded the weekly LEL and as such would qualify for SSP.

In the case of directors who are paid as a result of an annual voting of fees it is important to note that any money drawn in advance of the voting is not classified as earnings for the purposes of calculating average weekly earnings. Only the amount voted annually is included in the calculation and the date of the vote is the 'normal pay date' that must be used. If the director is paid contractually and by annual vote, the amount voted can be included in the average earnings calculation and treated in the same way as a bonus payment for an ordinary employee.

PAYE Settlement Agreements [6.24]

Items included in a PAYE Settlement Agreement (PSA) are not subject to Class 1 National Insurance but the employer has a Class 1B National Insurance liability. Such items should not normally be included in average earnings calculations. However, if:

(a) an employee's average earnings have been calculated as below the LEL; and

(b) he or she has earnings, which would otherwise attract a Class 1 NIC liability within the relevant period (see **6.17**) and these have been included in a PSA;

then average earnings should be recalculated to include the earnings that would have been subject to Class 1 NIC, if the PSA had not been in force.

> ***Example***
>
> Rae starts a PIW and her average weekly earnings are calculated as £73.23 for the tax year 2003/04. On the face of it she is excluded from SSP, as her average weekly earnings have not reached the LEL for NIC purposes. However, in the relevant period, Rae is also in receipt of a £50 Marks & Spencer voucher and her employer includes this ➡

within the scope of the company's PSA. But if the employer had not included this voucher in the PSA, it would have been treated as a non-cash voucher, which incurs a Class 1 NIC liability. Hence, her average weekly earnings are £79.48 and she satisfies the earnings condition for SSP.

Questions and Answers [6.25]

Question

Where do employers find out about the various changes in SSP payment rates?

Answer

The Inland Revenue publishes annually, free of charge, a guidance booklet E14 entitled 'What to do if your employee is sick'. This is sent automatically to all employers with a current PAYE Scheme Reference number. This booklet contains the current SSP daily rates tables. The weekly rate is usually announced in the November or December preceding the start of the relevant tax year and the figure is usually posted on the Inland Revenue web pages at www.inlandrevenue.gov.uk

Question

If an employee claims that he or she sick whilst on annual leave, do we have to let them retake their holiday at a later date?

Answer

Not if you don't want to. The employee is entitled to a statutory minimum period of annual leave, currently set at four weeks (pro-rated). However, there is no provision in statute for the employee to be able to retake holiday if they are ill for part or all of that leave period. Some employers view such a scenario sympathetically and allow the employee to take holiday later on within the same holiday year. Any payment of SSP can be offset against holiday pay paid for the same day(s) of incapacity.

Question

We have overpaid one of our employees; can we recover this from SSP now due for payment?

Answer

Yes, provided the contract of employment gives the employer the right to deduct any overpayment of wages or salary from such earnings. However, the Inland Revenue has pointed out that sickness is often a time of hardship and this is especially so if an employee does not enjoy the protection offered by an OSP scheme. In such circumstances, an Inland Revenue inspector might urge an employer to recover any earlier overpayment from the earnings due for the first full pay period falling after the employee has returned to work. Such a policy would avoid a sick employee possibly receiving no pay at all at the beginning of a period of sickness. The Inland Revenue adds, however, that there is no legal requirement to delay making recovery of an overpayment until the end of the PIW.

Question

Do employers have to deduct PAYE income tax and Class 1 NICs from payments of SSP?

Answer

Yes, in theory. Although given the current weekly rate of SSP (£64.35) compared to the weekly earnings and PAYE threshold (£89.00) for NIC and tax purposes, then no deduction may be due from SSP payments, where this is the only payment due to be made in a particular earnings period.

Question

Can we pay SSP as part of our flexible benefits system?

Answer

SSP can be paid by whatever means the employer prefers. However, it cannot be paid in kind, so the employee cannot opt to 'give up' any SSP entitlement in exchange, for say, enrolment in the employer's private healthcare scheme.

Question

Our Company operates an annual closure for three weeks during the summer. We pay holiday pay in advance for those weeks, in order that we are not required to run our normal payroll during that time. What should happen re employees that are sick during the closure?

Answer

If the employer is not running a payroll during the period of closure and it is known in advance that the employee will remain sick during that period, then SSP for that period should be paid on the last normal pay date prior to the closure. If the employer does not know in advance that the employee will remain sick, any SSP payment due for the weeks during the closure should be made on the first normal pay date after the business re-opens.

Question

We are a large firm of chartered accountants and all our employees earn well in excess of the LEL, so why do we need to bother about average earnings calculations?

Answer

It is true, that for most employees, it will be obvious to the employer if their earnings reach or exceed the LEL and therefore performing the detailed average earnings calculation is unnecessary for SSP eligibility purposes. However, sometimes employee's earnings vary, perhaps due to unpaid sickness or leave, so employers need to be aware of the average earnings rules to ensure no overpayment of SSP occurs to any individual employee.

Question

We have mutually agreed with one of our employees to terminate their employment contract immediately. There is no entitlement or option contained in the employment contract to make a payment in lieu of notice. We therefore intend to make a payment in lieu as damages for the breach. What should we do regarding our liability to pay SSP during the 'notional' period of notice?

➡

Answer

When an Employment Tribunal, a Court or parties to a termination settlement calculate damages they will often follow the principle that a person must not be placed in a better or worse position than if the contract had actually been carried out. For example, in this case the employer has failed to give proper notice of termination to an employee, and there is no contractual provision or expectation relating to payments in lieu of notice. The employer has breached the contract and the employee can claim damages.

The damages are first calculated by reference to the pay that the employee would have received during the notice period if proper notice had been given. Therefore, the minimum entitlement is the level of pay afforded under the SSP legislation. However, the contract has been terminated, so no SSP is actually payable. The main reason for terminating the employment contract must not be to avoid paying SSP, otherwise the employer will remain liable to pay SSP until the employee is excluded for some other reason.

7 Stopping SSP Payments

Introduction [7.1]

The employer's liability to pay SSP will usually end because the employee's incapacity for work under the contract ends, eg they return to work or stop sending doctor's statements. The liability to pay SSP ends after the last QD of the employee's sickness.

There are a number of other reasons for SSP liability to end.

Checklist: Ceasing SSP Payments

An employer does not have to pay SSP for any day after their:

(a) employee's contract of service ends (see **7.2**);

(b) employee has been due 28 weeks' SSP in a PIW or linked PIW (see **7.4**);

(c) employee's linked PIW with the same employer has run for three years (see **7.5**);

(d) employee's disqualifying period related to her pregnancy begins (see **5.6**);

(e) employee is taken into legal custody; (see **5.8**);

(f) employee goes outside the United Kingdom and the employer does not have a liability for Class 1 NICs, or would not if the employee's earnings were high enough; (see **5.10**);

(g) employee dies (see **11.4**).

Contract of Service Ends [7.2]

If the contract of employment has ended, other than because the employer has terminated it in order to avoid paying SSP (see **11.5**), there is no liability to pay SSP for any days after the termination date.

Where a worker has found work with a client through an employment agency (see **11.3**), the contract does not come to an end until the client no longer requires any worker. If they require a replacement for a sick worker then the contract continues.

Maximum SSP Liability in a PIW [7.3]

An employer is only liable to pay a maximum 28 weeks' SSP, ie 28 times the weekly rate, in any one PIW (or set of linked PIWs). After 28 weeks in a PIW the employee becomes excluded from the SSP scheme for the rest of that PIW. The 28-week limit relates only to a PIW or linked PIWs. If there has been a period of more than 56 days between two PIWs, the employer once again becomes liable for paying SSP up to the maximum 28 weeks. An employer's maximum liability cannot be less than 28 times the weekly rate unless:

(a) the employee becomes excluded from receiving SSP; or

(b) the liability is reduced because SSP paid by a previous employer has been deducted (see **7.6**); or

(c) the 'three-year cut-off' comes into effect (see **7.5**).

> ***Example***
>
> Maxine has been off work for 30 consecutive weeks, during which time she was paid 28 weeks' SSP. She returns to work on 9 June 2003. On 3 July 2003 she starts another PIW. As the two PIWs are linked (ie there are less than 57 days between them), Maxine is not entitled to SSP for the second period of absence.

If an employee's QDs remain constant throughout the PIW, then the calculation of the weeks and days of SSP paid and outstanding is straightforward.

> ***Example***
>
> Felix has been paid SSP for 58 days in a PIW. He has three QDs a week. The number of weeks and days for which he has been paid SSP is:
>
> 58 ÷ 3 = 19 weeks and one day
>
> The number of weeks and days which SSP liability continues to the maximum of 28 weeks is:
>
> 28 × 3 = 84 – 58 = 26 days (eight weeks and two days) ➡

This number of days can be expressed as a week and fraction of a week as follows:

$26 \div 3 = 8.6667$ weeks

Calculating Maximum SSP Liability [7.4]

The calculation of the amount needed to reach the maximum liability will be different if:

- an employee's QDs change in between PIWs, or from week to week (eg in a cycle of three weeks for varying shifts); or
- where the employee is due SSP at different weekly rates because the rates change (eg in a PIW spanning two or more tax years).

If the maximum has not been reached then a further day's SSP must be paid, even though the maximum would then be exceeded. The liability for SSP needs to be manually calculated in such cases is as follows.

Checklist: Manual SSP Calculation

(a) Isolate each period, in weeks or PIWs, as appropriate, in which the number of QDs in the week remained the same.

(b) With regard to each period, calculate how many QDs of SSP were due.

(c) Divide the total by the number of QDs in the week.

(d) Add the totals together and subtract from 28 to ascertain how many weeks of possible liability remain.

(e) To establish the odd days for which SSP can become due in any future week, take the number of QDs in the week and express one QD as a decimal fraction of a week.

Not all numbers of QDs in a week convert to precise, non-recurring decimals, so it is essential to use the decimals approximating to the required fraction in the calculation, which are issued by the Inland Revenue.

Qualifying days	Decimal fraction for one day
7	0.143
6	0.167
5	0.2
4	0.25
3	0.334
2	0.5
1	1.0

Case study: manual SSP calculation

Darren is an engineer, employed on a shift rotation basis, in a local manufacturing company. He is an intelligent, energetic young man, but unfortunately for his employer he has more interest in thinking about, watching and playing football, than pursuing his modern apprenticeship. As such he has a poor sickness record, with absence reasons including tiredness, general fatigue and a severe case of sunstroke (in May).

Darren is absent from work due to this incapacity from Monday 17 May 2004 returning to work on Monday 14 June 2004. In this PIW, his QDs are designated as being Monday to Thursday inclusive, including Bank Holidays. He is therefore entitled to SSP (taking into account three waiting days) for the following QDs:

20 May, 24–27 May, 31 May, 1–3 June, and 7–10 June – a total of 13 days.

SSP has therefore been payable for 3.25 weeks (ie 13 days ÷ 4). So he has received 3.25 × the applicable weekly rate, each QD during this period being paid at ¼ the weekly rate.

From 1 July, Darren's QDs are changed from four to five per week, in line with his rearranged work roster which is designed to ensure he has a more uniform work pattern and therefore feels less tired as result of changing shift patterns. Monday to Friday now become his QDs.

However, this doesn't work and Darren is ill again from Wednesday 21 July to Friday 3 September 2004, returning to work on 6 September 2004. The two periods of illness are separated by less than 56 days and so form part of a single PIW.

In the second PIW, there are no waiting days to be served, since this PIW links with the earlier PIW. He is therefore entitled to SSP on the following QDs:

21–23 July, 26–30 July, 2–6 August, 9–13 August, 16–20 August, 23–27 August, 30–31 August, 1–3 September – a total of 30 days.

SSP has therefore been payable for 6.6 weeks (ie 33 days ÷ 5). So he has received 6.6 × the applicable weekly rate, with each QD during this period being paid at ⅕ the weekly rate.

Therefore, the total number of weeks' SSP paid during these two linked PIWs is 9.85 weeks (ie 3.25 + 6.6). This therefore leaves the employee with 18.15 weeks (ie 28 – 9.85) before the maximum entitlement is reached.

If Darren continues to have five QDs per week, each QD is 0.2 of a week, therefore 18 weeks and one QD will take the employer to the maximum liability (18 weeks exactly is under the maximum). So 18 weeks and one QD (ie 18.2 weeks) is payable.

If Darren continues to have such a poor absence record, his employer may consider invoking the companies disciplinary rules regarding attendance, as contained in the staff handbook, issued to Darren on his first day of employment, for which he has acknowledged receipt.

PIW Exceeds Three Years [7.5]

An employee ceases to be entitled to SSP in a PIW which links with a series of PIWs with one employer extending back into the past for a period of more than three years. A period of entitlement will therefore end three years after the first day of incapacity, even if the employee has not yet received the maximum 28 weeks' SSP in any one PIW.

Example

Nigel is suffering from a recurring illness and has been absent from work regularly in the past three years. His first linked PIW started on 3 September 2000, with each subsequent PIW starting within 57 days of the end of the previous one. Nigel starts another PIW on 5 September 2003, which links to the previous PIW that ended on 31 July 2003. As the linked PIWs now extend beyond three years, Nigel's entitlement to SSP ceases on 2 September 2003.

Since PIWs can be linked and treated as one PIW, an employee who is sick during relatively short periods of incapacity for work which are never separated by more than 56 days will reach the three-year cut-off for a period of entitlement without having received the maximum 28 weeks' SSP. When the three-year cut-off is reached, the employee is excluded from SSP for the rest of that, and any linked, PIW. However, if a new unlinked PIW subsequently begins, that three-year cut-off no longer applies.

A PIW with a former employer does not count towards the three-year cut-off even if the new employer has taken account of the weeks of SSP indicated on any leaver's statement in calculating the 28-week maximum (see **7.6**).

Case study: three year rule

Fred has a PIW at Doldrum Motivators Ltd, which started on 15 February 2001. This PIW is made up of a very large number of short illnesses but all lasting at least four consecutive days and never separated by a gap of more than 56 days. On 15 February 2004, Doldrum Motivators has no further SSP liability to Fred during this particular PIW, even though Fred has received less than 28 times his weekly rate of SSP.

However, if Fred returned to work and had no further periods of illness lasting more than three days for a period of at least 57 days so that his next PIW did not link with the previous PIW, Doldrum Motivators' SSP liability to Fred at the beginning of this new PIW would once again be limited to 28 times Fred's weekly rate of SSP or a three-year linked PIW, whichever was achieved first.

Leaver's Statement SSP1(L) [7.6]

If an employee's contract of employment terminates (see **7.2**) and within the previous 56 days of that contract ending, the employee had a PIW for which SSP was payable for at least four days, the employer may need to supply that employee with Form SSP1(L). This is also known as a 'Leaver's Statement'.

The issue of Form SSP1(L) is not mandatory on the employer and need only be given where the employee so requests and SSP was payable for at least one week (more than three days) before the contract ended.

> **i** In practice, for odd days of sickness, three days or less are rounded down (and therefore disregarded), more than three days will be rounded up to a full week and therefore must be counted.

Examples

1. Brendan's contract of employment is due to end on 20 August. The last PIW, during which SSP was payable for more than a week, ended on 25 June. The period between 26 June (the day after the ending of the PIW) and 20 August (the day the contract of employment ends) is exactly 56 days. Therefore, a Leaver's Statement must be issued, if Brendan requests it.

2. Sheila has a Monday to Friday QD pattern and is ill from Monday to Saturday inclusive, four weeks before her contract of employment is due to end. Monday to Wednesday are waiting days (because there is no linking), and so only two days' SSP are payable and if this is the only relevant payment, no Leaver's Statement need be issued.

An employee starts employment with the same or new employer and falls sick again within 56 days of the last day on which SSP was payable under the former contract. The new employer should take into account the SSP shown on the Leaver's Statement in calculating maximum SSP liability for the PIW in the new employment.

In other words, an employer's maximum SSP liability can be reduced in these circumstances where SSP was paid to an employee in a previous job. This is the only effect of an employee's SSP record with a former employer on entitlement to SSP with a new employer. The usual rules about waiting days apply (see **1.7**). The question of SSP exclusion is determined by the new employer without reference to any information on the Leaver's Statement.

Therefore, if the Leaver's Statement presented by a new employee shows that he or she has received 28 weeks' SSP from their former employer, they are excluded from SSP for any PIW with the new employer falling within 56 days or less of the date indicated on the statement.

Issuing Form SSP1(L) [7.7]

With effect from 6 April 1996, the responsibility for initiating the Form SSP1(L) procedure was transferred from the employer to the employee. Formerly an employer had to issue a Leaver's Statement to an employer where the employee left their employment having had entitlement to SSP for four days or more within the preceding eight weeks. It was a criminal offence not to issue one. In general, the leaver's statement had to be issued by the former employer not later than the seventh calendar day after the end of that contract of employment.

The official Form SSP1(L) is in two sections, with the employer being required to give information about SSP and their employee in Section 1 and Section 2 containing information for the employee on how to use the form. Employers may use their own versions of Form SSP1(L), eg a computer printout. The employer should retain a photocopy of the completed Form SSP1(L) and pass the original to the ex-employee.

Whichever method the employer adopts, the form must contain a minimum amount of information.

Checklist: SSP1(L) Information

The information required on the Form SSP1(L) is:

(a) the employee's name, National Insurance number and payroll reference number;

(b) the date of the first day of incapacity, with linked PIWs are treated as one;

(c) the date of the last day for which SSP was paid;

(d) the number of weeks between the dates in (b) and (c) for which SSP was paid, taking into account the rounding rules (see **7.8**); and

(e) the date the statement was made and the employer's name, address and telephone number.

If account has been taken of any PIW with a previous employer shown on a Leaver's Statement issued by that employer, that PIW will be used for the first day of sickness in (b) and the SSP paid by that employer should be included in (d).

The employer should now give, or send the completed form, to the employee or former employee upon their making a request no later than:

(a) seven days after he or she requested it; or

(b) where the employer's procedures and arrangements are such that it is impracticable to issue it within seven days of the request, by the first pay day in the tax month following the one in which it was requested

Rounding Rules on Form SSP1(L) [7.8]

In determining whether SSP has been payable for at least one week, for SSP1(L) issuing purposes, employers may need to apply special rounding rules with fractions of a week rounded up if at least 0.50, or rounded down if less than 0.50.

Examples

1. Dee's QDs are Monday to Saturday inclusive. She was sick from 8 April 2004 to 28 April 2004 and received two weeks and three days' SSP. 8 to 10 April are waiting days.

3 days ÷ 6 QDs = 0.5 × 7 days = 3.5 days

3.5 days round up to a whole week.

Entry on Form SSP1(L): three weeks

2. Ian's QDs are Tuesday to Thursday inclusive. He was sick from 16 October to 30 November 2003 and receives five weeks and one day's SSP. 16, 21 and 22 October are waiting days.

1 day ÷ 3 QDs = 0.333 × 7 days = 2.331 days

2.331 days round down to nil

Entry on Form SSP1 (L): five weeks

Form SSP1(L) Received by New Employer [7.9]

There is no legal requirement for a new employee to hand the Leaver's Statement to the new employer. Also, there is no requirement on the employer to ask new employees whether they have been given Form SSP1(L) (and also whether they have received a linking letter from the Benefits Agency) (see **5.4**).

The employer must accept a Leaver's Statement given on or before the seventh calendar day after the first QD of a PIW occurring within the first eight weeks of the contract of employment. If it is posted to the employer properly addressed and stamped, the day of posting counts as the day of receipt. If the date of posting cannot be established, the employer may assume it was posted two days earlier than it was received, or three days earlier if it was received on Monday or Tuesday. The employer should make allowances for public holidays and any known local variations in postal arrangements.

Any in-house time limit cannot be stricter. There is an absolute limit of 91 days for acceptance of a Leaver's Statement after which the new employer cannot accept any reason for the delay, regardless of any in-house rules. Within the 91-day limit, a Leaver's Statement should be accepted, although late, if there is 'good cause' (see **4.3**) for the employee's delay in providing the form.

If the new employee has a PIW within 56 days (eight weeks) of the start of the new contract of employment and the employer has been handed a Leaver's Statement 'in time' as explained above, the employer must consider the information on the form.

If the gap between the last day for which SSP was payable with the former employer and the first day of the present PIW is 56 calendar days or less, the employer should take into account the weeks of SSP which are shown on the Leaver's Statement. If the gap is more than 56 days, the employer should keep the form but take no account of the weeks of SSP paid.

Example

Helen received two weeks and four days' SSP with Employer A in a PIW in July 2004. This linked with an earlier PIW. Her contract of employment ended on 23 July 2003 and she started work with Employer B on 26 July 2003. Helen was absent sick for the last two weeks of August.

Employer A issued a Leaver's Statement to the employee on 28 July showing a total of six weeks' SSP paid in the relevant PIW. Employer B asked Helen if she had a Leaver's Statement when the PIW began in August and was given it. As the first day of the PIW commenced within 56 days (eight weeks) of the last date that Helen was paid SSP for (Date 2 on Form SSP1(L)) then Employer B's maximum SSP liability is reduced from 28 to 22 weeks.

If the employee hands in more than one Leaver's Statement, perhaps where they have left more than one employment, the new employer should only take account of the one showing the greatest number of weeks of SSP paid.

If an employee is excluded from SSP during his or her PIW with a new employer and a Leaver's Statement has been handed to the new employer, the Leaver's Statement should be returned with the changeover Form SSP1 (see **7.10**). The employee should then hand both forms to the Benefits Agency office when claiming any State benefit.

If a new employee leaves within eight weeks of the start of his or her new contract of employment and no PIW has occurred, any Leaver's Statement should be handed back to the employee.

Change-over Form SSP1 [7.10]

There are two situations where an employer is required to complete Benefits Agency Form SSP1, known as the 'change-over' form.

The change-over form is issued if:

- the employee is sick for four days or more but no period of entitlement to SSP has arisen; or
- where an employee is to be transferred from receiving SSP to a State benefit because the employee remains ill after entitlement to SSP has come to an end. In other words, a period of entitlement is ending but the PIW is continuing.

In either case, the employee will normally be entitled to claim the relevant State benefit (see **13.2**) so long as the employer has provided him or her with a change-over form. This completed form must be sent or given to the employee, together with any Doctor's Statement and Leaver's Statements or linking letters which are still current, and which cover days for which the employer is not paying SSP. All the relevant boxes on the change-over form should be ticked. A change-over form is required to be issued for each PIW since an employee will be excluded during a PIW, which links with an earlier PIW in which the employee was previously excluded.

Checklist: Employer Information on Form SSP1

It includes:

(a) why SSP is no longer due;

(b) the date the PIW (linked or unlinked) began;

(c) the last date on which SSP will be payable;

(d) the number of QDs falling in the last week of payment of SSP;

(e) the dates of any linked PIWs; and

(f) where the entitlement ends before the 28-week maximum SSP, the number of weeks and days for which SSP has been paid.

In any case where the employer's liability is reduced because the employee had received SSP from a previous employer and handed the new employer a completed Leaver's Statement, the change-over form must also show the first day of the PIW as shown on the Leaver's Statement.

The employer must give or send the completed change-over Form SSP1 (see below) to the employee no later than:

- seven days after being notified that the employee's sickness would last at least four consecutive days; or
- the first pay date in the tax month following the one in which the reason for issuing the change-over form arose where the employer's payroll arrangements are such that it is impracticable for the employer to issue it within seven days.

In the case of an employee who is outside the UK, the change-over form should be given to the employee as soon as practicable after the fourth day of the PIW.

Copies of Form SSP1 are available on the CD-ROM which accompanies the employer's annual pack, issued to all employers with a PAYE scheme reference number. It can be printed off as an alternative to:

- ordering printed copies from Benefit Agency offices; or
- completing the form online or printing the form from the Department for Work and Pensions web pages at www.dwp.gov.uk/advisors/claimforms.htm

The employer completes the information in the first part of Form SSP1 clerically, while the second part of Form SSP1 is for the employee to complete if he or she wishes to make a claim for State Incapacity Benefit (see **13.2**).

Employers pressed for the right to supply the information covered by the first part of the SSP1 in the form of a computer printout and so gain greater flexibility and a reduction in administration costs. The Government agreed that computer printouts could be used with effect from 6 April 1996.

Form SSP1

SSP1 09/03

Statutory Sick Pay (SSP) and Incapacity Benefit

Claim form

About this form

Employers should complete this form when an employee is not entitled to Statutory Sick Pay (SSP), or when SSP has come to an end. Once completed the form should be given to the employee,who will then make a claim to Incapacity Benefit.

Section 1
is for the employer to give information about Statutory Sick Pay (SSP). The information will help the Department for Work and Pensions decide your employee's Incapacity Benefit claim.

- **Part A** asks for information about the employee and SSP.
- **Part B** tells the employee why the employer cannot pay SSP.
- **Part C** asks for further information about sickness and SSP.
- **Part D** is a declaration by the employer that all information is correct and complete.

Parts A, B and **D** must be completed by the employer. **Part C** should only be completed when the employee in question has already received SSP from the employer.

Section 2
are notes for the employee explaining how and where to claim Incapacity Benefit.

Statutory Sick Pay is money paid by employers to employees who are away from work for 4 days or more in a row because they have an illness or disability.

Incapacity Benefit is a social security benefit employees may be able to get because of their illness or disability when their SSP ends or if they cannot get SSP.

Section 1

About SSP and your employee

Part A

About your employee

Please tell us about your employee

Surname	
Other names	
National Insurance (NI) number	Letters / Numbers / Letter
Clock or payroll number	
Tax reference number	

(Substitute)(LexisNexis UK) 1

Form SSP1

Why you cannot get Statutory Sick Pay

Part B

I am filling in this form because

☐ I cannot pay you SSP

☐ I cannot pay you SSP after [/ /]

I have ticked a box to tell you why you cannot get SSP. The notes on **pages 6** and **7** explain the reasons in more detail.

I cannot pay you SSP because

A ☐ **You claimed Incapacity Benefit or Severe Disablement Allowance during the last 8 weeks, or you are entitled to the 52 week benefit protection so you may be able to get Incapacity Benefit or Severe Disablement Allowance instead of SSP.**

B ☐ **Your contract of employment has expired.**

C ☐ **Your contract of employment has been brought to an end.**

D ☐ **You will soon have been getting SSP for 28 weeks or you have already had SSP for 28 weeks.**

E ☐ **You have not earned enough money to qualify for SSP.**

F ☐ **You are aged 65 or over.**

G ☐ **You are expecting a baby soon or you have just had a baby.**

H ☐ **You have already been sick on and off for 3 years.**

I ☐ **You were away from work because of a trade dispute on the first day you were sick.**

J ☐ **You were in legal custody or you were serving a term of imprisonment when you became sick.**
Or you are now in legal custody or sentenced to a term of imprisonment.

K ☐ **You were working outside the UK on the day you first became sick.**

L ☐ **You have not started working for me yet.**

Notes on pages 6 and 7 explain the reasons in more detail

3

Form SSP1

More information we need

Part C

The employee's first day of sickness

To work out this date you will need to check

- your sick records for this employee, and
- any form **SSP1(L)** *Leaver's statement of SSP* from a previous employer.

If your employee has a form **SSP1(L)** from a previous employer and has been off work sick for 4 days or more within 8 weeks and one day of **date 2** on their **SSP1(L),** the first day of sickness is **date 1** on form SSP1(L).

If your employee has had 2 or more spells of sickness of 4 days or more in a row which were 8 weeks or less apart, the first day of sickness is the first day they were off work sick at the beginning of these linked spells of sickness.

For all other employees who have been off work sick for 4 days or more in a row, the first day of sickness is the first day they were off work sick.

The first day of sickness or first day of linked spell.   /   /

About the SSP that has been paid

How many weeks and days of SSP will have been paid to this employee when SSP ends?
Include all linked spells. Count from the first day you have paid SSP up to and including the date you have written on **page 3** of this form. If you are including any SSP paid by a previous employer, count from **date 1** on their form SSP1(L).   weeks   days

How many qualifying days are there in a week?   days
Count the number of qualifying days in the full week, not just the number of days they can get SSP for. Remember, for most employees qualifying days are the days of the week that they normally work.

Please tick which days of the week the employee normally works?

☐ Monday ☐ Tuesday ☐ Wednesday ☐ Thursday ☐ Friday

☐ Saturday ☐ Sunday

Provide dates of all periods of sick absences from the first date of sickness,in the current Period of Incapacity for Work (PIW).
Use a separate sheet of paper if necessary.

From	To	From	To
/ /	/ /	/ /	/ /
/ /	/ /	/ /	/ /
/ /	/ /	/ /	/ /
/ /	/ /	/ /	/ /
/ /	/ /	/ /	/ /
/ /	/ /	/ /	/ /
/ /	/ /	/ /	/ /

4

Form SSP1

Part D

Employer's declaration

I declare
that the information I have given is correct and complete.

I understand
that if this employee has been getting SSP, I must continue to pay SSP up to and including the date I have written on **page 3** of this form.

Employer's name	
Employer's Account Office reference number	
Signature	
Date	/ /
Position in firm	
Phone number and extension	extension
Fax number	
Address	
	Postcode
Business stamp	

What to do next

Please send this form to your employee with any medical certificates that cover a period you cannot pay SSP for.
Medical certificates are also called sick notes or doctor's statements.

Tick one of the following boxes

☐ I have enclosed Medical Certificates

☐ I have not enclosed Medical Certificates

In cases where a Form SSP1 must be issued, the employer can now supply the information on its own computer printout version of the form but must still give the employee a blank Form SSP1 so that he or she can complete a claim for Incapacity Benefit.

Issuing of Changeover Form SSP1 [7.11]

In cases where the exclusion relates to the maximum 28-week entitlement to SSP, the following procedure must be followed.

The employer must issue the change-over form to an employee in anticipation of the 28-week maximum period so that the employee may claim the relevant State benefit. The changeover form should be issued before the start of the 23rd week of entitlement to SSP (ie at least on or before the 42nd day before the 28-week maximum is reached). If an employee returns to work after the change-over form has been issued but before the 28-week maximum liability has been reached, the employer should issue another change-over form immediately. The employer must tick the box for 28 weeks SSP and giving the date SSP liability ends if there is a new linking PIW.

When completing the change-over form, any odd days of SSP, which are expressed as a decimal fraction of a week should be rounded up so that the total is given in whole days.

Weeks of SSP paid:	18.29
Number of QDs in the week in which SSP last paid:	7
Multiply the decimal part by the above number of QDs:	0.29 × 7 = 2.03 days
Round up to:	3 days
Enter on Form SSP1:	18 weeks and 3 days SSP paid

If the employer starts paying SSP, but there is a change of circumstances, the Form SSP1 must be issued within the following time limits:

- If the employer's liability is due to end before the 23rd week of SSP payments, two weeks before the date the liability is due to end.
- If the employer's liability ends unexpectedly before the 23rd week of SSP payment, as soon as the employer knows it will end or has ended.

Questions and Answers [7.12]

Question

I have worked in my employer's payroll office for several years and no one here has ever seen sight of a Form SSP1(L) Leaver's Statement. Are we omitting a procedure?

Answer

The average payroll person has more chance of seeing Lord Lucan riding Shergar past their office window than a Form SSP1(L) landing on their desk. The reasons behind this are that the issuing is only required on request from an employee, who probably doesn't know of their existence anyway. Even if the employee was aware, it is not to their advantage to have such a form issued, as any new employer can take into account the number of weeks stated on the form in order to reduce their maximum SSP liability for the employee. As regards procedures, with effect from 6 April 1996 there is no longer any statutory requirement for an employer to ask a new employee if they were given a Form SSP1(L) – another good reason why you have never seen Form SSP1(L).

Question

We have paid the maximum 28 weeks' SSP liability to an employee and issued change-over Form SSP1. However, our employee, who has had a Monday to Friday qualifying pattern throughout the PIW, is claiming that he has only been paid for 27 weeks and 2 days.

Answer

With a five-day qualifying week, the number of SSP days payable in a 28-week PIW (linked or otherwise) are 140 days. The first three QDs are waiting days and, therefore, will not count towards the employer's maximum SSP liability in a 28 week PIW.

Question

The time limit rules on issuing Forms SSP1 and SSP1(L) seem unnecessarily cumbersome; why not just have a straight seven-day rule of request?

Answer

The problem is that for some employers this would not be possible to meet, as often the payroll office would not have the information regarding the period of sickness to complete the form(s). SSP relating to a PIW in a particular pay period is often processed in the following pay period, because of the timing difficulties with the running of the employer's payroll.

Question

We have issued Form SSP1 by mistake, thinking we had already paid 28 weeks' SSP. What action should we take?

Answer

If an employer issues a Form SSP1 and then subsequently realises that they have made a mistake because SSP was due, they should pay the outstanding SSP to the employee at the earliest opportunity and immediately inform the employee and the Benefits Agency office, which deals with the employee's home address so that Social Security benefit is not wrongly paid. If the employer is not sure which Benefits Agency office deals with the employee's home address, advise the nearest BA office and they will pass on the information.

Question

One of our employees has had a number of short-term absences in the last three years, can we stop paying SSP?

Answer

The three-year cut-off rule can only be used if PIWs link. If there is a break in the links, the maximum liability of 28 weeks begins again. A PIW with a former employer does not count towards the three years, even if the employer has, unusually, been able to take into account any SSP shown on a Leaver's Statement.

Question

Do employers have to issue both Forms SSP1 and SSP1(L) when an employee is still sick when they finish work?

Answer

If a PIW continues after the end of the contract of employment with the employer, that employer is required to issue a change-over Form SSP1, where the employee's contract has been brought to an end, as well as any requested Leaver's Statement, SSP1(L).

8. How to Recover Payments from the State

Introduction [8.1]

The *Statutory Sick Pay Act 1994,* which came into effect on 6 April 1994, abolished the general right of employers to claim compensation from the State. In most cases, therefore, from 6 April 1994, employers must meet all the costs of providing SSP payments to their employees.

Immediately before 6 April 1994 qualifying employers could recover 100% of SSP paid after an employee had been sick for six weeks if the employer's annual NIC payments were £16,000 or less. For a further year after 6 April 1994 employers could recover 100% of SSP paid after an employee had been sick for four weeks if they paid £20,000 or less a year in NIC payments.

Employers may now potentially recover SSP paid to their employees from the Inland Revenue if they qualify under the Percentage Threshold Scheme (PTS). The PTS has been in existence since 6 April 1995 and applies to all employers, regardless of their size and number of employees.

Percentage Threshold Scheme [8.2]

The introduction of the PTS is based upon the fundamental principle of SSP, in that the State should accept at least a minimal responsibility for compensating workers during times of sickness.

In summary, the scheme operates as follows. If SSP paid in a month exceeds a percentage of the Class 1 NICs payable for a specified period, the excess amount is reimbursed to the employer. The specified period and the percentage to be used are to be determined by the Inland Revenue and can be varied by Statutory Instrument.

SSP legislation also gives the Inland Revenue the power to specify the following:

- the periods of reference to which the calculation is to be made;
- that amounts which would otherwise be recoverable but which do not exceed the specified minimum for recovery should not in fact be recoverable;

- the rounding up or down of any fraction of a pound which would otherwise result from a calculation; and
- that any deduction from NIC payments may be disregarded for specified purposes.

Unless an employer qualifies under the PTS, they are not entitled to recover any SSP paid to their employees.

Calculation of the SSP Recoverable Amount [8.3]

The amount of SSP to be reclaimed must be calculated for each tax month and the eligibility to recover SSP is determined as follows:

Checklist: SSP Recovery Calculation

(a) Establish the gross employees' and employer's NICs due for the tax month, excluding Class 1A (arising on the majority of taxable benefits in kind) and Class 1B employer only NIC liabilities.

(b) Add the figures in (a) to give the total Class 1 NIC liability for the same income tax month.

(c) Multiply the total figure in (b) by 13%. Fractions of a penny should be rounded down.

(d) Establish the total SSP payable in the same income tax month for all eligible employees.

(e) If the amount at (d) is greater than at (c), SSP can be recovered based on the difference between the two figures, if however (c) is greater than (d) no SSP can be recovered.

The 13% rate used has remained fixed since the PTS first started and this specified percentage still remains current in tax year 2003/04. The reference to the liability for NICs refers to the primary and secondary (ie the employees' and employer's) Class 1 NICs. The contracted-out rebate, for relevant employees in contracted-out money purchase or salary related schemes must be deducted from the total for the relevant tax month. This NIC contracted-out rebate does not need to be claimed back each month. However, employers can only offset the NIC rebate due for that month when calculating whether they are entitled to recover any sums under the PTS, even if they have claimed a rebate covering, for example, three months.

'SSP payments' means the amount actually paid to relevant employees during the tax month, not what is due for days of incapacity in that tax month.

> *i* In practice, an employer's Class 1 NIC liability for a tax month is based on the payments made to employees in that month.

'Income tax month' means the period beginning on the sixth day of any calendar month and ending on the fifth of the following month. In calculating the amount that the employer is entitled to recover, any payment of SSP must be excluded if it was not made:

- in the income tax month in which the employer received notice from the employee that he or she had a day or days of incapacity for work to which the payment of SSP related; or
- in a case where it would have been impracticable to make the SSP payment in that income tax month in view of the employer's methods of accounting for and paying remuneration, in the following tax month; or
- in a case where a decision has been made by an officer of Board of Inland Revenue or Tax Appeal Commissioner that the employee was entitled to that payment of SSP, within the statutory time limits (see **10.6**).

An intention of these conditions is to prevent an employer deliberately delaying payment of SSP until such time that the payment will lead to an unjustified recovery under the PTS.

If the SSP is excluded from an income tax month for any of the above reasons, the employer can:

- re-visit the PTS calculations for the earlier income tax month to which the SSP properly relates; and
- re-perform the calculations under the PTS for that month; and
- make recovery under the PTS if the threshold is exceeded for that month.

> ***Example***
>
> In tax month 5 (6 August to 5 September 2004), the total employee's NICs are £1,056.79 and the employer's liability is £1,890.90. The SSP payable is £559.80. The calculation is: (£1.056.79 + £1,890.90) × ➡

13% = £ 383.1997 (£383.19 rounded down). As this is less than the SSP figure of £559.80, the total SSP that can be recovered is £176.61.

! It is unlikely that many employers will be able to recover any SSP, as it will require a high proportion of the workforce to be absent at any one time.

Small employers who pay their tax and NICs quarterly (and so will recover any SSP quarterly) must, however, calculate the amount they are entitled to recover monthly. Large employers with more than one PAYE scheme must add together the NICs liability and the SSP payments for all their PAYE schemes in calculating if they are entitled to reimbursement for that month under the PTS eg where an employee's and director's payroll is operated.

! An employer who qualifies under the PTS in one tax month will not automatically qualify in the next tax month.

In cases of any PIW spanning two or more tax months, the employer must perform a separate calculation for each tax month.

Example

Jennifer is sick from 22 April to 14 May 2003 and is paid calendar monthly on the last day of the month. The employer must compare the SSP payments on:

(a) 30 April with 13% of its NIC liability for tax month 1 (6 April to 5 May 2003); and

(b) 31 May with 13% of its NIC liability for the tax month 2 (6 May to 5 June 2003).

Recovery of SSP from the Collector of Taxes [8.4]

If there is an amount of SSP that can be recovered under the PTS, this can be deducted from the next available remittance to the Inland Revenue Accounts Office. The employer can deduct the amount recoverable under the PTS from the NIC payments for the tax month in which the SSP was paid, or later in the same tax year, if the employer wishes.

If SSP was paid in a previous tax year but was not recovered by the employer, for whatever reason, the employer must complete Form SSP/

SMP32 (see below), available from the employer's order line: 0845 7 646 646. This form is used to obtain reimbursement and should be sent to the nearest Inland Revenue office. Recovery of SSP paid in a previous tax year cannot be claimed directly from the Accounts Office.

If the amount of SSP which the employer is entitled to recover is more than the Class 1 NICs due in a particular tax month, the excess can be deducted from the PAYE income tax due that month. The employer's payroll should enter the excess in the National Insurance box of the payslip P30BC preceded by the letter 'M', for 'minus'. Payroll should not alter the amount entered for PAYE tax.

Example

An employer qualifies under the PTS and is entitled to recover £248.80 of the SSP that it has paid. The employer is also due to pay £143.79 NICs and £229.76 income tax.

The entries on the payslip P30BC would therefore be:

Income tax	=	£229.76
National Insurance contributions	=	£105.01
(ie £143.79 NICs – £248.80 SSP)		
Total to pay	=	£124.75

If the amount of SSP that an employer is entitled to recover is more than the sum of the Class 1 NICs and income tax due, the employer can deduct the excess from the following month's payment. However, employers can never deduct the excess due for month 12 from month 1 as it is in a different tax year.

Example

An employer qualifies under the PTS and is entitled to recover £415.75 of the SSP that it has paid. The employer is also due to pay £166.29 NICs and £179.10 income tax.

A balance of £70.36 cannot be recovered during that month. The employer's payroll should send the payslip P30BC to the Inland Revenue Accounts Office showing 'NIL'. The employer can recover the remaining £70.36 next month and total the figures for the two months at that stage.

Form SP32

Late claim for SSP/SMP/SPP/SAP

Inland Revenue

Inland Revenue
National Insurance Contributions Office
Contributor Group
Employer's Refunds
BP2001, Benton Park View
Longbenton
Newcastle upon Tyne NE98 1ZZ

Late claim for Statutory Sick Pay (SSP)/Statutory Maternity Pay (SMP)/ Statutory Paternity Pay (SPP)/Statutory Adoption Pay (SAP) recovery and NIC compensation on SMP/SPP/SAP

1 When to use this form

Only use this form if you have paid SSP/SMP/SPP/SAP to employees in a previous tax year but

- you failed to recover the statutory payments
- you have failed to claim NIC compensation on SMP/SPP/SAP.

To find out if you are entitled to NIC compensation on SMP see the Employer's Help Book *Pay and time off work for parents, E15,* or the Employer's Help Book *Pay and time off work for adoptive parents, E16.*

Do not use this form if you have paid SSP and/or SMP/SPP/SAP in the current tax year, even if the statutory payment is due for a previous tax year, see the Employers Help Book *What to do if your employee is sick, E14,* or the Employer's Help Books *E15* and *E16*.

2 How to fill in this form

You must enter your PAYE reference number in the box overleaf.

Late recovery of SMP/SPP/SAP and/or NIC compensation

If your claim is for the recovery of

- SMP, SPP or SAP, fill in columns 1 to 7 in Part 3 overleaf
- NIC compensation, fill in columns 1 to 6 and 8, in Part 3 overleaf.

Column 4 is the last complete tax year before the 15th week before the week baby due, or the week when the adoption agency told the adopter that they had been matched with a child. See the Employer's Help Books *E15* or *E16*, for help in working out these dates. Take the information for column 6 from your *SMP/SPP/SAP record sheets,* forms *SMP2, SPP2, SAP2* or equivalent.

Late recovery of SSP

If your claim is for the recovery of SSP

- fill in all the columns in Part 4 overleaf
- take the information for columns 5 and 6 from form *SSP2* or equivalent
- fill in all the columns in Part 5 overleaf, **but only for the month(s) in which the late SSP you are recovering was actually paid.**

please turn over ▶

Form SP32

Your claim

What is your PAYE reference number? *(See your paying in slip)*

3 Late recovery of SMP/SPP/SAP or NIC compensation on SMP/SPP/SAP

Recovery may only be made within six years of the end of the tax year payment was made.

1 Employee's name	2 National Insurance number	3 Employee's date of birth	4 Qualifying tax year	5 Tax year in which SMP/SPP/SAP was paid	6 Amount of SMP/SPP/SAP paid	7 Amount of SMP/SPP/SAP you are claiming	8 Amount of NIC compensation you are claiming
		/ /	/	/	£	£	£
		/ /	/	/	£	£	£
		/ /	/	/	£	£	£
		/ /	/	/	£	£	£
		/ /	/	/	£	£	£
		/ /	/	/	£	£	£
		/ /	/	/	£	£	£
		/ /	/	/	£	£	£
		/ /	/	/	£	£	£
		/ /	/	/	£	£	£
		/ /	/	/	£	£	£
		/ /	/	/	£	£	£
				Totals	£	£	£

2

Form SP32

4 Late recovery of SSP

1 Employee's name	2 National Insurance number	3 Tax year in which SSP was due	4 Tax year in which SSP was paid	5 Month in which SSP was paid	6 Amount of SSP paid
		/	/		£
		/	/		£
		/	/		£
		/	/		£
		/	/		£
		/	/		£
		/	/		£
		/	/		£
		/	/		£
		/	/		£
		/	/		£
		/	/		£
				Total	£

5 Gross NIC and SSP payments

1 Tax month	2 Total Gross NIC liability for each tax month	3 SSP Payments made to all employees in each tax month	4 SSP already recovered under Percentage Threshold Scheme (PTS)	5 Amount of SSP you are claiming
April	£	£	£	£
May	£	£	£	£
June	£	£	£	£
July	£	£	£	£
August	£	£	£	£
September	£	£	£	£
October	£	£	£	£
November	£	£	£	£
December	£	£	£	£
January	£	£	£	£
February	£	£	£	£
March	£	£	£	£

3

please turn over ▶

Form SP32

6 What to do now

Please sign below, fill in the necessary details and send this form to your nearest Inland Revenue office.

Declaration

I/ We claim SSP/SMP/SPP/SAP reimbursement/NIC compensation for SMP/SPP/SAP of £ ______ shown in Parts 3 and 5 of this form.

I/We declare that the particulars on this form are correct to the best of my/our knowledge and belief and that the amounts shown have not been, and will not be shown on the *Employer's Annual Return,* form *P35* for any tax year, and have not been previously reimbursed or credited.

I/We understand that the information submitted is subject to checking by the Inland Revenue and if the claim is found to be incorrect any subsequent over recovery will need to be repaid.

Employer's signature(s)

Employer's stamp

Business name

Address

Postcode

Daytime telephone number *(including national dialling code)*

Date / /

Further information

You can get further information about SSP/SMP/SPP/SAP by telephoning the Employers Helpline on **0845 7 143 143** - calls will be charged at local rates - or from the Employer's Help Books *E14, E15* and *E16.*

You can get further stocks of this form by telephoning the Employer's Orderline on **0845 7 646 646.**
The form is also available on the Inland Revenue website at www.inlandrevenue.gov.uk

For official use

Type of refund	Amount of refund	Type of refund	Amount of refund
Statutory Sick Pay	£	NIC compensation on SMP/SPP/SAP	£
Statutory Maternity Pay	£	**Total refund**	£
Statutory Paternity Pay	£		
Statutory Adoption Pay	£		

I confirm that the refund has been checked and authorised.

Signed ______________________ Name ______________________

Refunds ______________________ Telephone ______________________

Date / / File reference ______________________

4

If the employer needs to recover the amount more quickly, it should apply in writing to the Inland Revenue Accounts Office. Such exceptional circumstances could arise where the employer's only employee is absent on sick leave and the employer is not liable to pay NICs or PAYE tax each month. Any written request should include the following points:

Checklist: Direct SSP Recovery

(a) The amount of SSP that has been paid to the relevant employees.

(b) The amount to be recovered, that is set out the calculation method used in arriving at the recoverable amount under the PTS.

(c) Direct reimbursement is required because you as the employer will not be able to recover it from the payments of NICs and PAYE in the normal way for some time and as such, this is causing cash flow difficulties, and immediate reimbursement is required.

An employer can recover amounts of SSP within six years from the end of the tax year in which they first became entitled to make the recovery.

Questions and Answers [8.5]

Question

We receive a payroll report each month, which shows on the update and error report a percentage figure for SSP compared to the Class 1 NIC liability. It is usually between 2–3% – do we need to do anything with this figure?

Answer

No, not unless the figure exceeds 13% in any one particular tax month. This is the current threshold set for recovering SSP payment based on the PTS. As the figure quoted from the calculation performed by your payroll software is so far below the relevant percentage figure, this would seem unlikely, unless the bubonic plague makes a sudden unexpected reappearance at your workplace. Generally only very small employers with fewer than 20 employees can make SSP recovery under the PTS.

➡

Question

What records does an employer need to keep when seeking to recover SSP from the Inland Revenue?

Answer

If an employer is paying SSP to its employees, they should record details of the total gross Class 1 NICs liability and the SSP payments in each month on the inside page of the Inland Revenue payslip booklet (P30BC), Form P32, or in their supporting pay records.

Question

Why is the Percentage Threshold Scheme used to calculate SSP reimbursement from the State?

Answer

At the time of introducing the legislation, there was considerable concern within Parliament that any employer could face an excessive cost burden, perhaps even being forced into liquidation, if a high proportion of the workforce were sick at the same time. Hence, the opening up of the scheme to all employers in theory, although in practice it remains only the very smallest of employers that qualify for any reimbursement under the scheme. The scheme governs any payment made in respect of a PIW starting on or after 6 April 1995.

9. Correcting Mistakes and Keeping Records

Introduction [9.1]

The DSS announced a number of changes, which took effect from 6 April 1996, in respect of the record keeping of employers in relation to SSP.

On 6 April 1996 the requirement to maintain the following previously mandatory SSP records was abolished:

- a record of days for which SSP is not paid with reasons for non-payment;
- records of QDs;
- records of SSP paid on deductions working sheets, Form P11 or computerised equivalent;
- any Leaver's Statements (Form SSP1(L)) which had been given to the employer by a new employee and taken into account in calculating the employer's maximum 28-week liability to pay SSP; and
- end-of-year records on Form P35 of the totals of SSP paid and recovered unless SSP is being recovered under the PTS.

Mandatory SSP Records [9.2]

From the start of the tax year 1996/97 the following SSP records must be kept:

- dates of sickness lasting at least four consecutive calendar days which are reported by employees (ie any PIW); and
- details of SSP paid during any PIW.

Employers are required to keep the above records for a period of at least three years after the end of the tax year to which they relate. The employer may keep these records in any way which it finds convenient but they must be accessible to Inland Revenue inspectors on request within a reasonable time.

The Inland Revenue can supply employers with an SSP record sheet, Form SSP2, free of charge. The form was designed for the needs of smaller employers. A copy of Form SSP2 can be found in booklet E14 'What to do if your employee is sick', available from www.inlandrevenue.gov.uk. However, this form can be cumbersome to use and most employers now tend to store the information using computer software rather than keeping the original documents, provided all the information contained on the record is retained. Many commercial SSP record-keeping systems are also available.

In relation to computerised records, the Inland Revenue accepts that employers can format and produce data in the cheapest and easiest way possible on the proviso that the employer also provides the means to read the data; this includes printing and viewing records.

> *i* In practice, the Inland Revenue supply several forms to help small employers operate the SSP scheme. Form SSP2 (see below) is a record sheet and Form SSP33 contains a self-certificate and tells the employer how to pay, record and recover SSP. Supplies of these forms can be obtained from the employer's order line, telephone 0845 7 646 646.

Optional SSP Records [9.3]

Employers may find it useful to keep the following records even though there is no statutory requirement to do so:

- records of QDs in each PIW, since an employer might need this information if the employee seeks to appeal against the employer's decision on SSP entitlement. The employer also needs to state on change-over form SSP1 how many QDs there were in the last week for which it paid SSP to the employee in question;
- records of days for which the employer did not pay SSP and the reason or reasons for not paying it, since an employee who disagrees with the employer's decision is entitled to ask the employer for a written statement (see **10.3**). The employer may also need this information if the employee seeks a formal decision on SSP entitlement;
- copies of any SSP1(L) Leaver's Statements (see **7.6**) which the employer had taken into account, since these may be useful in resolving any query over the amount of SSP it has paid; and
- copies of any SSP1(L) Leaver's Statements that the employer has issued.

Form SSP2

Inland Revenue

Statutory Sick Pay (SSP)

Statutory Sick Pay record sheet

1 About this form

This form is for you, the employer, to use to record details of your employee's sick absences.

Keeping an accurate record of each absence will help make sure you pay the correct amount of Statutory Sick Pay (SSP).

You do not have to use this form, but you may find it helpful.
You can keep other records if you wish. However, you must keep SSP records for at least 3 years after the end of the tax year to which they relate.

You are required by law to keep:

- records of dates of sickness lasting at least four calendar days in a row, that is Periods of Incapacity for Work (PIW), reported by your employees
- records of all payments of SSP you make during a PIW.

2 What to do now

Please:

- read the guidance notes at part 4, and
- fill in part 5.

3 Further information

For further information see Help Book E14 *What to do if your employee is sick*.
You can get more copies of form SSP1, SSP2 and Help Book E14 from either:

our website. Go to www.inlandrevenue.gov.uk
and click on 'Employers', or
the Employers Orderline on **0845 7 646 646**.

▸ *please turn over*

Form SSP2

4 How to use this Statutory Sick Pay record sheet

Boxes A - D - Information brought forward

For existing employees take the information you hold from the previous year's record.
For new employees use form SSP1(L) *Leaver's Statement of Statutory Sick Pay* and fill in boxes A and C, if appropriate.

Box 1 √ the qualifying days, and write in the date of any change.

Box 2 Write in the maximum liability. Remember that you have to pay 28 weeks in a PIW. But if linked PIW's with you run longer than 3 years, your liability stops.

Week 1 Week 1 will be the first calendar week or part-week of the new tax year, from 6 April to the Saturday of that week.

Box 3 Use the following code letters to note the days of sickness:

- **W** Waiting days.
- **N** Non-qualifying days.
- **C** Change-over days for which SSP is not due. Give the reasons in Box 6. Remember to issue Change-over form SSP1 *Statutory Sick Pay and Incapacity Benefit*.
- **X** Sickness in doubt, or late notification. Give the reasons in Box 6.
- **P** SSP is due. Only use '**P**' where the qualifying days vary. If they do not vary, write in the numbers. Always note 4 days or more sickness, whether or not SSP is due.

Box 4 SSP due in week/month.

Box 5 Running total of SSP.

Box 6 Remarks.

If the qualifying days are the same each week:
- use the '**Days**' parts of Box 2
- note the days of SSP due in numbers. Write 1,2,3,4,5 etc in Box 3
- if the qualifying days change, write the new details in Boxes 1 and 2.

If the qualifying days are not the same each week:
- use the '**Money**' parts of Box 2
- write '**P**' in Box 3 for each day SSP is due
- keep a running total of SSP in Box 5.

At the beginning of a new tax year, start a new record sheet.
Write in any new details for Box 2.

If a new employee gives you form SSP1(L) *Leaver's Statement of Statutory Sick Pay (SSP)*, transfer the information to Box 2, if appropriate.

If SSP is due after a gap of more than 8 weeks since the end of the last PIW, work out new details for Box 2.

2

▸ *please see opposite page*

Form SSP2

5 Employee details

Surname	
First forename	
Other forename(s)	

Information brought forward		D		1 √ the qualifying days Sun	Mon	Tue	Wed	Thu	Fri	Sat	Date
A First day of PIW	/ /	Waiting days in PIW with you	1 ☐	☐	☐	☐	☐	☐	☐	☐	/ /
B Date SSP1 change-over form issued	/ /		2 ☐	☐	☐	☐	☐	☐	☐	☐	/ /
C Last day of PIW	/ /		3 ☐	☐	☐	☐	☐	☐	☐	☐	/ /

2 Maximum SSP Liability								
	Days							
	Money	£	£	£	£	£	£	£

Week ending Saturday	Week	3 Record of sickness and SSP Sun	Mon	Tue	Wed	Thu	Fri	Sat	4 SSP due in week/month	5 Running total of SSP	6 Remarks
	1								£	£	
	2								£	£	
	3								£	£	
	4								£	£	
	5								£	£	
	6								£	£	
	7								£	£	
	8								£	£	
	9								£	£	
	10								£	£	
	11								£	£	
	12								£	£	
	13								£	£	
	14								£	£	
	15								£	£	
	16								£	£	
	17								£	£	
	18								£	£	
	19								£	£	
	20								£	£	
	21								£	£	
									Carried forward	£	

3

▸ *please turn over*

Form SSP2

5 Employee details (continued)

Week ending Saturday	Week	3 Record of sickness and SSP Sun	Mon	Tue	Wed	Thu	Fri	Sat	4 SSP due in week/month	5 Running total of SSP	6 Remarks
	22								£	£	
	23								£	£	
	24								£	£	
	25								£	£	
	26								£	£	
	27								£	£	
	28								£	£	
	29								£	£	
	30								£	£	
	31								£	£	
	32								£	£	
	33								£	£	
	34								£	£	
	35								£	£	
	36								£	£	
	37								£	£	
	38								£	£	
	39								£	£	
	40								£	£	
	41								£	£	
	42								£	£	
	43								£	£	
	44								£	£	
	45								£	£	
	46								£	£	
	47								£	£	
	48								£	£	
	49								£	£	
	50								£	£	
	51								£	£	
	52								£	£	
	*								£	£	

*Use the last line if sickness at the end of the tax year includes part of the 53rd week.

4

In addition, the Inland Revenue and, previously, the Benefits Agency have long recommended that employers keep the following additional records:

Checklist: Useful Records to Keep for SSP Purposes

(a) any doctor's statements or sick notes (or essential details taken from them, especially the date the doctor signed the statement, the date the employer received it, the period it covers and the nature of the illness);

(b) self-certification forms: if an employee is dismissed for frequent or long-term absence or for misuse of the self-certification procedure, these forms will be essential evidence in any unfair dismissal proceedings;

(c) details of the employer's rules about notification of sickness;

(d) a record of the dates when employees actually notified sickness as this will be important for SSP purposes if SSP is withheld for late notification;

(e) any doctor's statements or other medical evidence; and

(f) full details of cases referred to an adjudicating authority, for decision or appeal, and the results of such referral.

These records may be needed to either:

- resolve any query over the amount of SSP paid; or
- provide information to the Inland Revenue if the employee makes a claim that payment of SSP has been withheld.

Although absences of three days or less are not within the scope of SSP, it is strongly recommended that an employer keep a record of all absences from work, for whatever reason. This will enable adequate sickness monitoring for the employer's internal procedures (see **12.2**).

Employers can use the official SC2 self-certification form to record absences for up to seven calendar days. Form SC2 can be viewed and printed from www.ir.gov.uk/pdfs/emp2002/sc2.pdf

Tax-year-end Records [9.4]

From 6 April 1996 employers do not need to record details of SSP paid on Form P14, or its substitutes, nor give any details of SSP paid during the tax year on Form P35 provided the employer has not recovered any SSP during the tax year under the PTS.

The employer is also not required to record the SSP paid to its employees separately on Form P11, or its computerised equivalent, although the employer may wish to do so, especially where they are paying sums from their own OSP scheme, for the avoidance of doubt. All payments of SSP must be included in the employee's gross pay for the purposes of operating statutory deductions eg PAYE and Class 1 NIC.

If the employer has recovered any SSP during the tax year under the PTS, the employer must give certain information when making its annual end-of-year returns of pay, tax and contributions to the Inland Revenue Accounts Office. The information required is:

- the total amount of SSP paid to each employee in any tax month(s) for which recovery is made, which must be entered on Form P14, or its substitute; and
- the total amount of SSP which has been recovered during the year, which must be entered on Form P35, or its substitute.

The NIC liability and SSP payment cannot be netted off against each other, in order to ensure that the individual's NIC record reflects the actual contribution liability paid by the employee.

Example

The employer's NIC liability and SSP payments are as follows for the tax year 2003/2004:

Tax month	NIC liability	SSP payments	SSP recovered under PTS
1	£564	£12.87	—
2	£510	—	
3	£527	—	
4	£471	—	
5	£498	—	

Tax month	NIC liability	SSP payments	SSP recovered under PTS
6	£490	£167.31	£103.61
7	£567	£64.35	—
8	£527	£90.09	£21.58
9	£492	—	
10	£510	—	
11	£419	—	
12	£524	—	

At the end of the year, the employer should only enter:

- the details of the SSP paid to employees in tax months 6 and 8 on Form P14, or its substitutes; and
- the total amount of SSP recovered during the year (ie £125.19) on Form P35, or its substitutes.

! Where an employee is in receipt of SSP in pay periods where the employer is entitled to recover SSP under the PTS, and also in periods where recovery is not possible, it is only the SSP paid in the periods where recovery is permissible under the PTS that have to be recorded and detailed on Forms P14 and P35.

SSP Mistakes [9.5]

From time to time an employer may make an error in calculating and recording SSP payments. Indeed, mistakes are uncomfortably common. The Inland Revenue NI Contributions Office (NICO) (and formerly the Contributions Agency) employs inspectors to make visits to check employers' administration of SSP. The inspectors have consistently found monetary errors in 25% to 30% of SSP examined.

In some cases, in view of the restricted recovery of SSP, the reduction in requirements for record keeping and reporting and the fact that SSP and contractual pay may have been fully offset, there may be no need for the employer to take any action to correct the mistake. If there is any doubt as to what action to take to remedy the mistake, the local NICO should be contacted.

If the Inland Revenue itself discovers an error, it will advise the employer how to proceed. An employer who disagrees with the Inland Revenue's decision on an overpayment or underpayment of SSP need not do anything until they receive formal notification. It is for the Inland Revenue officer who disagrees to ask for a formal decision (see **10.4**). If the employer is formally notified of a positive decision, the payment must be corrected unless the employer wishes to appeal. If the employer agrees that there has been an error, it should be corrected immediately.

SSP Overpaid [9.6]

Checklist: Issues to Consider with SSP Overpayments

(a) If, for the income tax month in which the overpayment of SSP occurred, recovery under the PTS was made, the amount recoverable under the PTS must be recalculated. Any adjustment must be included in the next available remittance to the Inland Revenue Accounts Office, provided this falls within the same tax year.

(b) Records must be amended, even if recovery is not made from the employee. This should be done for records in the current year by drawing a line through the relevant figure on the Form P11 or alternative pay records, so that the figure can still be read, and then inserting the correct figure, or by keeping appropriate computer records.

(c) If the overpayment of SSP means that the employee has been overpaid wages, then the procedures and law pertaining to deductions from wages and restitution apply (see **6.13**).

(d) If the employee has been paid SSP for a period in which he or she had no entitlement to it, eg maximum entitlement in the PIW reached, then the employee's local Benefits Agency office should be informed as the employee may be entitled to State Social Security benefit instead (see **Chapter 13**). The Benefits Agency will need details of the employee and the period concerned, normally given by the employer by completion of Form SSP30.

> *i* In practice, the overpayment of SSP may represent a technicality, as the overpaid SSP has not actually affected the overall gross payment given to the employee and only the level of reimbursement from the Accounts Office needs to be paid back.

Example

An employer qualifies to recover SSP payments under the PTS in June 2003 and deducts £47.98 from the PAYE remittance made to the Inland Revenue Accounts Office.

However, the employer later realises that they have overpaid SSP to their employees because they forgot that the first three QDs are waiting days. The employer must therefore reassess the SSP payments for June 2003 and check if they still qualify under the PTS.

- The gross Class 1 NIC liability is £785.98.
- £785.98 × 13% = £102.17 (£102.1774 rounded down).
- The revised SSP payments are £115.83.
- £115.83 is greater than £102.17 by £13.66 so the employer should adjust their sickness and wage records and repay the amount incorrectly recovered: £47.98 – £13.66 = £34.32.

SSP Underpaid [9.7]

If an employee has been paid too little SSP, any additional amount due should be paid to that employee as soon as the mistake is discovered. The employer merely has to pay the employee the correct amount of arrears owing. These arrears must be recorded in the normal way. Where appropriate, it may be necessary to recalculate the amount due to be recovered under the PTS (see **8.2**).

However, if the employer has also issued incorrectly Form SSP1 (see **7.10**), the employee's local Benefits Agency office must be informed to check whether there has been a resulting overpayment of State benefit. If the employer is not sure, which Benefits Agency office deals with the employee's home address, advise the nearest Benefits Agency office and they will pass on the information. The Benefits Agency will need details of the employee and the period concerned, normally given by the employer on completion of Form SSP30.

SSP Mistakes in Previous Tax Years [9.8]

If a mistake is discovered after the end-of-year tax returns have been sent, the employer should contact the Inland Revenue Accounts Office to find out if the returns have been sent on to the National Insurance Contributions Office (NICO) in Newcastle. If they have not, an adjustment may still be possible to the returns. If they have, the employer should seek advice from the local Inland Revenue office. There is a six-year time limit for making any adjustments in cases where the employer believes that it is entitled to any unclaimed reimbursement in an earlier tax year.

> **!** Under no circumstances should an error in a previous tax year be corrected in the payments or records for the current tax year.

If SSP was paid in a previous tax year but was not recovered by the employer, for whatever reason, the employer must complete Form SSP32 (available from the employer's orderline) to obtain reimbursement and send to their nearest Inland Revenue office. Recovery of SSP paid in a previous tax year cannot be claimed directly from the Accounts Office.

Questions and Answers [9.9]

Question

Can I recover an overpayment from SSP payments, if this is the only payment due?

Answer

Provided the recovery of the overpayment is lawful, the deduction can be made from the employee's SSP, even if that is the only earnings receivable by the employee for that later period. It is common practice for the contract of employment to specifically provide for such recovery.

However, the Inland Revenue has pointed out that sickness is a time of hardship and this is especially so if an employee does not enjoy the protection offered by an OSP scheme. In such circumstances, an Inland Revenue Inspector might urge an employer to recover any earlier overpayment from the earnings due for the first full pay period falling after the employee has returned to work. Such a policy would avoid a sick employee possibly receiving no pay at all at the beginning of a period of sickness.

Question

We now realise that one of our employees was not entitled to SSP as their PIW linked back to a previous PIW, when they were not entitled to SSP and had been given Form SSP1. As a result of this SSP payment we recovered part of this sum under the PTS for tax month 2. What should we do?

Answer

Do not panic. Firstly, calculate the revised SSP payment for the employee, which in this instance will be Nil. Then contact the employee's nearest Benefits Agency Office regarding the overpayment. Adjust the employee's payroll record to reflect the SSP adjustment, and repay the amount incorrectly recovered in the PAYE remittance for tax month 3.

Question

Do we need to record SSP payments on the employee certificate of pay, Form P60?

Answer

Form P60 is effectively the 'under copy' of Form P14. Employers do not need to record details of SSP paid on Form P14/P60, or its substitutes, nor provide any details of SSP paid during the tax year on Form P35 provided the employer has not recovered any SSP during the tax year. However, if the employer has recovered any SSP during the tax year, the employer must give certain information when making its annual end-of-year returns of pay, tax and contributions to the Inland Revenue Accounts Office. The information required is:

- the total amount of SSP paid to each employee in any tax month(s) for which recovery is made, which must be entered on Form P14/P60, or its substitute; and
- the total amount of SSP which has been recovered during the year, which must be entered on Form P35, or its substitute.

Question

We operate a generous occupational sick pay scheme which gives employees 20 weeks at full pay and then a further 20 weeks at half pay. Currently all employees earn a salary which when calculated at half pay is in excess of the current rate of SSP. In these circumstances we have decided not to operate any SSP rules. Is this acceptable? ➡

Answer

If you decide to opt out of operating the rules of SSP, you are still required to keep sufficient records to complete Form SSP1, or your own computerised version, to allow employees to transfer onto State Benefit when they receive their maximum entitlement of 28 weeks' SSP.

Employers must also record the following details: the first and last day of any sickness liability for SSP; the number of weeks and days of SSP entitlement and the number of qualifying days.

Most employers operating a contractual sick pay scheme would be able to supply this information as standard practice rather than having to keep separate records.

10. Dealing with Disputes, Offences and Penalties

Introduction [10.1]

The regime governing disputes, appeals and reviews changed extensively as a result of the merger of the Contributions Agency and Inland Revenue in April 1999. Notably, responsibility for deciding questions relating to SSP passed from the Department of Social Security to the Inland Revenue, and responsibility for hearing appeals against such decisions passed from the Social Security appeal tribunal and Social Security Commissioners to the Tax Commissioners.

Disputes [10.2]

If an employee disputes an employer's decision not to pay SSP, or disputes the amount that is due, it is usually best for the dispute to be processed through the employer's own grievance procedures in case it can be resolved at this stage. An airing of the issues in this way may be useful to both parties in any event. However, an employee has a right to ask the Inland Revenue for a formal decision (see **10.4**). The Board of the Inland Revenue is the first of the authorities that decide questions about entitlement to SSP.

> *i* In practice, such decisions are given judicially by authorised officers acting on behalf of the Board of the Inland Revenue. They work from local Inland Revenue offices and their decisions are given strictly in accordance with the facts and the law.

Prior to asking for a formal decision from the Inland Revenue, the employer will be expected to have requested a written statement (see **10.3**) about their SSP position.

Checklist: SSP Disputes Procedure

(a) Before the employee can approach the Inland Revenue he or she must ask their employer for a written statement about their SSP situation.

(b) If the employee does not agree with the decision made by the employer he or she can ask the Inland Revenue for a formal decision, the employer cannot approach the Inland Revenue.

(c) The Inland Revenue will then ask both parties to state their views on the case in writing but neither will have to appear in person.

(d) From this information the Inland Revenue will make a decision and written notification will be sent to both the employer and the employee.

(e) If the decision is made in favour of the employee, the employer must pay the SSP due within the time scale fixed unless he or she appeals against the decision.

(f) If the decision is made in favour of the employer, the employee may appeal against it.

(g) Both the employer and the employee have the right to appeal against the decision to the Tax Appeal Commissioners.

Employee Right to a Written Statement [10.3]

Employees are entitled to ask their employers to provide a written statement giving certain specific information, and they are expected to ask for one if they are planning to refer a dispute to the Inland Revenue for a formal decision. The employer is required to comply 'to the extent to which the request was reasonable'. If the request was reasonable, the statement must be supplied within reasonable time, for example within seven days of the request.

In the case of SSP the specific information to be given in the written statement may be one or more of the following:

- which days (if any) within the period concerned the employer regards as days for which SSP is payable;
- the employer's opinion as to the amount of SSP to which the employee is entitled in respect of each of those days; and
- the reasons the employer does not consider SSP to be payable for the other days in the period concerned.

Formal Decisions on SSP [10.4]

If an employer refuses to pay an employee SSP, or the employee feels the appropriate amount has not been paid, the employee may apply to the

Inland Revenue, which has the power to overrule the employer's decision. Only the employee can apply, as the employer has no such right, although the employer will be able to appeal against the Inland Revenue's decision. Inland Revenue officers may also request a formal decision.

An employee who disputes his or her employer's decision must, in order for questions to be considered, apply to the Inland Revenue within six months of the earliest day for which SSP is in dispute. The application must be in writing and state the grounds (if any) on which the employer has refused to make payments and specify the period to which that refusal relates.

The Inland Revenue officer will ask both the employer and the employee for their observations in writing before reaching a decision. Each party can also provide written evidence in support of its position. If there is a subsequent appeal, each party's evidence will be sent to the other. Neither party will be called to give evidence in person. When the Inland Revenue has reached its decision it will notify both parties, giving a time limit by which any SSP due must be paid and also explaining how to appeal against the decision.

In some cases, decisions are required under law to be made by the Board of Inland Revenue. These include:

- whether a person is or was an employer or employee of another (see **Chapter 3**);
- the employer's entitlement to recover SSP (see **8.2**);
- whether two or more employers are treated as one for SSP purposes (see **3.2**); and
- whether earnings under separate contracts should be aggregated.

SSP Appeals [10.5]

Either party can appeal against the formal decision of an Inland Revenue officer. Information about the procedure will be contained in the written notification of the formal decision, which will be sent to each party.

There is a time limit for making an appeal. This is 30 days from the date when the notice of the formal decision was issued, on Form DAA3. The time limit may be extended if the applicant can establish that there were good reasons for the delay and that he or she has taken action as soon as reasonably possible.

On receipt of a notice to appeal, the Inland Revenue officer who made the formal decision will first contact the parties to see if the subject of the appeal can be resolved by agreement. However, before reaching an agreement with the appellant the Inland Revenue will try to take into account the interests of any non-appellant. The Inland Revenue will not normally enter into an agreement to vary the decision where it is believed that it will not be acceptable to a person who has not appealed without making that person aware of their view of the correct position first.

> ***Example***
>
> The Inland Revenue may be prepared to agree with an employer that SSP is not payable in circumstances where it is unlikely that the employee will readily accept that conclusion. The Inland Revenue will therefore try and ensure the employee accepts the decision before determining the appeal.

If agreement is not possible, the appeal will go to the Tax Commissioners. Both parties have the right to appear in person and/or be represented at the hearing. The Tax Appeal Commissioners are an independent tribunal.

There are two bodies – the General Commissioners and the Special Commissioners. The General Commissioners hold confidential proceedings in private and deal with cases arising in particular areas or 'Divisions'. These commissioners are, like magistrates, unpaid lay people, assisted by a clerk who is usually a solicitor. The Special Commissioners are appointed full-time and generally hold their appeal hearings in public. Applicants normally have a choice whether to appeal to the General or Special Commissioners.

Appeals to the General Commissioners will usually be heard in the Division that covers the employer's address, although an employee may be able to choose for it to be heard in the Division in which he or she lives. The Special Commissioners normally hear appeals in London but they also hear appeals in other major cities.

The hearing will normally be informal. Applicants present the facts of their case and their arguments and may call witnesses. After hearing the parties' representations, the Commissioners may come to a decision immediately or they may issue a written decision at a later date.

If there is a point of law of general importance to be decided, a claimant or the Inland Revenue may appeal, with leave, to the Court of Appeal, or in

Scotland, to the Court of Session. For more detailed information concerning the appeals procedure see Inland Revenue Booklet IR37, 'Appeals against tax, NICs, SSP and SMP' – see www.inlandrevenue.gov.uk/pdfs/ir37.htm.

Instead of appealing against an Inland Revenue formal decision and if new facts come to light, a party affected by the decision may ask to have the decision reviewed. If a party affected by the decision is dissatisfied, he or she may appeal against it.

> ! It is in everyone's interest to put all the facts before the officer making the decision in the first place.

Enforcement [10.6]

If the Inland Revenue or Tax Commissioners issue a formal decision that the employee is entitled to an amount of SSP, the employer must pay it by a certain date. The SSP must be paid not later than the first normal pay day following:

- where an appeal has been brought, the day on which the employer receives notification of the decision;
- where leave to appeal has been refused (and there remains no further opportunity to apply for leave), the day on which the employer receives notification of the refusal; or
- in any other case, the day on which the time for bringing an appeal expires.

If payment on the first normal pay date is not practicable, then the SSP is to be paid on the next pay date. Where the pay is not yet due, it need not be paid until the date it is due.

A 'normal pay date' is defined as either the:

- pay date specified in the contract; or
- day on which it is the practice in the employee's employment for them to be paid if:
  - they have no contract; or
  - their contracts do not specify when they should be paid; or

- if there is no agreement or normal practice, the last day of the calendar month.

SSP Offences [10.7]

If the employer fails to pay the SSP by the required date and has failed to appeal, liability to make the payment for the days in the PIW may be assumed by the Inland Revenue and a penalty imposed upon the employer.

In such cases of default by the employer to pay SSP, the Inland Revenue will become liable to pay SSP to the employee to the extent that the employee remains unpaid for any further days of incapacity for work which fall within the same spell of incapacity for work. 'Spell of incapacity for work' means a period of consecutive days of incapacity for work, with no day of the week being disregarded. This means that an employee who is entitled to receive payment from the Inland Revenue under this provision cannot receive payment for days of incapacity which are in the same PIW, but are separated (even by a day) from the original days referred to in the determination.

There are a number of other offences in connection with the operation of SSP. These are broadly as follows:

Checklist: SSP Offences

(a) Failure to pay SSP within the time allowed, when the Board of Inland Revenue has given a formal decision that it is payable.

(b) Failure to keep the required records in connection with SSP.

(c) Failure by an employer to provide information as required by the Inland Revenue in connection with the determination of questions.

(d) Failure by an employer to provide information eg Form SSP1 to their employees in relation to their entitlement to SSP (see **7.10**).

(e) Failure by an employer to provide a statement eg Form SSP1(L) in relation to the payment of SSP (see **7.6**).

Any person who, without reasonable excuse, contravenes or fails to comply with any of the above provisions shall be guilty of an offence.

SSP Penalties [10.8]

There are various criminal offences in relation to SSP and provision is made for the recovery, on summary conviction of any such offence, of penalties. In some cases a prison sentence may also be imposed.

Checklist: SSP Penalties

(a) Failure to pay SSP within the time allowed incurs a penalty of a maximum fine up to £1,000 for any one offence. For continued failure to pay SSP after conviction, a further fine of up to £40 for each day of such failure.

(b) Failure to maintain the statutory records incurs a penalty for any one offence, of a maximum fine up to £1,000. For continued failure to keep records after conviction, a fine of up to £40 for each day of such failure.

(c) Failure to provide information required by the Inland Revenue a penalty for one offence, of a maximum fine up to £1,000. For continued failure to provide such information after conviction, a fine of up to £40 for each day of such failure.

(d) Failure by an employer to provide an employee with Form SSP1 incurs a penalty of a maximum fine up to £1,000 for any one offence. For continued failure to provide such information after conviction, a fine of up to £40 for each day of such failure.

A more serious penalty is exacted for producing, furnishing or causing or knowingly allowing to be produced or furnished, any document or information which is known to be false in a material particular, when purporting to recover amounts by way of SSP. A penalty of a maximum fine not exceeding £5,000 or a term of imprisonment not exceeding three months or both can be imposed.

Employer Insolvency [10.9]

If the employer is declared insolvent within the terms of the *SSP (General) Regulations 1982 (SI 1982 No 894)* and the employees' contracts are terminated, entitlement to SSP ends when the employee's contracts end. Where the employer has ceased to trade, entitlement to SSP ends only when the employee's contracts ends. Any employee who was sick when the contract ends cannot get SSP from that date, but can claim Incapacity Benefit from the Benefits Agency instead (see **13.2**).

However, if the employees' contracts are not terminated on insolvency, any SSP due in that employment from the date of the insolvency becomes the liability of the Inland Revenue. Any SSP due for the period before the date of insolvency remains the liability of the employer.

If the employee asks the Inland Revenue to decide formally if SSP is payable, assuming there is no appeal and payment is not made, the Inland Revenue will assume liability for paying the SSP.

In England and Wales the employer will be deemed to be insolvent if and only if:

- the employer has been adjudged bankrupt or has made a composition or arrangement with creditors;
- the employer has died and the estate falls to be administered under the *Insolvency Act 1986, s 421*; or in the case of a company:
  - a winding-up or administration order is made;
  - a resolution for voluntary winding-up is passed;
  - a receiver or manager is appointed;
  - the holders of any debenture secured by a floating charge or any property comprising or being subject to it, take possession; or
  - a voluntary arrangement proposed for the purposes of the *Insolvency Act 1986, Part I* is approved under that Part.

In Scotland, an employer is taken as insolvent if and only if:

- an award of sequestration is made on the employer's estate, or he or she executes a trust deed for his or her creditors or enters into a composition contract;
- the employer has died and a judicial factor appointed under the *Judicial Factors (Scotland) Act 1889, s 11A* is required by that section to divide the insolvent estate among the creditors; or
- where the employer is a company, a winding-up order or an administration order is made or a resolution for voluntary winding-up is passed with respect to it or a receiver of its undertaking is duly appointed or a voluntary arrangement proposed for the purposes of the *Insolvency Act 1986, Part I* is approved under that Part.

Questions and Answers [10.10]

Question

Do many disagreements relating to SSP ever get beyond the internal dispute stage between employee and employer?

Answer

Very rarely. Most disagreements can be settled without recourse to a formal decision from the Inland Revenue. Cases that are considered by the Tax Appeal Commissioners and the higher courts are usually where the point of law being contested is ambiguous and liable to affect a group of workers rather than a single employee eg paying SSP to agency workers.

Question

Are the penalty provisions within SSP law regularly enforced?

Answer

The Inland Revenue general policy is to encourage compliance amongst employers, rather than impose financial penalties in relation to the operation of SSP. The fines are maximum amounts and are usually only imposed where there is clear evidence of fraudulent conduct or wilful neglect on the part of the employer.

11. Special Employment Situations

Introduction [11.1]

This section deals with a number of special employment situations which affect SSP entitlement.

Accidents [11.2]

Employees who are absent as a result of an accident (even if self-inflicted, for example, an injury whilst taking part in a sporting activity outside of work) are entitled to SSP if they are incapable of doing their job. However, if an employee has, for example, his or her left arm in plaster but is right-handed and attends the employer's offices to do a normal job (even if more slowly) entitlement to SSP would cease.

If, as a result of a work accident, the employee was subsequently sent home later the same day because he or she could not perform their job, that day would not count as a QD for SSP purposes since the employee had undertaken some work on that day (see **1.3**).

If the employee, as a result of the accident, remains absent from work, he or she would have to wait three more waiting days unless he or she had already qualified for SSP in an earlier linking PIW.

In other words, incapacity for work, which results from an accident, is treated no differently for SSP purposes from an incapacity for work that arises from any other cause.

Accidents at work must be investigated and employers with 10 or more employees should keep an accident book or record equivalent information by electronic means. The book or record must be easily available to employees and be kept for at least three years after the date of the last entry in it.

Where a work-based accident or prescribed industrial disease causes serious disablement, the employee may be in a position to claim Industrial Injuries Disablement Benefit from the State (see **13.6**) in addition to any long-term permanent health insurance benefit or ill-health pension via arrangements sponsored by the employer (see **12.10**).

If the employee successfully sues the employer for damages as a result of personal injury, any compensation payments awarded by the civil courts may be reduced by a deduction payable to the State for any Industrial Injuries Disablement Benefit that has been paid.

The employer is required by law to give the Department for Work and Pensions any information requested about:

- any accident or alleged accident, where benefit might be payable; and
- the type of job and any relevant facts connected with it.

Agency Workers [11.3]

Although in law an agency worker may or may not be an employee, the responsibility for paying SSP falls on whoever is responsible for paying the Class 1 NICs liability on his or her earnings as required by the *Social Security (Categorisation of Earners) Regulations 1978* (*SI 1978 No 1689*). Usually the responsibility falls on the agency, unless it has acted merely to introduce the worker to a client who then contracts (whether a contract for services or of services) directly with the client without the agency's further involvement in which event the responsibility may fall on the client.

Typically, agency workers work under short-term or fixed-term contracts and were ineligible for SSP because of the exclusions provisions (see **5.3** above) in the *Social Security Contributions and Benefits Act 1992*. These exclusions were removed by the *Fixed Term Employees (Prevention of Less Favourable Treatment) Regulations 2002* (*SI 2002 No 2034*), which came into force on 1 October 2002.

Agency workers are eligible for SSP if:

- they satisfy the remaining qualifying conditions; and
- Class 1 NICs are payable in respect of their earnings.

Contract of Employment [11.4]

Generally, a contract of employment is a 'contract of service', as opposed to a 'contract for services' (ie self-employment). Any arrangement providing for the terms of appointment of an employee may amount to a contract, which need not be in writing but may be verbal or implied. Workers employed under a contract of service are employees for Class 1 NIC purposes and therefore also for SSP purposes. Whoever is liable to pay the employer's share of Class 1 NICs is the employer.

If a new employee has done no work under a contract of employment and so has not actually commenced work, he or she is excluded from SSP.

Death [11.5]

The death of an employee causes the employment contract to be terminated and therefore the employer no longer has to pay SSP from the day after the date of death. If an employee dies during a PIW, the employer's liability to pay SSP does not transfer to the employee's estate.

An employee may well be ill due to bereavement, for example, shock or depression. The employer must make a judgement call whether the incapacity can be accepted or not for SSP purposes.

Dismissal [11.6]

If an employee is dismissed and so ceases to be employed, SSP will not be payable after the date of termination, even if the event occurs during a PIW. However, the ending of a contract of employment solely or mainly to avoid paying SSP is of no effect for SSP purposes. Where a contract is ended in order to avoid payment of SSP, and the employee is incapable of work and entitled to receive SSP on the date of termination, the employer will be liable to continue paying SSP in the ordinary way. This means that payments must continue until the employee's PIW ceases or the employee reaches the 28-week maximum entitlement or (if earlier) the date when the contract of employment would, ordinarily, have come to an end.

Employment of Spouse [11.7]

A wife or husband will be entitled to SSP if one spouse employs the other, for the purpose of the spouse's employment. This is because they are treated as an 'employed earner' for Class 1 NIC purposes, regardless of the actual agreement between them.

Holidays and SSP [11.8]

If an employer makes no special arrangements with its employees about sickness on holidays, the normal rules will apply. QDs will be as in a normal working week, and procedures on notification and production of evidence will remain unchanged although some leniency on time limits because of illness away from home might be expected.

Some employers with OSP schemes (see **12.5**) pay for illness during holidays (providing proper evidence is produced), treat it as absence through sickness, and allow the employee to take his or her holiday again later in the leave year. In these circumstances, the normal QDs per week should remain unchanged. Problems in control of sickness absence may arise for the employer because sickness absence while on holiday is hard to police. Employers will need to consider carefully what notification and medical evidence they require from an employee to establish illness on holiday. For example, self-certification may not be felt to be sufficient for an employee who is ill on holiday. However, medical evidence cannot be required for SSP purposes for the first seven calendar days of illness. Whatever the employer decides is acceptable policy, this should be made clear to employees.

It may also be felt that public holidays should be excluded as QDs for SSP purposes. If so, such exclusion must be specifically agreed with the employees or their representatives. Certain industries, such as the construction and engineering industries, have special holiday pay schemes where funding takes place, through the use of special stamps or credits during the course of a tax year. Such schemes do not give rise to a Class 1 NIC liability as the payment is administered through a centrally controlled holiday pay fund, managed through a third party. Therefore, the holiday pay generated does not count for SSP offsetting purposes (see **6.6**) or the average earnings calculation (see **6.15**).

Linking PIWs [11.9]

Any two PIWs for the same employee which are separated by eight weeks, that is 56 days or less, 'link' and are treated as one PIW. For an example of the linking tables for tax year 2003/04 see section **1.5**.

An employee can have any number of PIWs which can link together and form one PIW, providing the gap between each one is eight weeks, that is 56 days, or less.

> **!** A PIW must always be formed before there can be a link, that is the employee must be sick for at least another four days in a row. Odd days of sickness do not form a PIW and so cannot link.

Case study: linking PIWs

Mandy, Roger and Mary are three friends who work together at the local supermarket. They work Monday to Friday each week and each receive a salary of £14,000 a year, paid in even monthly instalments. During tax year 2003/04, the weekly rate of SSP is £64.35 and QDs are established as working days.

Mandy is ill during the period 15 to 22 September 2003 inclusive and again falls ill during the period 18 to 24 November 2003 inclusive.

15–17 September serve as waiting days and SSP is payable for 18, 19 and 22 September. Three days' SSP is payable in a week with five QDs so Mandy's SSP entitlement is £38.61 (£12.87 × 3).

The PIW beginning on 18 November 2002 links with the earlier PIW because the gap between them, 23 September to 18 November, is no more than 56 calendar days. (In fact, in this example, it is exactly 56 calendar days.) Therefore, there are no further waiting days and Mandy's SSP entitlement begins immediately on the first QD. Mandy is ill for five QDs in this linked PIW and so has an SSP entitlement of £64.35.

Roger is also ill during the period 15 to 22 September 2003 inclusive, falling ill during the period 19 to 24 November 2003 inclusive. Mary is highly suspicious of these 'coincidental' dates of sickness and suspects they are having an extra-marital affair.

As is the case with Mandy, 15–17 September serve as waiting days and SSP is payable for 18, 19 and 22 September. Three days' SSP is payable in a week with five QDs, therefore Roger's SSP entitlement is £38.61 (£12.87 × 3).

The PIW beginning on 19 November 2002 does not link with the earlier PIW because the gap between them, 23 September to 19 November, is more than 56 calendar days. (In fact, in this example, it is exactly 57 calendar days.) Therefore, Roger must serve three further waiting days and his SSP entitlement thus begins on Monday, 24 November. Roger is ill for one QD in this new PIW and so has an SSP entitlement of £12.87 for 24 November.

Mandy and Roger both return to work on Tuesday, 25 November looking very happy.

Mary herself was ill during the period 8 to 12 September; she also falls ill during the period 8 to 10 October inclusive and again falls ill during the period 1 to 5 December 2003 inclusive.

As with Mandy and Roger, three waiting days are served and SSP is payable for 11 and 12 September. Two days' SSP is payable in a week with five QDs so Mary's SSP entitlement is £25.74.

The period 8 to 10 October does not form a PIW, as it is less than four days. Mary therefore does not have any SSP entitlement over this period.

The PIW beginning on 1 December 2003 does not link with the earlier PIW because the gap between them, 13 September to 1 December, is more than 56 calendar days. Therefore, Mary must serve three further waiting days and her SSP entitlement begins on 4 December 2003. Mary is ill for two QDs in this new PIW and so has an SSP entitlement of £25.74.

Since Mandy, Roger and Mary are all covered by the supermarket's OSP scheme, they each receive normal monthly salaries for each of the months in which they have been sick.

Furthermore, since the employer does not qualify under the PTS, the company cannot recover any of the SSP cost from its Class 1 NICs. The computational exercise is therefore a complete formality.

Mary returns to work on 8 December, to find Mandy and Roger in a state of undress at the back of the bakery department, they both look embarrassed but say they are just changing into their bakery overalls. Mary walks away, only to stop suddenly, with the realisation that Mandy and Roger are both on the checkouts today!

Night Shift Workers [11.10]

Any work done in a shift which extends over midnight is treated for SSP purposes as if it were done entirely on the first of the two days. Therefore, if the employee becomes sick later during the second day, and does no other work on that day after the nightshift has ended, that second day can be taken as a day of incapacity for work (see **1.3**).

> ***Case study: night-shift worker — day of incapacity for work***
>
> Bob works night shifts from 9 pm to 7 am on Mondays, Tuesdays, Wednesdays and Thursdays each week. All other days are designated as rest days. He falls sick on Tuesday lunchtime and telephones his employer to inform them that he will not be working that night's shift, as he has a sore throat and runny nose.
>
> Bob returns to work on Wednesday, and works that Wednesday/Thursday's night shift as per his normal shift pattern. Tuesday is therefore a day of incapacity for work for SSP purposes, however Wednesday is not.

In many cases a manual worker, paid by an hourly rate, will not be paid when they take an odd day off sick with a cold, unless this is covered in the contract of employment by an OSP provision (see **12.5**). However, if they have the flu and the sickness lasts the required four or more consecutive days to form a PIW (see **1.4**), they will be eligible for the payment of SSP.

Part-time Employees [11.11]

SSP is payable to part-time employees on the same basis as they are paid to full-time employees. Some part-time employees may, in practice, not be eligible because their average earnings are less than the weekly LEL, currently £77 per week for tax year 2003/04.

Redundancy [11.12]

If an employee is made redundant and so ceases to be an employee, SSP will not be payable after the date of termination, even if that occurs during a PIW. However, if the redundancy is simply a dismissal solely or mainly to avoid paying SSP, it has no effect for SSP purposes and the employer continues to have a SSP liability – this situation is unlikely in practice.

If the employee is dismissed by reason of redundancy and the notice period is not worked, the effective date of termination, for liability to pay SSP, is the date the employment ends, not the end date of the notice period had it been worked by the employee (see **11.5**).

Retirement [11.13]

SSP ceases when an employee retires, as the employer no longer employs him or her after the date of retirement. If an employee continues in employment after he or she reaches age 65, SSP remains payable provided the PIW or linked PIW began before that date.

> ***Example***
>
> Peter, after a fortnight's illness, returns to work to celebrate his 65th birthday and then is away ill for another two weeks. SSP must be considered for the second, linked PIW, subject to the normal rules. An employee who is aged 65 or over on the first day of a PIW that does not link to a previous PIW is not entitled to SSP.

The fact that a female employee has reached age 60 and therefore attained State Pension Age is of no significance for SSP purposes. Prior to 6 April 1994 women over 60 were excluded from receiving SSP but now SSP continues to be payable until she reaches 65 under the normal rules.

Statutory Adoption Pay [11.14]

An employee absent from work on adoption leave may be entitled to Statutory Adoption Pay (SAP) (see **Chapter 29**). However, if he or she commences a PIW during or before the adoption pay period, generally SSP is to be paid and not SAP for the PIW.

Where the PIW commences during the APP, SAP cannot be paid for any SAP week in which SSP is payable for any day. For this purpose, a SAP week is a period of seven consecutive days beginning with the day of the week on which the APP commenced.

SAP is payable in any SAP week during the PIW where SSP is not payable for one or more days. SSP is not payable for:

- waiting days; or
- non-qualifying days.

Where the PIW begins before the start date of the employee's adoption leave, the leave and therefore the APP should be delayed until the PIW ends.

If the employee is excluded from SSP, SAP can continue to be paid. If SSP is paid, SAP becomes payable again when the PIW ends.

Statutory Paternity Pay [11.15]

An employee absent from work on paternity leave may be entitled to Statutory Paternity Pay (SPP). (See **Chapter 28**.) However, if he or she commences a PIW during or before the paternity pay period (PPP), generally SSP is to be paid and not SPP for the PIW.

Where the PIW commences during the PPP, SPP cannot be paid for any SPP week in which SSP is payable for any day. For this purpose, a SPP week is a period of seven consecutive days beginning with the day of the week on which the PPP commenced.

SPP is payable in any SPP week during the PIW where SSP is not payable for one or more days. SSP is not payable for:

- waiting days; or
- non-qualifying days.

Where the PIW begins before the start date of the employee's paternity leave, the leave and therefore the PPP should be delayed until the PIW ends.

If the employee is excluded from SSP, SPP can continue to be paid. If SSP is paid, SPP becomes payable again when the PIW ends.

Questions and Answers [11.16]

Question

What details need to be recorded where an accident occurs in the workplace?

Answer

The following details should be recorded: name of employee, date and time of accident, where the accident happened, how it happened and what caused it and the type of injury sustained by the employee.

Question

Do waiting days always have to be served by an employee?

Answer

SSP is never payable for waiting days and waiting days are the first three QDs in a PIW. However, if the PIW links to an earlier PIW, then provided all three waiting days have been served, then SSP is payable from the first QD in the latest PIW. The waiting days do not have to be served again.

12. Occupational Sick Pay

Introduction [12.1]

It is for the individual employer to decide how to control, record and monitor sickness absence for Occupational Sick Pay (OSP) purposes. The employer is in the best position to know whether repeated short absences for minor illnesses may be masking a more serious problem or some difficulty at work. Employers undertaking personnel or management initiatives to address such problems have seen significant reductions in sickness absence levels.

The employer may have reason to think that an employee that claims to be sick and incapable of work is, in fact, capable of doing their job and should therefore return to work. If so, the employer may wish to consider withholding OSP and to have their incapacity reviewed by a doctor.

Controlling Sickness Absence [12.2]

Any loss of working time through sickness is likely to result in both higher direct and indirect costs on the employer. Direct costs can take the form of:

- non-productive wages or salary;
- additional costs associated with increased overtime;
- hiring of temporary replacement staff; or
- outsourcing of work to a third party provider.

Indirect costs may result from the loss of customers to the business because of the failure to provide a satisfactory level of service or to meet production targets.

Certain areas are more prone to sickness absence than others, for example traditionally the hotel and leisure industry has one of the highest rates of sickness absence, whereas lower rates are normally found in the financial and professional service sectors.

Employers should be aware of the following sickness patterns in attempting to reduce staff absenteeism.

Checklist: Absence Patterns

(a) Young people tend to have more frequent, short periods of sickness, while older people have less frequent but longer periods of absence.

(b) Sick leave due to workplace accidents is greater for new and/or inexperienced employees; they also tend to be more often absent for other reasons.

(c) Absence can also increase when high levels of overtime, or shift patterns, which rotate frequently, are worked.

(d) Absence is likely to be greater in larger working groups than in small groups where individuals or shift groups are interdependent.

Poor working conditions and a lax approach to health and safety are likely to result in a high incidence of sickness absence. Employers have in the past cited poor motivation, work-related stress, family responsibilities and job insecurity as contributory factors towards unauthorised absences from work.

All employers should put in place an absence policy and the following points should be adhered to, wherever practical and possible.

Checklist: Absence Policies

(a) An effective recording of each and every sickness absence.

(b) Effective analysis of absence trends to identify where particular absence problems are developing.

(c) Involving middle and senior managers in monitoring sickness absence; this should include taking an interest in employees' health and welfare.

(d) Clearly communicating any absence policy to all employees, ensuring sufficient training is given for new recruits on company health and safety standards.

(e) Providing good physical working conditions and a flexible approach to working hours to cater for individual employee requirements.

(f) Providing an occupational health service for periodic general checks to prevent illness and for the examination of employees that are frequently sick.

(g) Conducting return-to-work interviews with employees after a period of sickness.

(h) Proper enforcement of disciplinary procedures in cases where absence becomes a disciplinary matter.

(i) More effective recruitment checks before new employees are taken on the payroll, including pre-employment medical checks.

An employer who wishes to apply to an employee's own doctor for a medical report must secure that employee's consent in writing (see **12.3**). The procedure is strictly controlled by the *Access to Medical Reports Act 1988*. Similarly, an employer who wishes to see an employee's existing health or medical reports kept by health professionals with a duty of care to that employee must go through the procedures stipulated by the *Access to Health Records Act 1990*. Again the employee must give his or her consent.

Repeated Self-certificate Absences [12.3]

If an employer needs to obtain medical advice about how to deal with an employee who is frequently absent for short periods, it is possible to obtain help from the Medical Services. For frequent absences, the Inland Revenue stipulates that the employee must have been sick for four or more short periods during a twelve-month period before it is able to offer assistance. The employer should first write to the Inland Revenue at their local NICO seeking help. The employer may do this, even if the employee has subsequently returned to work.

Checklist: Information to Medical Services re: Short Absences from Work

(a) Employee's full name, address, date of birth, sex and National Insurance number, date the latest period of sickness began and the nature of the illness certified by the doctor.

(b) The employee's written consent.

(c) Copies of any medical certificates submitted by the employee over the last 12 months, making sure the doctor's name and address are clear.

(d) Employee's occupation and main activities involved in doing the job.

(e) Reason for requesting an opinion.

(f) Outcome of any control action already taken by the employer during the present spell of sickness (see **12.2**).

(g) Dates of any sick absences of at least four days over the past 12 months (details of the past two years, if known).

(h) Course of incapacity given on each occasion.

(i) The four or more self-certificates.

From there the Inland Revenue will forward the case to Medical Services.

Checklist: Procedural Review by Medical Services

(a) The Medical Services contacts the doctor who issued the latest medical certificate asking for a report.

(b) Once this report is returned, if the Medical Services comes to the conclusion that the employee is incapable of work, it will inform the Inland Revenue who will in turn contact the employer.

(c) In the alternative, where the Medical Services feels it necessary for one of its doctors to examine the employee before it can give an opinion, the employee will be asked to attend for an examination. After the examination, the Medical Services will send a report to the Inland Revenue. The report will state whether or not the employee is incapable of work. The Inland Revenue will write to the employer setting out the Medical Services's overall conclusion but will not disclose the actual report to the employer.

(d) The employer then decides whether or not SSP should be payable.

If the employer decides that SSP is no longer payable, the employee is entitled to a written statement from the employer and can ask for a formal decision, currently given by the Inland Revenue (see **10.4**). The Inland Revenue will have access to the medical report from the Medical Services to help form a judgement as to whether or not SSP should be paid. They will give a decision and inform both parties.

To obtain medical advice from the Medical Services, the employer must obtain the employee's written consent. The employee may choose not to give his or her consent, in which case the employer cannot use the Medical Services sickness control system. Where the employee is willing to give consent, the Inland Revenue suggests that the following pro-forma be completed.

Sample form

Form of written consent

Name of employer ....

Full name of employee ....

Full address of employee ....

....

....

I agree that my employer may obtain a medical opinion about my incapacity for work from the Inland Revenue in connection with my entitlement to Statutory Sick Pay. I agree that my doctor may give relevant medical information to a doctor acting on behalf of the Inland Revenue and agree that, if necessary, a doctor acting on behalf of the Inland Revenue may medically examine me and send a report in confidence to the Inland Revenue.

Employee's signature ....

Date ....

If the employee refuses to give his or her consent then the onus is placed on the employer to decide whether the refusal is sufficient grounds to doubt that the incapacity is genuine and, therefore, to cease paying him or her SSP.

Advice on Lengthy Medical Absences [12.4]

Where the employee's absence lasts longer than would normally be expected, the employer can:

- stop paying SSP, and explain the reasons for this decision to the employee;
- continue paying SSP but seek medical advice;
- accept the incapacity as genuine and continue paying SSP.

Medical advice may be sought through the employer's own medical adviser, or via a report from the employee's doctor or by writing to Medical Services. If the employer chooses the latter then he must write to the Inland Revenue local NICO asking for an opinion on whether the employee is or is not capable of work in connection with SSP. The procedure to be followed by the employer and Medical Services is as illustrated in the checklists in section **12.3**.

The Inland Revenue has produced a useful list of illnesses commonly diagnosed by doctors and suggests a period of work after which the employer may wish to consider seeking advice. See Appendix 3 for the full list.

> ***Example***
>
> The employee is diagnosed as being absence from work due to tonsillitis. This would fall within the general heading 'mouth and throat disorders'. Therefore, it would be reasonable to seek advice after one month. If the employer wishes to consult Medical Services, they should not do so earlier than one month after the sickness started.

Occupational Sick Pay (OSP) Schemes [12.5]

There are generally two different types of occupational sick scheme. One scheme deals with short-term absences, say up to one year, the other with long-term disability provision (see **12.10**).

Under an OSP scheme the employer and employee can agree any terms and conditions they wish, and these are usually included in the contract of employment, or a separate sickness policy document. The employer should appraise any new employee of the OSP arrangement, for the avoidance of doubt and subsequent disputes.

> ***Sample clause: Occupational Sick Pay***
>
> The employment contract could stipulate that:
>
> 'Occupational Sick Pay is discretionary but will not be unreasonably withheld by the company. Entitlement to OSP is subject to a qualifying period of continuous service. This is set at three months, regardless of the number of days or hours worked. The employee must also have satisfied the company notification and evidence requirements relating to the absence.
>
> The maximum entitlement to OSP is as follows:
>
> (a) Up to three months' service = SSP only.
>
> (b) Three months up to one year's service = 2 weeks on full pay.
>
> (c) One to four years' service = 4 weeks' full pay and 2 weeks' half pay.

> (d) Over four years' service = 8 weeks' full pay and 4 weeks' half pay.
>
> When OSP entitlement is finished the employee will be entitled to SSP only, subject to satisfying the necessary qualifying conditions. Where the company makes full payment during sickness the payment includes SSP, shown as an offset against basic pay. Where the company pays half pay, SSP will be paid in addition, except basic pay and SSP cannot exceed the standard basic wage or salary'.

OSP Eligibility Conditions [12.6]

The following is a summary of the key features of an employer OSP scheme with regard to eligibility.

Checklist: Eligibility for OSP

(a) Any qualifying period of service before entitlement to OSP begins and how this is calculated, eg rules on breaks in service.

(b) Information on conditions which are excluded from OSP, eg injuries or illnesses which are self-inflicted or suffered through playing dangerous sports.

(c) Results of failing to comply with the rules of the OSP scheme, eg late notification.

(d) Requirement for medical evidence for payment of OSP to continue ,eg doctor's statements.

(e) Details of what conditions are or are not treated as sickness for OSP purposes, eg bereavement.

(f) When the employee will not be covered by the OSP scheme rules, eg sickness during holidays or industrial action.

Employers need to ensure their scheme is applied equally across their workforce as any special conditions and especially exclusions for certain classes of employee, part-time staff for instance, could well result in claims of indirect sex discrimination. *The Part-time Workers (Prevention of Less Favourable Treatment) Regulations 2000 (SI 2000 No 1551)* provide that a part-time worker has the right not to be treated less favourably than comparable full-time workers as regards, for example, his or her pay and conditions of employment.

The Regulations apply directly to contractual sick pay. The benefits that a full-timer receives must also apply to part-timers pro rata. The only exception will be if the different treatment is justified on objective grounds.

OSP Payment Structures [12.7]

OSP is invariably limited to a maximum entitlement over a stated period. Those employees that have worked with the company for longer tend to have a longer period of sickness entitlement. OSP is subject to PAYE income tax and Class 1 NIC and OSP usually brings the employee's entitlement to SSP up to a guaranteed level, ie a percentage of basic pay, say 50% or 100%. Any legal deductions can be made from OSP, such as Court Orders or student loans.

Some employers use a sliding scale of waiting days before paying OSP, with the more days' sickness taken in the recent past, say twelve months, the more waiting days will have to elapse before OSP becomes payable in a new spell of sickness.

The OSP scheme year may vary between employers and, in some cases, will not be a fixed twelve-month period but instead will be a rolling twelve months for each employee. In the latter instance, entitlement to OSP is by reference to absence in the twelve months preceding the first day of the current period of absence. The following scheme illustrates the principles:

Sample clause: rolling sick pay scheme

Service	Allowance
During first year	25 days' full pay and, after completing six months' service, 50 days at half pay.
During second year	50 days' full pay and 50 days' half pay.
During third year	75 days' full pay and 75 days' half pay.
During fourth and successive years of service	100 days' full pay and 100 days' half pay.

All days referred to above are working days and as can be seen the level of pay changes after a stated period of time.

The above sample scheme rules provide that the sick pay allowance is granted for the year beginning 1 April. When an employee is absent due to sickness on 31 March the new entitlement to sick pay does not commence until he or she has returned to work. The period of sickness from 1 April is then deemed part of the previous sickness year.

Offsetting OSP [12.8]

If an employer has an OSP scheme in operation he may offset OSP against SSP provided that:

- the OSP payment must count as earnings for Class 1 NIC purposes (see **6.6**);
- the amount of SSP payable is the minimum due to an employee. Therefore, if the amount of OSP (or any other form of contractual remuneration) that is paid is less than the amount of SSP due, the balance must be paid;
- the offsetting rules only apply if the OSP is due for the same day as SSP; and
- OSP which derives from the employee's own contributions cannot be used to offset SSP.

OSP Treated as a Loan [12.9]

Some OSP schemes carry provisions to the effect that where the employee has suffered a personal injury the sick pay paid in respect of the related absence from work is to be treated as a 'loan' or advance of damages. The OSP to be repaid to the employer upon damages or compensation, being awarded against a third party or the employer.

Case law

Facts

In the case of (*British Railways Board v Franklin [1993] IRLR 441 (CA)*), the employee was paid OSP after a work-related injury. PAYE tax and Class 1 was deducted from the OSP. The employer subsequently paid compensation for the injury and this included the net amount of the sick pay already paid.

Findings

Under the contract of employment the employee was required to refund the sick pay to the employer upon receipt of compensation and the employee duly repaid the net amount of OSP received. The employer claimed that the employee was obliged to refund the tax and NI deducted from the sick pay. The Court of Appeal held that the employee was not obliged to do this. The value of the loan repayable in such circumstances is the net pay, not including any SSP (ie after deductions of tax and Class 1 NIC). An employer can apply directly to the Inland Revenue for a refund of the income tax and both the employees and employer's NICs previously deducted from the OSP.

Long Term Disability Provisions [12.10]

Where an employee suffers a long-term sickness or disability and OSP or SSP provisions have been exhausted, the employer has a number of options to consider.

The employee could be kept on the employer's payroll and a Group Permanent Health Insurance (PHI) scheme or long-term Group Disability Insurance scheme can continue to provide the employee with a level of income.

Group PHI schemes are sometimes known as 'salary continuance schemes'. If the Group PHI scheme is insured, the insurer will assess whether or not a benefit becomes payable under the insurance contract, whatever the employer may have promised to the employee under the contract of employment. This could result in an employer having a liability to pay salary continuance to a sick employee but being refused reimbursement from the insurance company. Employers may opt for a self-insured scheme where the company bears the cost of benefits and no insurance contract is taken out with a third party.

Many insurers will not offer a group PHI policy if a minimum number of employees are not to be covered, say, ten employees. The insurer will also insist that all relevant employees must be covered by the group PHI policy, in order to avoid the employer selecting only high-risk category employees with poor attendance records. Pre-existing medical conditions relating to employees in the group PHI policy must also be disclosed in advance of the policy being brought into force. The definitions of 'disability' are not always generous and there are usually exclusions, for example, incapacity resulting from alcohol or drug abuse, dangerous sports or travel to certain parts of the world.

The employer will specify the period of absence from work due to sickness or disability before any benefits become payable under the policy. The shorter the period of deferment the higher the insurance premium; periods of 28 weeks (in line with maximum SSP entitlement) are commonly used by employers. Once benefits are provided they remain payable until the employee reaches company retirement age (when an occupational pension becomes due), provided the employee remains unable to return to work.

Where a third party insurer is involved benefits are paid direct from the insurance company to the employer not the employee. The employer pays the amount of benefit to the employee under deduction of Class 1 NIC and PAYE Income tax. The employee normally remains on the payroll, whilst benefits are paid, even though it may be several years since they actually performed any work for the employer.

> ***Example***
>
> Ron is covered under his employer's group PHI policy taken out with a third party insurer. The benefits payable after a period of 28 week's sickness are 75% of gross salary (£500 per week) less the State Incapacity Benefit payable to a single claimant (£64.35 per week 2003/04 tax year). The insurer accepts the claim and pays the employer a cheque of £310.65. This sum is then paid to Ron as a gross payment under deduction of PAYE tax and Class 1 NIC in the next pay period.

> *i* In practice, PHI claims usually involve an arrears calculation for the first payment due to the amount of time taken to settle any claim made on behalf of the employee.

Alternatively, the employee may be granted early retirement from an occupational pension scheme. Normally, the trustees of the scheme may have discretion under the trust deed and rules of the scheme to pay an early retirement pension. In this situation the long-term sick person retires and ceases to be on the employer's payroll.

With the number of final salary pension schemes diminishing this approach may no longer be feasible with a defined contribution scheme. Employers may wish to offer Group Income Protection cover as an alternative, to ensure that those struck down with a disability are provided with an income. Most Income Protection plans provide cover after a qualifying period of service, usually six months and provide the employee with up to 75% of their salary until they are able to return to work or for a limited period, say five years.

Questions and Answers [12.11]

Question

We as an employer cannot afford an expensive insurance policy to cover employees unable to work due to long-term sickness – can we not just sack them instead?

Answer

One option the employer has to consider is terminating the employment contract. Absence as a result of illness or injury is potentially grounds for a fair dismissal at any time provided proper consultation and consideration of the medical evidence has been carried out. The employer must look at the reasons for the absence, the likelihood of the employee resuming work within a reasonable time scale (taking into account the needs of the business) and whether alternative employment could be offered instead. Terminating employment in these circumstances must be undertaken in a reasonable manner and in line with company procedure, to avert the possibility of a case being brought before an Employment Tribunal. An employment specialist should be consulted prior to contemplating any such action.

Question

What is a good OSP scheme?

Answer

Whatever scheme works for the employer and employee. The rules of an OSP scheme can be as complex or as simple as both parties agreed on. Obviously, the more nuances included, the more time spent on administration, but where the scheme is not properly thought out, employees have been known to explore loopholes in abusing their level of sickness, to the extent they regard spells of sickness as additional paid holiday! An effective absence policy is a first step, aligned to a strong management commitment to tackle sickness absence. The rules should be fair, easy to understand and apply and meet the needs of both employee and employer.

Question

I am sure one of my employees is deliberately taking time off work, with no good reason. What can I do about it?

Answer

Firstly, how are you sure? What prima facie evidence do you have to support the accusation? Employers must tread warily before levelling unsubstantiated accusations at employees. If an employer believes that an employee who claims to be sick is capable of doing their job and should return to work, then the employer may wish to have a doctor review the incapacity. The employer can approach their local Inland Revenue office for help, but the employer should first discuss the issue with the employee in case there is an explanation for the absence which has not been previously made known. The employer can with the employee's consent ask for an examination from another doctor (known to the employer) and the employer will be liable for any associated costs.

Question

One of our employees has been absent on long-term sick leave. He is now claiming unpaid holiday pay – is he entitled to any payment?

Answer

Employers have sought to argue that holiday is leave from work and therefore as no work is being performed whilst an employee is sick, therefore no holiday can accrue during this time. However, a recent Employment Appeal Tribunal case *[Kigass Aero Components Ltd v Brown [2002] IRLR 312] All ER (D) 341 Feb]* examined the provisions of the *Working Time Regulations 1998* (*S.I 1998 No 1833*) and concluded that:

- there is no pre-condition for the worker to be in work prior to taking holiday leave;
- the regulations do require a period of notice to be given to the employer to take holiday leave. Employers can make agreements with their employees regarding notice periods instead of following the procedure set out in the regulations; and
- therefore, a worker absent from work on medical grounds may give notice to take paid holiday leave and, on completion of that leave, return to sick leave.

So, a worker that has exhausted their paid sick leave entitlement may apply to take holiday and receive payment for that leave. The amount of leave is currently subject to a minimum provision of four weeks' paid leave per leave year.

Question

We wish to make a lump-sum payment to compensate one of our employees for the loss of their employment through a disability, which prevents them carrying out the duties of their employment. What are the tax and NIC consequences in making such a payment?

Answer

An employer compensating an employee for the loss of his or her job following an injury, disability or ill health by awarding the employee an *ex gratia* lump sum payment can make any such payment free of PAYE income tax. The lump sum is also not included in gross pay for Class 1 NIC purposes. This tax treatment is unaffected by the payment of early retirement benefits under a tax approved pension scheme.

Question

Do employers need to keep certain records for OSP purposes?

Answer

There is no formal record keeping required for the payment of OSP. However, where OSP is paid for less than 28 weeks, the employer may have to consider making payments of SSP when the OSP ceases to be payable. The employer should also keep records of OSP, as this information may be required for a third party, eg where a claim is made for loss of earnings in the case of a road traffic accident.

13. State Benefits

Introduction [13.1]

An employee who becomes long-term sick or disabled and is unable to work may become entitled to one or more of the State benefits designed to support disabled people. The *Welfare Reform and Pensions Act 1999* introduced a number of changes to the benefits structure for the long-term sick and disabled including:

- replacing the 'all work test' for Incapacity Benefit with a 'Personal Capability Assessment'. For more information see leaflet IB 214 'Personal Capability Assessment';
- amending the entitlement rules for Incapacity Benefit so that, in most cases, it is only paid to those who have recently worked and satisfy two NIC conditions;
- abolishing Severe Disablement Allowance from April 2001 for new claimants. If the claimant is aged under 20 (25 if in education or training before age 20) they may receive Incapacity Benefit even if there is a shortfall in their NIC record.

The main State benefits payable to long-term sick and disabled people of working age are:

- Incapacity Benefit;
- Severe Disablement Allowance;
- Disability Living Allowance; and
- Industrial Injuries Disablement Benefit.

Incapacity Benefit [13.2]

Incapacity Benefit (IB) is a contributory (based on a person's NIC record) non-means-tested benefit, which provides financial assistance to people that are sick or disabled and unable to work. IB is available to those under State Pension age and who are employed, self-employed or unemployed. IB can also be claimed by persons under age 20 (or 25 if in education or training before age 20), under the youth provisions.

The two NIC contributory conditions that must be satisfied in order to qualify for IB are as follows:

- the person must have paid, or be treated as having paid, Class 1, or equivalent Class 2 contributions of at least 25 times the weekly LEL in any one tax year; and
- the claimant must have paid or been credited with Class 1, or equivalent Class 2 contributions on earnings of at least 50 times the weekly LEL in both the last two complete tax years before the beginning of the year in which the benefit claim falls due.

The claimant must complete one of two forms:

- IB(Y)1 claim form, where the claim is being made under the youth provisions; or
- SC1 claim form where the claimant is self-employed, unemployed or cannot get SSP (unless the person is claiming under the youth provisions).

The SSP1 form was revised and reissued in 2003 and does not now include an IB claim form.

Where an employer has paid the maximum SSP entitlement, the employee should claim IB. The Form SSP1 should be completed prior to the 28-week SSP period ending in order that entitlement to IB can be established before that date.

Incapacity Benefit is paid at one of three rates:

- short-term (lower) IB;
- short-term (higher) IB; and
- long-term IB.

The short-term, lower rate is payable for the first 28 weeks of incapacity. In 2003/04 the weekly rate is £54.40 and is not taxable. It is not paid to employees who are entitled to SSP from their employer.

IB is paid at the short-term, higher rate to an eligible claimant for weeks 29 to 52 of incapacity. In 2003/04 the weekly rate is £64.35 and is taxable, i e it is the same as the SSP weekly rate.

IB is paid at the long-term rate to those under State pension age who have been sick for more than 52 weeks and is taxable. An age addition is paid with the long-term rate provided the claimant was less than age 45 when the incapacity began – there are two rates of the age addition depending on the age of the claimant when the PIW began. Increases may be payable for an adult dependant (spouse) who is aged 60 or over and in receipt of Child Benefit for a child or children.

In 2003/04 the basic weekly rate of long-term incapacity is £72.15. If the claimant was aged 35 to 44 inclusive when the incapacity began, a lower age addition of £7.60 is also payable. If the claimant was aged under 35 when the incapacity began, a higher age addition of £15.15 is payable. For more information, see leaflet GL23 Social Security Benefit Rates – www.dwp.gov.uk.

Medical Evidence for IB **[13.3]**

Claims for IB must be supported by medical evidence. If the claimant is employed and claiming IB because their SSP has stopped or they ceased to be entitled to SSP, the employer may also need to see the sick certificate. It is the claimant's responsibility that the sick certificate is sent to the Benefits Agency office dealing with the claim and not the employer's.

There are four types of sick certificate issued by a doctor.

Checklist: Appropriate Medical Evidence for IB

(a) A white form (Med 3) on which the doctor records a diagnosis of the condition and the advice given regarding the person's capacity to work.

(b) A green form (Med 4) only issued in cases of Personal Capability Assessment (see **13.1**).

(c) A pink form (Med 5) on which the doctor can, in special circumstances, confirm the diagnosis and that the person was incapable of work for a past period.

(d) A yellow form (Med 10) issued by a hospital to confirm that the person has been, or is, in hospital.

Doctors have to issue medical certificates of incapacity free of charge to their National Health Service patients. The sick certificate will either be an open or closed certificate. An open certificate will cover a period when the claimant should go back to see a doctor again, usually two or four weeks. A closed certificate will be issued when the person is ready to return to work, or will be ready to return in the next 14 days.

Severe Disablement Allowance [13.4]

Severe Disablement Allowance (SDA) is a non-contributory, non-means-tested, non-taxable benefit payable to those who are incapable of work for at least 28 weeks, because of illness or disability and who do not satisfy the NI contribution tests for IB.

There are three groups who continue to receive, or be entitled to receive SDA:

- those actually in receipt as at 5 April 2001;
- those who can establish entitlement using the linking rules (ie may not be receiving SDA on 5 April 2001 but become entitled again after this and within eight weeks of previously being entitled; up to 52 weeks for Welfare to Work cases); and
- those who established entitlement using the backdating rules (claims for SDA can be backdated three months in certain cases and if this took entitlement back to 5 April 2001 then SDA will have been and will continue to be paid).

Everyone else and any new claimants have to rely on long-term IB, which retains its contributory test. In 2003/04 the rates for SDA were increased to £43.60 for the basic weekly rate with age additions of £15.15, £9.70 and £4.85 respectively where the claimant first became incapable of work under 40 years of age, between 40 and 50 and between 50 and 60.

> ! This is a social security benefit; as such employers should not attempt to answer questions relating to entitlement but refer their employee or ex-employee to their local Benefits Agency office.

Disability Living Allowance [13.5]

Disability Living Allowance is a non-contributory, non-means-tested, non-taxable benefit payable to those who become disabled and have claimed before age 65. It is payable to disabled people who need personal care (the care component) and/or need help in getting around (the mobility component) or both because they are severely disabled. The claimant must have needed help for three months and be expected to need help for at least a further six months (unless it is recognised that the claimant is terminally ill, when it is immediately payable). However, the three-month qualifying period does not need to be completed prior to their 65th birthday.

There are three rates of the care component and two rates of the mobility component depending on the level of help needed. In 2003/04 the three-weekly care component rates are £57.20, £38.30 and £15.15. The two-weekly mobility component rates are £39.95 and £15.15.

Industrial Injuries Disablement Benefit [13.6]

Industrial Injuries Disablement Benefit is a non-contributory, non-means-tested, non-taxable benefit. It is payable to those who have been disabled because of an industrial accident or prescribed industrial disease. The claimant cannot receive the benefit until 90 days after the date of the accident or the date of the onset of the prescribed disease. To be entitled the claimant needs to be medically assessed on the degree of his or her disablement. The degree of disablement also determines the weekly rate of disablement pension that is paid. Constant attendance allowance and Exceptionally Severe Disablement Allowance may also be payable to a claimant who is in receipt of Industrial Injuries Disablement Benefit and who needs constant care and attention because of the effects of the industrial injury or disease.

In tax year 2003/04 the weekly rate payable to a person assessed at 100% disabled is £116.80. If the person is also entitled to Exceptionally Severe Disablement Allowance, set at £46.80, and to the highest level of constant Attendance Allowance, set at £93.60, the claimant would receive a further £140.40 per week.

Disabled Person's Tax Credit [13.7]

The Disabled Person's Tax Credit (DPTC) replaced the former social security benefit, Disability Working Allowance from 5 October 1999. The DPTC was paid through the payroll from 6 April 2000 to working people with an illness or disability. Recipients of DPTC were aged 16 or over, worked an average of at least 16 hours a week and were restricted in the work they did, or the number of hours they worked, because of illness or disability, which limited their earning capacity.

The Inland Revenue had responsibility for working out the amount of DPTC an employee was entitled to receive, and informed employers when to start and stop credit payments. The amount of the credit depended on whether the claimant had a partner, the age and number of children living with them, their weekly income and savings (there was an upper capital limit of £16,000). Some of the costs related to childcare were taken into account and an additional credit was payable if the claimant worked 30 hours or more a week.

The DPTC was replaced from 7 April 2003, when a new Working Tax Credit became available to those in full-time employment with low incomes, whether or not they have dependent children or a disability.

Questions and Answers [13.8]

Questions

Why do employers need to know about State benefits?

Answer

The short answer is they don't. However, when paying OSP it is worth noting that the employee may also be receiving a State benefit, especially where SSP entitlement has finished. Hence, many employers factor in any State benefit payment to ensure that the total payment from both sources does not exceed the basic rate of pay. For example, the appropriate State benefit is made up to the employee's basic rate of pay by OSP.

Question

Where can an employer find out more about State benefits?

Answer

There is a lot of information on the DWP web pages at www.dwp.gov.uk or employers can add their name to the Benefits Agency publicity register on 0845 602 4444 to receive a full catalogue of social security material.

14. Introduction to SMP

Introduction [14.1]

In comparison to SSP, SMP is a very exciting subject for payroll. This may on the face of it seem odd, as there are a lot more people that fall sick than become pregnant. However, the interest is that unlike with SSP, all employers are able to make recovery from the State of SMP (in full or in part) and the calculations of average earnings can have a very material effect on the level of pay received by the employee. Also, SMP somehow seems so much more tangible than SSP.

Nevertheless, SMP is on a par with SSP, when it comes to the importance of employers getting it right first time. The rules are just as complex and esoteric in places and the penalties just as severe if the employer errs in the application of the law.

SMP was first introduced by the *Social Security Act 1986* in respect of babies expected on or after 21 June 1987. It replaced the existing Maternity Benefit payable by the State from the maternity fund. SMP is a Social Security benefit, which is administered by employers. Employers must pay SMP to employees who satisfy the statutory eligibility criteria. It is irrelevant that the employee may not intend to continue to work for the employer after the birth of her baby. In some cases, employers offer contractual maternity benefits that are more generous than SMP (see **25.3**).

Although entirely separate from the Social Security legislation governing SMP, employers must also take into account the employment protection measures relating to pregnant employees and employees who have recently given birth. These are now found in the *Employment Rights Act 1996* and the *Employment Relations Act 1999.*

The *Employment Act 2002* made significant changes to the law providing employment protection to women who are pregnant or have recently given birth.

Terms of Reference [14.2]

There are four key terms and abbreviations commonly used in considering payment of SMP:

- Expected week of confinement (or childbirth) (EWC).
- Qualifying and/or Notification Week (QW).
- Maternity Pay Period (MPP).
- Lower Earnings Limit (LEL).

Expected Week of Confinement [14.3]

Confinement (or childbirth) itself is defined as any labour resulting in a live birth, or any labour resulting in a still birth after at least 24 weeks of pregnancy ie after the start of the 16th week before the Expected Week of Confinement (EWC). The EWC is simply the calendar week running from Sunday to Saturday, which in the opinion of the medical practitioner is when the woman is expected to give birth. The EWC is the date given on the Maternity Certificate MAT B1 or other like maternity form as issued by a doctor or midwife.

> ***Example***
>
> Karen is expecting a baby on 18 August 2004. The EWC begins on 18 August 2004, the Sunday of that week.

Since 28 September 2001, the earliest date that the certificate MATB1 can be issued is the beginning of the 20th week before the EWC (previously certificates could not be issued prior to the 14th week before the EWC). This means that certificates can now be issued at scheduled antenatal appointments. The date of issue is the date the certificate is signed by the doctor or midwife (see **17.3**).

> *i* In practice, the EWC is the key determining date for establishing entitlement to SMP and the level of payment. This is usually so even if the baby is born earlier or later than the EWC stated on the maternity certificate.

Qualifying Week [14.4]

The qualifying week is the 15th calendar week running from Sunday to Saturday before the EWC. Most payroll software can calculate this date, from the EWC (see **15.4**).

Example

We have established Karen's EWC is the week commencing 15 August 2004. Her Qualifying Week is therefore the week commencing 2 May 2004.

In order to be eligible for SMP from her current employer, an employee must either have been employed, or be treated as having been employed by that employer, for some time during the Qualifying Week (QW). 'Employed by' means that the employer must have a liability for employers' Class 1 NICs, or would have if her earnings were high enough. A woman can be 'treated as having been employed' in the QW in certain circumstances, for example the baby was born early or she was absent for a specific reason (see **17.5**).

Even if the employer only employed the woman for part of the QW, for example the Sunday, the QW week still counts as a full week of continuous employment.

Example

Penelope is expecting her baby during the week running from Sunday 4 July to Saturday 10 July 2004. This is her EWC. Her QW is the week beginning on Sunday 21 March 2004. To qualify for SMP, Penelope must have been employed, or able to be treated as employed, at some time during the week beginning Sunday 21 March 2004.

! An employer remains liable to make SMP payments to any employee if her contract was brought to an end solely or mainly for the purpose of avoiding liability for SMP.

Maternity Pay Period [14.5]

SMP is payable for a maximum period of 26 weeks, known as the Maternity Pay Period (MPP). The *Employment Act 2002* extended the payment period of SMP from 18 to 26 weeks.

Although it is normal for the MPP to start on the Sunday of the week following the week in which the employee ceases to work, the *Employment Act 2002* has radically altered this long-standing principle. Now, in certain circumstances, the MPP starts on the day following the day on which she:

- gives birth; or
- is absent from work due to a pregnancy-related reason after the beginning of the fourth week before the EWC.

The MPP may start, if the employee wishes, at any time beginning with the Sunday of the 11th week before the EWC. The MPP must start if the employee is absent from work because of a pregnancy-related illness or confinement in the four weeks before the EWC.

> *i* A 'week' is a period of seven consecutive days. It can also mean a week commencing on a Sunday, eg in the context of the qualifying week.

If the baby is born before the MPP is due to start, the MPP commences on the day following the actual date of birth.

The MPP can end early where there is a change in the employee's circumstances (see **Chapter 18**).

Lower Earnings Limit [14.6]

A woman does not qualify for SMP if her average weekly earnings 'are less than the lower earnings limit (LEL) in force ...immediately before the commencement of the 14th week before the EWC'.

In other words, the employee is entitled to SMP if her average weekly earnings are at or above the LEL that applies on the Saturday of the QW. She does not have to have paid a Class 1 NI contribution on those earnings. The LEL for tax year 2003/04 is set at £77 per week (£75 per week tax year 2002/03).

Questions and Answers [14.7]

Question

What happens to payments of SMP if the employee decides not to return to work after the baby is born?

Answer

SMP remains payable for the full duration of the MPP. The exercise or otherwise of the employee's maternity employment rights is irrelevant. ➡

Question

If the employee's MPP starts on a day of the week other than a Sunday, does this mean that a daily rate of SMP applies?

Answer

No, SMP is a weekly payment and cannot be adjusted to a daily rate. A week for SMP purposes is in this context seven consecutive days. So, where the SMP week begins on a day other than a Sunday it ends seven days later, eg starts Wednesday and ends Tuesday. This is a fundamental change to the SMP rules.

15. Statutory Maternity Pay

Operating the SMP Scheme [15.1]

Nearly all employers in the UK are required to participate in the Statutory Maternity Pay (SMP) scheme. For SMP purposes an employer is any person liable to pay secondary (employer's) Class 1 NICs; there does not have to be a written contract of service. Furthermore, any agreement between an employer and an employee to exclude, limit or otherwise modify the statutory requirements governing SMP is automatically void. An employer may not require an employee to contribute, either directly or indirectly, towards any cost incurred by the employer in providing SMP.

Excluded Employers [15.2]

Certain employers are specifically excluded from the scope of the SMP scheme.

- *Mariners* — Employers of foreign-going mariners, for whom a special rate of secondary (employer) Class 1 NICs is payable, are outside the scheme.
- *Foreign organisations* — Certain foreign or international organisations, which, as employers, do not meet the conditions of residence or presence in Great Britain, are not required to pay SMP. Basically these are employers who do not have a liability to pay secondary Class 1 NICs.

Mariners are not covered by the SMP scheme if they are:

- employed on a foreign-going ship, or
- their employer does not have a place of business in the United Kingdom.

If the employee is a continental shelf worker or a mariner employed by a UK employer who has a place of business in the United Kingdom, trading within the near continental limits they are covered by the SMP scheme. Moreover, if the baby is born early or the employee cannot be returned to the mainland when the MPP is due to start, the employee will be regarded as if they are in the UK.

SMP Tables [15.3]

In order to assist employers in operating the SMP scheme the Inland Revenue has produced a set of SMP Tables, as contained in Booklet E15 'What to do if your employee is pregnant'. These tables are no longer automatically included in the employer's annual pack issued to all employers with a current PAYE scheme reference number.

SMP Tables – 2004/05

Expected week of confinement (EWC) commencing Sunday	Qualifying week (QW) commencing Sunday	Latest start date for 26 weeks' employment	11th week before the EWC commencing Sunday	4th week before the EWC commencing Sunday
04/04/04 to 10/04/04	21/12/03	05/07/03	18/01/04	07/03/04
11/04/04 to 17/04/04	28/12/03	12/07/03	25/01/04	14/03/04
18/04/04 to 24/04/04	04/01/04	19/07/03	01/02/04	21/03/04
25/04/04 to 01/05/04	11/01/04	26/07/03	08/02/04	28/03/04
02/03/04 to 08/05/04	18/01/04	02/08/03	15/02/04	04/0404
09//0504 to 15/05/04	25/01/04	09/08/03	22/02/04	11/04/04
16/05/04 to 22/05/04	01/02/04	16/08/03	29/02/04	18/04/04
23/05/04 to 29/05/04	08/02/04	23/08/03	07/03/04	25/04/04
30/05/04 to 05/06/04	15/02/04	30/08/03	14/03/04	02/05/04
06/06/04 to 12/06/04	22/02/04	06/09/03	21/03/04	09/05/04
13/06/04 to 19/06/04	29/02/04	13/09/03	28/03/04	16/05/04

Expected week of confinement (EWC) commencing Sunday	Qualifying week (QW) commencing Sunday	Latest start date for 26 weeks' employment	11th week before the EWC commencing Sunday	4th week before the EWC commencing Sunday
20/06/04 to 26/06/04	07/03/04	20/09/03	04/04/04	23/05/04
27/06/04 to 03/07/04	14/03/04	27/09/03	11/04/04	30/05/04
04/07/04 to 10/07/04	21/03/04	04/10/03	18/04/04	06/06/04
11/07/04 to 17/07/04	28/03/04	11/10/03	25/04/04	13/06/04
18/07/04 to 24/07/04	04/04/04	18/10/03	02/05/04	20/06/04
25/07/04 to 31/07/04	11/04/04	25/10/03	09/05/04	27/06/04
01/08/04 to 07/08/04	18/04/04	01/11/03	16/05/04	04/07/04
08/08/04 to 14/08/04	25/04/04	08/11/03	23/05/04	11/07/04
15/08/04 to 21/08/04	02/05/04	15/11/03	30/05/04	18/07/04
22/08/04 to 28/08/04	09/05/04	22/11/03	06/06/04	25/07/04
29/08/04 to 04/09/04	16/05/04	29/11/03	13/06/04	01/08/04
05/09/04 to 11/09/04	23/05/04	06/12/03	20/06/04	08/08/04
12/09/04 to 18/09/04	30/05/04	13/12/03	27/06/04	15/08/04
19/09/04 to 25/09/04	06/06/04	20/12/03	04/07/04	22/08/04
26/09/04 to 02/10/04	13/06/04	27/12/03	11/07/04	29/08/04

Expected week of confinement (EWC) commencing Sunday	Qualifying week (QW) commencing Sunday	Latest start date for 26 weeks' employment	11th week before the EWC commencing Sunday	4th week before the EWC commencing Sunday
03/10/04 to 09/10/04	20/06/04	03/01/04	18/07/04	05/09/04
10/10/04 to 16/10/04	27/06/04	10/0104	25/07/04	12/0904
17/10/04 to 23/10/04	04/07/04	17/01/04	01/08/04	19/09/04
24/10/04 to 30/10/04	11/07/04	24/01/04	08/08/04	26/09/04
31/10/04 to 06/11/04	18/07/04	31/01/04	15/08/04	03/10/04
07/11/04 to 13/11/04	25/07/04	07/02/04	22/08/04	10/10/04
14/11/04 to 20/11/04	01/08/04	14/03/04	29/08/04	17/10/04
21/11/04 to 27/11/04	08/08/04	21/02/04	05/09/04	24/10/04
28/11/04 to 04/12/04	15/08/04	28/02/04	12/09/04	31/10/04
05/12/04 to 11/12/04	22/08/04	06/03/04	19/09/04	07/11/04
12/12/04 to 18/12/04	29/08/04	13/03/04	26/09/04	14/11/04
19/12/04 to 25/12/04	05/09/04	20/03/04	03/10/04	21/11/04
26/12/04 to 01/01/05	12/09/04	27/03/04	10/10/04	28/11/04
02/01/05 to 08/01/05	19/09/04	03/04/04	17/10/04	05/12/04
09/01/05 to 15/01/05	26/09/04	10/04/04	24/10/04	12/12/04

Expected week of confinement (EWC) commencing Sunday	Qualifying week (QW) commencing Sunday	Latest start date for 26 weeks' employment	11th week before the EWC commencing Sunday	4th week before the EWC commencing Sunday
16/01/05 to 22/01/05	03/10/04	17/04/04	31/10/04	19/12/04
23/01/05 to 29/01/05	10/10/04	24/04/04	07/11/04	26/12/04
30/01/05 to 05/02/05	17/10/04	01/05/04	14/11/04	02/01/05
06/02/05 to 12/02/05	24/10/04	08/05/04	21/11/04	09/01/05
13/02/05 to 19/02/05	31/10/04	15/05/04	28/11/04	16/01/05
20/02/05 to 26/02/05	07/11/04	22/05/04	05/12/04	23/01/05
27/02/05 to 05/03/05	14/11/04	29/05/04	12/12/04	30/01/05
06/03/05 to 12/03/05	21/11/04	05/06/04	19/12/04	06/02/05
13/03/05 to 19/03/05	28/11/04	12/06/04	26/12/04	13/02/05
20/03/05 to 26/03/05	05/12/04	19/06/04	02/02/05	20/02/05
27/03/05 to 02/04/05	12/12/04	26/06/04	09/01/05	27/02/05
03/04/05 to 09/04/05	19/12/04	03/07/04	16/01/05	06/03/05
10/04/05 to 16/04/05	26/12/04	10/07/04	23/01/05	13/03/05
17/05/05 to 23/04/05	02/01/05	17/07/04	30/01/05	20/03/05
24/04/05 to 30/04/05	09/01/05	24/07/04	06/02/05	27/03/05

Expected week of confinement (EWC) commencing Sunday	Qualifying week (QW) commencing Sunday	Latest start date for 26 weeks' employment	11th week before the EWC commencing Sunday	4th week before the EWC commencing Sunday
01/05/05 to 07/05/05	16/01/05	31/07/04	13/02/05	03/05/05
08/05/05 to 14/05/05	23/01/05	07/08/04	20/02/05	10/04/05
15/05/05 to 21/05/05	30/01/05	14/08/04	27/02/05	17/04/05
22/05/05 to 28/05/05	06/02/05	21/08/04	06/03/05	24/04/05
29/05/05 to 04/06/05	13/11/05	28/08/04	13/03/05	01/05/05
05/06/05 to 11/06/05	20/02/05	04/09/04	20/03/05	08/05/05
12/06/05 to 18/06/05	27/02/05	11/09/04	27/03/05	15/05/05
19/06/05 to 25/06/05	06/03/05	18/09/04	03/04/05	22/05/05
26/06/05 to 02/07/05	13/03/05	25/09/04	10/04/05	29/09/05
03/07/05 to 09/07/05	20/03/05	02/10/04	17/04/05	05/06/05
10/07/05 to 16/07/05	27/03/05	09/10/04	24/04/05	12/06/05
17/07/05 to 23/07/05	03/04/05	16/10/04	01/05/05	19/06/05
24/07/05 to 30/07/05	10/04/05	23/10/04	08/05/05	26/06/05
31/07/05 to 06/08/05	17/04/05	30/10/04	15/05/05	03/07/05

The tables can be used to establish entitlement to SMP.

Example

An employee who starts work for an employer on 5 January 2004 is pregnant and has an EWC beginning 17 October 2004. If the employee had started work at any time on or after 18 January 2004 then the 26 weeks' employment criterion would not have been met and she would not be eligible for SMP.

(a) Using the Tables look up the EWC in column 1: 17/10/04 to 23/10/04.

(b) Using the Tables find in the second column the date of the start of the QW: Sunday 4/07/04.

(c) Using the Tables find in the third column the date of the latest start date for 26 weeks' employment: Saturday 17/01/04.

(d) Compare the date found in the third column to the actual start date of employment of Monday 5/01/04.

(e) Determine whether the 26-week continuous employment rule is met.

(f) In this case, the criterion has been satisfied as 5 January is before the latest start date found, 17 January 2004.

Inland Revenue Guidance [15.4]

The Inland Revenue publishes each year, just prior to the start of the tax year, a Booklet CA 29 'Manual for Employers — Statutory Maternity Pay'. Overall guidance on maternity rights, including the employment legislation governing maternity leave and other statutory rights, is available by going to www.dti.gov.uk/er/maternity.htm. For interactive information see www.-tiger.gov.uk. A guide to Maternity Benefits, booklet NI17A is available from www.dwp.gov.uk or from local Benefits Agency offices.

Questions and Answers [15.5]

Question

Why isn't the official guidance relating to SMP and maternity-related employment rights covered in one manual?

Answer

The operational responsibility for SMP and maternity leave and its associated employment rights are split between two separate departments. The Department of Trade and Industry is the governing body ➡

for issues relating to the pregnant employee's employment protection rights, including maternity leave. The responsibility for administering SMP transferred from the Contributions Agency, an executive agency of the DSS, to the Inland Revenue NICO, in April 1999. As a consequence, the Inland Revenue is the first of the authorities, who decide questions relating to an employee's entitlement to SMP.

Question

What does the term 'place of business' mean?

Answer

There is no definition of the phrase 'place of business' in Social Security legislation. Whether an employer has a place of business is a question of fact and may depend on how the employer's business operates. Generally, an employer can be said to have a place of business in the United Kingdom if:

- they have a fixed address or occupy premises where they are, or are present with the consent of, the lawful owner or tenant, and
- an activity takes place, which need not necessarily be remunerative in itself, but is in furtherance of the purposes of the business. The business does not need to be of a trading or commercial nature.

16. Who is Eligible?

Employee's Eligibility to SMP [16.1]

To be entitled to receive SMP, the woman must be, or have been, an employee. An employee for the purposes of SMP means a woman over the age of 16 who is gainfully employed in Great Britain either under a contract of service or in an office (including elective office) with general earnings as defined by the *Income Tax (Earnings and Pensions) Act 2003* (*ITEPA 2003*), *s* 7. 'General earnings' are defined in *ITEPA 2003, s 62* as:

- any salary, wages or fee;
- any gratuity or other profit or incidental benefit of any kind obtained by the employee if it is money or money's worth; or
- anything else that constitutes an emolument of the employment.

Where a woman over age 16 is treated as an employed earner by virtue of the *Social Security (Categorisation of Earners) Regulations 1978* (*SI 1978 No 1689*), she is treated as an employee. If she is not treated as an employed earner by virtue of these Regulations, she is not treated as an employee for SMP purposes. Any woman who is in employed earner's employment under a contract of apprenticeship is treated as an employee.

A wholly self-employed woman will not qualify for SMP, as her earnings will never attract an employer Class 1 NIC liability, as she has no employer.

Eligibility conditions [16.2]

In order to qualify for SMP the pregnant employee must satisfy certain criteria as set out in Social Security law.

Checklist: SMP Qualification Rules

The pregnant employee must:

(a) have been employed by the same employer for a continuous period of 26 weeks into the employee's QW. The QW is the fifteenth week before the employee's EWC (see **14.4**);

(b) have average gross weekly earnings for Class 1 NIC purposes (see **19.4**) in the relevant period of not less than the LEL immediately prior to the end of the QW;

(c) still be pregnant at the beginning of the eleventh week before the EWC, or have had the baby by then. Give her employer at least 28 days' notice (in writing if her employer requests it) of the date from which she expects his liability to pay her SMP is to begin. If it is not reasonably practicable for her to give 28 days' notice before that date, the notice must be given as soon as is reasonable practicable;

(d) give her employer at least 28 days' notice (in writing if her employer requests it) of the date from which she expects his liability to pay her SMP is to begin. If it is not reasonably practicable for her to give 28 days' notice before that date, the notice must be given as soon as is reasonable practicable; and

(e) have stopped working for her employer (see **17.4**).

All the above conditions must be met in order for a woman to qualify for SMP.

Continuous Employment **[16.3]**

The first question the employer needs to consider in determining whether a woman is eligible to receive SMP is whether she has had continuous employment with the same employer for a period of at least 26 weeks continuing into the QW (see **14.4**).

> *i* In practice, the employee must have been in employment for a continuous period of at least 26 weeks ending with the week immediately preceding the 14th week before the EWC to qualify for SMP.

The employee must therefore have been employed into the 15th week before the EWC or she will not be eligible for SMP. She may have worked for only part of that 15th week: it need not have been for the entire week, but she must have been liable to perform some work during that week.

The continuous employment rule is satisfied if:

- the employee's baby is born before or during the QW, and
- she would have completed 26 weeks' employment with the employer into the QW if the baby had not been born early.

> ***Example***
>
> Daphne began working for her employer on 15 September 2003. Her EWC is the week of 20 to 26 June 2004. Her QW is therefore the week beginning 7 March 2004. She gives birth early on 1 March 2004. Although her current employer has not continuously employed Daphne for at least 26 weeks by 1 March 2004, she would have been employed for at least 26 weeks by 13 March 2004. Daphne therefore qualifies for SMP.

Interruptions of Work [16.4]

Where in any week a woman is for the whole or part of the week incapable or absent from work for any of the reasons listed below, and returns to work for her employer after the incapacity for, or absence from, work, that week is treated as part of a continuous period of employment with that employer, notwithstanding that no contract of service exists with that employer in respect of that week:

Checklist: Allowable Breaks in Calculating Continuous Employment

(a) The employee is incapable of work in consequence of sickness or injury. However, incapacity for work that lasts for more than 26 consecutive weeks is not counted for continuous employment.

(b) She is absent from work on account of a temporary cessation of work.

(c) She is absent from work in circumstances such that, by arrangement or custom, she is regarded as continuing in the employment of her employer for all or any purpose.

(d) She is absent from work wholly or partly because of pregnancy or confinement. This only applies to a woman who has a contract of service with the same employer both before and after the confinement, but not during any period of absence from work due to her confinement, and the period between those contracts does not exceed 26 weeks.

(e) She is absent from work in consequence of taking paternity leave, adoption leave or parental leave as provided under the *Employment Rights Act 1996*.

(f) In the case where an employee complains of unfair dismissal and is subsequently re-instated through an order of an Employment Tribunal, a compromise agreement under the employment protection legislation or an agreement brokered by ACAS, all the weeks between dismissal and re-instatement (see **24.4**).

(g) In the case of an employee who returns to her employment after a spell in the Armed Forces under the *Reserve Forces (Safeguard of Employment) Act 1985*, her previous employment can be treated as continuous with her current employment although the period of military service is excluded.

(h) In the case of an employee who has been on strike, her period of employment before she went on strike can be treated as continuous with her current employment although any week or part week while she was on strike is excluded. Any week or part week during which an employee is 'locked-out' counts towards meeting the 26 weeks' continuous employment rule.

Example

Kim is employed for 30 weeks into the QW. During that period, she was on strike for five weeks. Although continuity of service has not been broken, the employer can count only 25 weeks' continuous employment and so she does not qualify for SMP.

There are special rules for agency workers. There may be complete weeks when an employee is not working for that agency. This does not necessarily mean that continuity of employment is broken.

Employment Agencies [16.5]

If a woman has worked through an employment agency in each of the 26 weeks into the 15th week before the EWC (the QW), she may be eligible for SMP from the agency. Even if there were complete weeks in which the woman did not work, she may still qualify if she was unable to work for example because of sickness, injury, leave under the *Working Time Regulations 1998 (SI 1998 No 1833)*, pregnancy or because the agency was unable to offer work.

If there was no employment in the QW itself, the woman can still be treated as employed in that week if all the following conditions are satisfied:

- the agency had no work for her;

- she was not intending to start her maternity absence at that time and was available for work after the QW; and
- she did in fact have further employment with the agency before starting her maternity absence. A woman, intending to go on working but who is sick must actually resume work within 26 weeks of stopping before she can be regarded as working into her QW.

Spasmodic Employment [16.6]

A pregnant employee who is only employed spasmodically for fixed periods whenever and wherever the need for her service arises may nevertheless qualify for SMP; such workers could include supply teachers or seasonal workers.

Interruptions of work do not necessarily mean the continuous employment test cannot be satisfied. However, if the employee is absent from work due to sickness (whether the sickness is connected to the pregnancy or not) during the 15th week before the EWC, she can be treated as having worked into the QW even if she does not resume work before starting maternity leave.

For continuity of employment to exist all the following conditions must apply:

- it is the employer's practice to offer work for a fixed period of not more than 26 consecutive weeks;
- such work is offered on two or more occasions during the year and the periods of work do not overlap; and
- the work is offered to the same people that worked during the last such period.

More than One Employment [16.7]

An employee may work under two or more separate contracts of employment for the same employer. In such a case SMP liability may arise separately under each contract of employment provided the employer's Class 1 NICs are paid separately for each contract. The employee may have a different MPP for each contract but SMP is only payable if she is not working under either contract.

If, however, the employee's gross wages are aggregated for Class 1 NIC purposes, there is only one SMP liability. If earnings are aggregated, the employee must have stopped work under both contracts before any SMP can be paid under either contract.

The decision whether two or more employers should be treated as one for SMP may be resolved by an Inland Revenue formal decision (see **23.4**).

Where an employee works under separate contracts for different employers, each employer must consider only its own SMP liability and take no account of the other contract or contracts. As long as the employee is entitled to SMP under at least one contract, State MA (see **26.2**) is not payable.

Example

Polly has a part-time job as a cleaner in a factory in the mornings and as a school dinner lady at lunchtimes. She satisfies the qualifying rules with both employers, so she can receive SMP from each of them and choose a different MPP with each employer.

! Employers should be aware that where an employee starts work or returns to work after the baby is born, for an employer that did not employ her in the QW, their liability to pay SMP will cease (see **18.5**).

Change of Employers **[16.8]**

Where the *Transfer of Undertakings (Protection of Employment) Regulations 1981* (*SI 1981 No 1794*) apply on the taking over of a business and the business or trade is transferred as a going concern, the employee's contract of employment (see **24.2**) is not broken. This means that for SMP purposes the employment is continuous and the new employer must take account of:

- the employee's length of service;
- any earnings with the previous employer; and
- any SMP already paid by the previous employer.

i In practice, the test as to whether the business or trade has been transferred as a going concern is the 'second' employer must see whether the effect of the transfer is to put them in possession of a going concern which they can then carry on without interruption.

Example

If Business B takes over the contracts of employment of all those employed in the Business A immediately before the transfer of undertakings and all rights and obligations arising from those contracts, except occupational pension rights, then the business has been transferred as a going concern.

Checklist: Transfer not Covered by the Regulations

(a) Transfers by share take-over. This is a transfer of ownership of the company, not the business.

(b) Transfers of a contract to provide goods or services if this does not involve the transfer of the business, or part of the business.

(c) Transfers of assets only.

(d) Transfers of undertakings situated outside the United Kingdom.

If the regulations do not apply, continuity is broken and any SMP remains the liability of the original employer.

The following situations will not break the continuity of employment:

Checklist: Change of Employer – Where Service is Treated as Continuous Employment

(a) If by or under an Act of Parliament one corporate body takes over from another as the employer.

(b) If the employer dies and his or her personal representatives or trustees keep on the employee in employment.

(c) If there is a change in the partners, personal representatives or trustees who employ the employee.

(d) If an employee moves from one employer to another where, at the time of the move, the two employers are associated employers, that is if one is a company of which the other, directly or indirectly, has control or if both are companies over which a third company, directly or indirectly, has control.

(e) If a teacher in a school maintained by a local education authority moves to another school maintained by the same authority (including maintained schools where the governors of that school rather than the local education authority are the teacher's employer).

(f) If an employee of a health service employer moves to another health service while undergoing training.

Outside the European Economic Area [16.9]

An employee who qualifies for SMP is not excluded from SMP if she goes outside the EEA during the MPP. Furthermore, an employee who satisfies the qualifying conditions but who is working outside the EEA can qualify for SMP if she is working for an employer who is liable to pay Class 1 NICs on her earnings throughout the period.

Where the employee has worked in the UK and within the EEA for the same employer, and that employer is liable to pay Class 1 NICs for her in the qualifying week, employment within the EEA can count towards the 26-week continuous employment rule. This rule applies even though the employer may not have been liable to pay Class 1 NICs for some of the 26-week continuous employment period.

Checklist: EEA countries

Austria, Belgium, Denmark, Finland, France, Germany, Gibraltar, Greece, Iceland, Eire, Italy, Liechtenstein, Luxembourg, Netherlands, Norway, Portugal, Spain, Sweden and the United Kingdom.

Case study: employee working outside the UK

Roxanne is seconded by her employer to work in Australia as a sports advisor from Sunday 28 March 2004. Upon arriving she meets a 'Crocodile Dundee' hunk of a man from the outback. One thing leads to another and she falls pregnant. She returns to the UK on unpaid leave from 31 May 2004 to 17 June 2004 to tell her family and friends the news. Her EWC is subsequently established as falling in the week 30 January 2005 to 5 February 2005.

Her QW begins 17 October 2004. For Roxanne to satisfy the 26-week continuous employment test her employer must have been liable to pay secondary Class 1 NICs from week ending 1 May 2004 to week ending Saturday 23 October 2004.

> Even though Roxanne took unpaid leave during this time period and therefore no Class 1 liability arose as there were no earnings, the employer still had an underlying liability to pay Class 1. This, therefore, does not break her continuous employment.
>
> Upon returning to Australia in mid-June, her man seems to have gone 'walkabout' and cannot be found. After vainly searching for him, she accepts that she is to be a single mum and returns to the UK in September 2004.
>
> Liability for Class 1 NICs ceases after an employee has worked abroad for 52 contribution weeks, as there is no bilateral treaty agreement with Australia. However, as she returns to work to the UK on or before Saturday 27 March 2005, the liability for Class 1 NICs has remained, and her continuous employment has not been broken.
>
> If Roxanne had became pregnant towards the end of 2004, such that her QW fell some time after the end of the 52-week period and she had still been working abroad after 27 March 2005, her employer would no longer have been liable to pay employers' Class 1 NICs. Therefore, her continuous employment, for SMP purposes, would have been broken.
>
> Roxanne gives birth to a baby boy in February 2004, and SMP is paid.

Domestic Employees [16.10]

There are no special rules governing payment of SMP for female employees in domestic service. If satisfying all the relevant qualifying criteria they are eligible to receive SMP. However, it is not uncommon for nannies to be supplied, in the first instance, by a specialist Nursing Agency and where the person proves acceptable to the family they may subsequently employ the nanny direct.

> *i* In practice, this may often happen, as it can reduce the labour costs and increase the family's' control over the worker.

Although the nanny may continue to work at the same premises, doing the same work at approximately the same rate of pay, such a 'transfer of employer' does not constitute a change of employer within the meaning of the SMP and Transfer of Undertakings regulations (see **16.8**).

Hence, any previous service with the agency is ignored as the nanny has effectively moved to a 'new' employer. Therefore, in order to determine if SMP is payable only the service and level of earnings with the 'new' employer should be taken into account. If the nanny is not eligible to receive SMP she may be eligible to claim a State benefit (see **26.2**).

Government Training Schemes [16.11]

SMP may be payable to a woman employed under a contract of service as part of a Government training scheme.

If the person is placed with an employer by a training agent and the contract is directly between the employer and the agent then no employment status exists and no SMP can be payable. However, if circumstances change during the placement, such that the woman is treated as an employee, then she may be eligible for SMP.

The period of continuous service for SMP purposes only counts from the start of the employment and not from the start of the training period.

Example

Becky is placed with an employer for six months as part of a Government training scheme. She originally receives only a training allowance, but after two months the employer decides that as her work is excellent he will take her on as a full-time employee. For the purpose of continuous service, the two months prior to her attaining employee status are ignored.

National Health Service Trusts [16.12]

The establishment of National Health Service Trusts means that an employee who worked for a Health Authority under a single contract at more than one hospital or unit, one or more of which becomes a Trust, will then have two or more, separate contracts of employment.

Regulations provide for these employees to make an election: to have the contracts treated as one for SMP purposes if it would benefit them. The election lasts until the end of the MPP. Separate elections can be made for each pregnancy, if the employee wishes to exercise that choice.

The special rules only apply to employees that were employed by a Health Authority at the time the contract was split between the Health Authority and Trust(s), or between Trusts. Employees who start working for the Trust(s) after the split:

- are not entitled to make this election;
- will only qualify for SMP from their employers if the conditions are satisfied; and
- does not affect the rules where an employee has more than one contract with the same employer (see **16.7**)

An employee who wants all her contracts to be treated as one must tell all her employers, to make sure that none of them issue a Form SMP1 (see **20.9**) if she does not qualify for SMP under that contract.

> ***Example***
>
> Alice has average weekly earnings (see **19.4**) from the following:
>
> - Trust (Hospital 'A') of £59.20.
> - Health Authority (aggregating her earnings from Hospitals 'B' and 'C') are £62.90.
>
> Under the normal rules she would not qualify for SMP from the Trust or the Health Authority.
>
> However, because the Health Authority employed Alice at the time her contracts were split, she can elect to have her SMP entitlement calculated as though the split had not taken place.
>
> If Alice makes an election, she will be entitled to:
>
> - £109.89 ((£59.20 + £62.90) × 90%) for the first six weeks; and
> - up to £900.00 (£75.00 × 12).
>
> This gives a maximum SMP liability of £2,199.34.
>
> If she does not make an election, Hospital A and the Health Authority will each issue a Form SMP1 (see **20.9**).

Questions and Answers [16.13]

Question

We are an employment agency and one of our regular 'temps' has made a claim for SMP. Are we required to pay her SMP as she doesn't work all the time?

Answer

If an agency was unable to offer the worker work for any particular week, continuity of employment is not necessarily broken. If the agency did offer work, but the worker was not available, the period of absence can count as continuous employment only if she was unable to work because of sickness, injury, annual leave under the *Working Time Regulations 1998 (SI 1998 No 1833)*, or pregnancy. Therefore, it is good practice to record a note of explanation as to why a worker is not available for work, in order to determine any future questions relating to SMP entitlement. If the agency did offer work and this was turned down due to the person not wishing to work, there would be a break in continuity of service.

If there is a complete week from Sunday to Saturday in which a worker is not working for the agency, the agency must consider the reason why she was not working in order to answer the question of continuous employment.

Question

We have received no official notification that an employee is pregnant, but have heard 'on the grapevine' that she is. We do not want to go to the time and trouble of paying her SMP, as she only started a few months ago and she is next to useless anyway. Can we dismiss her before she reaches the 26-week continuous service period?

Answer

SMP legislation offers a degree of protection against unscrupulous employers wishing to take the sort of action you are contemplating. A former employer is liable to pay SMP to any employee who has been employed for a continuous period of eight weeks but who was then dismissed by the employer solely or mainly for the purpose of avoiding liability for SMP.

The employee is considered as employed by her employer until the end of the 15th week before the EWC. Therefore, if she would have qualified for SMP but for the dismissal, she is still deemed to be eligible. For the purposes of calculating her average earnings, the eight weeks immediately prior to the termination of her contract of employment is used as the basis of the calculation.

An employee can be dismissed fairly on the grounds of capability, but under the provisions of the *Employment Rights Act 1996*, dismissal of an employee on the grounds of pregnancy is automatically unfair dismissal.

Question

We have a casual employee who has worked for us on an ad hoc basis for the past year. She has just informed us that she is pregnant. Over the past nine months she has worked for us about 50% of the time. We have not issued a P45 each time she completed her assignment but kept her on the payroll until we have had more work for her to do. She also works for another employer on an ad hoc basis. Will she be eligible for SMP from us?

Answer

If the employee concerned has had 26 weeks' continuous employment into the qualifying week and her average earnings are at, or above the LEL, the employer must consider paying SMP. However, if during the 26-week period into the QW, there were times when work was offered but the employee declined due to her commitments for another employer then this will constitute a break in service for the purpose of the continuous employment test. If the employee was unable to work because of sickness; injury; leave such as paternity leave, adoption leave, parental leave or under the *Working Time Regulations 1998* (*SI 1998 No 1833*); pregnancy; or confinement, such periods of absence will still count as continuous service and the employer must consider paying SMP.

Question

Our workforce consists of a large number of part-time employees. We have one lady who works one day each week for us and for another employer for two days each week. Her average earnings are above the LEL for the relevant period. Do we have to pay SMP as she will be getting it from her main employer?

Answer

If a woman fulfils the qualifying conditions for SMP she can receive payment from all of her employers provided her earnings in each employment exceeded the LEL in the relevant period.

17. Notification and Evidence Requirements

Introduction [17.1]

The right of a woman to receive SMP not only depends on her satisfying the eligibility conditions (see **16.2**) The right is also contingent upon the employee complying with certain conditions regarding notification and provision of medical evidence.

The various rights under the employment legislation given to pregnant workers and those who have recently given birth also depend on the employee giving proper notification and medical evidence (see **27.5**).

Checklist: Notice and Evidence Requirements

Generally, a woman is not entitled to SMP unless she fulfils certain notification and evidence conditions. The main conditions are as follows.

(a) She must give her employer notice of either her confinement or the date from which she expects his liability to pay her SMP to begin (see **17.2**).

(b) She must provide written notice if her employer requires it.

(c) She must give her employer medical evidence (see **17.3**) of the EWC or the confinement.

Notice Periods [17.2]

The principal notice requirement is that the woman must give her employer 28 days' notice of the date from which she expects his liability to pay her SMP to begin. If it is not reasonably practicable for her to give 28 days' notice the notice must be given as soon as is reasonably practicable.

A woman who leaves her employment after the beginning of the week immediately preceding the 14th week before the EWC is not required to give her employer such notice. However, if she is confined before the 11th week before the EWC she is only entitled to SMP if she gives her employer notice, specifying the date she was confined.

Where a woman gives her employer 28 days' notice but is confined before the date on which she expects her employer's liability to pay SMP is to begin, she is entitled to SMP only if she gives her employer a further notice (in writing, if he requests it) specifying the date she was confined and the date her absence from work began. This further notice must be given within 28 days of the date she was confined or, if in the particular circumstances that is not practicable, as soon as is reasonably practicable thereafter.

However, where the woman is confined before the beginning of the 14th week before the EWC, she must give her employer notice (in writing, if he requests it) of the date on which she was confined. This notice must be given within 28 days of the date she was confined or, if in the particular circumstances that is not practicable, as soon as is reasonably practicable thereafter.

A notice contained in an envelope, which is properly addressed and sent by pre-paid post, is deemed as given on the date on which it is posted.

Example

Paula intends to start her MPP on Sunday, 6 June 2004 after ceasing work on Friday, 4 June. However, she goes into early labour on Saturday, 24 April before she has had a chance to give her employer notice of the start date of her MPP. After the birth, which occurred in the early hours of Sunday, 25 April, Paula has other things to occupy her and forgets that she must give her employer notice of the confinement. However, on Saturday, 23 May her monthly payslip turns up in the post and she sees that she has not been paid SMP. Aware that her employer does not work on Saturdays, Paula hurries down to the local post office and puts the required notice in the midday post, thereby fulfilling the requirement to notify her employer within 28 days of the confinement.

If the employee does not provide her employer with the required notice, the employer is not obliged to pay her SMP. The initial decision as to whether there was good cause for the delay in giving the requisite notice lies with the employer.

However, if the employer decides that her explanation of the cause of the delay is unconvincing and refuses to pay her SMP, she has the right to demand a written statement from the employer. This should detail the basis of the employer's refusal to pay SMP, to enable her to appeal against this initial decision (see **23.5**).

Form SMP1 (see **20.9**) can be treated as the written statement, where the employer decides not to pay SMP and the employee requests a written statement about their entitlement.

> **!** The employee's notice does not have to be given in writing unless so requested by her employer. This notice and the notice required to be given by the employee indicating when she wants to start her maternity leave are usually given together (see **27.5**).

Medical Evidence [17.3]

It is a statutory requirement that the employee provides medical evidence of the EWC (or confinement) and that the employer retains such evidence. Medical evidence is normally given by means of the Maternity Certificate MATB1, which is issued by a doctor or registered midwife but cannot be issued earlier than the beginning of the 20th week before the EWC.

The MATB1 states the due date (and so by implication the dates of the EWC) (see **14.3**) and must be an original, not a photocopy. Alternative medical evidence 'in a form substantially to the like effect with such variations as the circumstances may require' can be accepted provided it is not issued before the beginning of the 20th week before the EWC and it states the date the baby is due.

The certificate or other alternative medical evidence, must bear the address of the doctor, which must be stamped on the form or, if signed by a registered midwife, his or her United Kingdom Central Council for Nursing, Midwifery and Health Visiting (UKCC) personal identification number.

Every maternity certificate shall provide the following detail:

Checklist: Medical Evidence Detail

(a) the woman's full name, address and postcode;

(b) the EWC;

(c) if the certificate is given after confinement, the actual date of birth and the EWC;

(d) the signature of the person giving the maternity certificate; and

(e) the date of the examination on which the maternity certificate has been based.

If the employee's baby is born before she has been able to hand over certificate MATB1 (see below), she must, if reasonably practicable, give her employer suitable medical evidence within 21 days of the birth. This time limit can be extended to the end of the 13th week of the MPP, if the employer accepts the employee's reasons for the delay. The medical evidence is normally given on certificate MATB1 (Part A) but in this case it will specify the date the baby was due and the date the baby was actually born (Part B).

i In practice, an employer should also accept a birth certificate as evidence of the date of a birth where the woman's entitlement to SMP depends upon the fact of her already having given birth. If an employer is provided with an original of a birth certificate as evidence of the confinement, this must not be retained but should be returned to the employee. It is sufficient for the employer to retain a record of the date of the birth.

If an employee is eligible to SMP from more than one employer, only one maternity certificate will normally be issued. As such the other employer will have to advise the employee what other medical evidence is acceptable.

Stopping Work [17.4]

In order to be eligible to receive SMP from her employer, the employee must have stopped working for that employer. The *Employment Act 2002* removed the words 'wholly or partly because of pregnancy or confinement' from the *Social Security Contributions and Benefits Act 1992, s 164(2)(a)*. The woman must have actually ceased to work to receive SMP. SMP is not payable by an employer for any week in which the employee works for that employer in the MPP (see **18.4**).

Where a woman leaves her employment at any time after the beginning of the 11th week before the EWC and before the start of the MPP but not later than the week immediately following the week in which she is confined, the first week of the MPP is the week after the week in which her employment ends.

A former employer is liable to pay SMP to a woman who was employed by him for a continuous period of at least eight weeks and whose employment was brought to an end by the former employer solely or mainly for the

Form MATB1

This is your

MATERNITY CERTIFICATE

Use this certificate if you want to claim
Statutory Maternity Pay (SMP)
or Maternity Benefits

Before you use the certificate, please fill in your name and address below

Your full name ______________________

Your address and postcode ______________________

____

____

More information

There is more information in leaflet **FB8** *Babies and Benefits*. You can get this leaflet from ante-natal clinics, or any Social Security office.

You can make free phone calls for general advice about maternity benefits. Ring Freeline Social Security — just dial 0800 666 555.

There are time limits for claiming. You may lose money if your claim is late.

Statutory Maternity Pay (SMP)

You may be entitled to payments from your employer if

- you have worked for the same employer from the beginning of your pregnancy into the 15th week before the week when you expect to have your baby (your 26th week of pregnancy).

Ask your employer if you can get SMP. Do this now.

Maternity Allowance

This is a benefit you may be entitled to if

- you are self-employed
- you do not have an employer
- your employer cannot pay you SMP.

If you think you may be entitled to to Maternity Allowance get form **MA1** from a Social Security office, a maternity clinic or a child health clinic.

Maternity Payment from the Social Fund

You may be able to get this payment if you or your partner

- are getting Income Support or Family Credit.
- get Income Support or Family Credit within 3 months of the birth of your baby.

Ask for form **SF100** from your ante-natal clinic or Social Security office. When you claim you may use this certificate or some other proof, like your clinic appointment card, if it shows when you expect to have your baby.

Child Benefit

You can claim this benefit when your baby is born. Use the coupon in leaflet **FB8** *Babies and Benefits* to get a claim form.

Or write to your Social Security office for one — they will need to know if you are already getting Child Benefit for another child.

(Substitute)(LexisNexis Butterworths Tolley)

Form MATB1

MAT B1

MATERNITY CERTIFICATE

Please fill in this form in ink

Name of patient

TO THE PATIENT
Please read the notes on the back of this form ▶

Part A

Fill in this part if you are giving the certificate ***before*** *the confinement.*

Do not fill this in more than 14 weeks before the week when the baby is expected.

I certify that I examined you on the date given below. In my opinion you can expect to have your baby in the week that includes ....../......./......

We use ***week*** *to mean the 7 days starting on a Sunday and ending on a Saturday.*

Part B

Fill in this part if you are giving the certificate ***after*** *the confinement.*

I certify that I attended you in connection with the birth which took place on ....../......./...... when you were delivered of a child [ ] children

In my opinion your baby was expected in the week that includes ....../......./......

Date of examination ....../......./......

Date of signing ....../......./......

Signature

Registered midwives

Please give your UKCC PIN here

Doctors
Please stamp your name and address here if the form has not been stamped by the Family Practitioner Committee.

purpose of avoiding liability for SMP.Prior to the *Employment Act 2002* removing the words 'wholly or partly because of pregnancy or confinement' from the *Social Security Contributions and Benefits Act 1992, s 164(2)(a)*, women with an EWC before 6 April 2003 who left *voluntarily* for reasons wholly unconnected with pregnancy were not entitled to SMP. As a consequence, there were a small number of women who did not qualify for SMP if they left their employment after the start of the 15th week before the EWC but before the MPP commenced. Prior to a decision of a Social Security Commissioner in 2000 it was always understood that women who left their employment after the start of the 15th week before the EWC for whatever reason, would still receive SMP. However, the Social Security Commissioner determined that if a woman ceased to work for her employer for reasons that were not wholly or partly due to her pregnancy, she would not qualify for SMP.

Secondary legislation was introduced in 2000 to restore SMP in many of these cases where the woman left work involuntarily for reasons wholly unconnected with the pregnancy and their EWC was on or after 4 March 2001. However, the primary powers were insufficient to restore SMP to those few women who leave work voluntarily for reasons wholly unrelated to their pregnancy. This has now been corrected.

> ! The *Social Security Contributions and Benefits Act 1992* now safeguards the employee's entitlement to SMP from the 15th week before the EWC on her satisfying the employment and earnings tests and giving notice where appropriate. This will be the case even if should happen that, for whatever reason, her employment ends after this point. This applies for all women with an EWC on or after 6 April 2003.

Early Births [17.5]

If an employee gives birth early, before the woman has given notice, she is entitled to SMP only if:

- she gives notice to her employer of the date on which she was confined (see **17.2**);
- that notice is given within 28 days of the date she was confined, or if in the particular circumstances that is not practicable, as soon as it is reasonably practicable; and
- if the employer so requests, the notice is in writing.

If the employee has already given her employer notice but in the event she gives birth before the date stated in the notice, the employee is entitled to SMP only if:

- she gives further notice to her employer specifying the date she was confined and the date her absence from work began;
- that further notice is given within 28 days of the date she gave birth or if in the particular circumstances that is not practicable, as soon as it is reasonably practicable; and
- if the employer so requests, the notice is in writing (see **17.2**).

In the above situations any notice which is posted in a properly addressed stamped envelope is taken as being given on the date it is posted.

Where a woman having given the requisite notice to her employer ceases to work for him in a week which is later than the 12th week before the EWC, then the first week in the MPP is the earlier of:

- the week following the week in which she ceased to work, or
- the week immediately following the week in which she is confined.

In this context a week is seven days beginning on Sunday.

Where a woman is confined either before the 11th week before the EWC or after the 12th week before the EWC, and the confinement occurs in a week which precedes that mentioned in a notice given to her employer as being the week she intends to give up work, the first week in the MPP is the week commencing on the day after the day on which she is confined.

Pregnancy Related Illnesses [17.6]

Although in the normal course of events, the earliest that the employee's MPP can begin is the 11th week before the EWC, a woman has a certain amount of discretion as to when her MPP should begin, provided sufficient notice and adequate medical evidence (see **17.3**) is given to the employer. However, if she is absent from work wholly or partly because of pregnancy or confinement on any day which falls on or after the beginning of the fourth week before the EWC, but not later than the week immediately following the week in which she is confined, the first week of the MPP is the week beginning on the day following the day on which she is so absent.

The following examples (and those given in **5.6**) illustrate the treatment.

Examples

1. Pauline has been absent from work because of a pregnancy-related illness since 14 January 2004. Her EWC is the week beginning Sunday, 2 May 2004, and she had given her employer notice that she would finish work on Friday, 16 April. However, because she is incapable of work on Sunday, 4 April, which is the first day of the fourth week before the EWC, the first week of her MPP begins on 5 April.

2. Lorraine had notified her employer that she would cease work on Friday, 25 June 2004 just before the start of her EWC commencing Sunday, 27 June. However, as Lorraine is first incapable of work for a pregnancy-related reason on Wednesday, 9 June, her MPP begins on Thursday, 10 June.

Questions and Answers [17.7]

Question

How does an employer know whether an illness is pregnancy-related or not – we are not all General Practitioners?

Answer

Deciding if an employee's absence from work in the four weeks prior to her EWC is wholly or partly due to pregnancy may not always be easy for an employer to establish. The Inland Revenue has access to Medical Services and can provide an employer with advice about whether or not the employee's incapacity is related to her pregnancy. If the employer wishes to seek advice from Medical Services the employer should contact their nearest Inland Revenue National Insurance Contributions office. In the mid 1990s the Benefits Agency produced a useful little booklet, NI 200, which gave a list of illnesses and the likelihood of their being pregnancy-related; however, this has not been updated and is no longer listed as an available resource for employers.

Question

One of our employees has lost the MATB1 certificate given to her by the midwife. What can she do about it and can we accept her word for the EWC date in order to start her SMP?

Answer

The simple rule is no medical evidence means no SMP payment for the employee. Once a maternity certificate has been given, no further maternity certificate based on the same examination can be furnished other than a replacement of an original which has been lost or mislaid, in which case it must be clearly marked 'duplicate'.

Question

If the illness is pregnancy-related, how do I work out the fourth week before the EWC?

Answer

The Inland Revenue publishes annually a set of SMP tables in the Employer's Help Book E15 entitled 'Pay and time off work for parents'. The tables give the date of the first day (Sunday) of the fourth week before the EWC. These table are reproduced in the book in Chapter 15 or can be requested from the employer's order line 0845 7 646 646 or by visiting www.inlandrevenue.gov.uk

Question

Our company is having financial problems, such that one of our pregnant female employees and other members of staff are being made redundant on 4 June 2004. Her QW is the week beginning 11 April 2004 and she has already given us written notice that she wishes to start her maternity leave after Friday, 9 July 2004. What happens about SMP in this situation?

Answer

Provided the pregnant employee has satisfied the employment rule of at least 26 weeks' continuous service into the QW and the other eligibility criteria she is entitled to SMP. However, her MPP will start from Sunday, 6 June 2004, five weeks earlier than she originally intended.

18. Who is Excluded?

Introduction [18.1]

Some employees are ineligible to receive SMP from their employer but may be able to claim a Social Security Benefit, normally MA (see **26.2**). The following employees are not entitled to SMP.

Checklist: Employees not Entitled to SMP

Employees who:

(a) are not employed by an employer during the QW (see **16.2**);

(b) do not satisfy the continuous employment rule (see **16.3**);

(c) with average weekly earnings below the LEL for Class 1 National Insurance purposes (see **19.4**);

(d) give late notification (see **17.2**);

(e) do not give the employer relevant medical evidence (see **17.3**); and

(f) are in legal custody (see **18.3**).

Stillbirths [18.2]

A condition of entitlement to SMP is that the woman has reached or been confined before reaching the commencement of the 11th week before the EWC. Confinement for this purpose means:

- labour resulting in the issue of a living child; or
- labour after 24 weeks of pregnancy resulting in the issue of a child whether alive or dead.

Accordingly, in cases of a stillbirth, provided that confinement takes place after the start of the 25th week of pregnancy (ie the 16th week before the EWC), then SMP is payable and the MPP will begin at the beginning of the week immediately following the confinement.

If stillbirth takes place earlier than the 25th week of pregnancy (ie the 16th week before the EWC), SMP is not due but the woman may be due SSP. If the baby survives the birth for only an instant, it is a live birth, not a stillbirth.

Where a woman's labour results in the issue of twins or a greater number of children, for the purposes of SMP she is treated as confined on the day of the issue of the last of them.

Legal Custody [18.3]

An employee will lose her entitlement to SMP if she is taken into legal custody, detained or otherwise sentenced to a term of imprisonment, unless the sentence is suspended. SMP stops at the end of the last week before she is taken into custody and will not resume even if she is released from custody during the MPP. Legal custody does not mean voluntarily helping police with their enquiries.

Working During the MPP [18.4]

SMP is not payable for any SMP week in which an employee works for her employer. If an employee returns to work for an employer paying her SMP after the MPP has started, either before or after the baby is born, she will lose one week's SMP for each week or part week worked in the MPP. There is no daily rate of SMP, so even if the employee only comes in to attend work for just one day, she loses a week's SMP.

The MPP is not extended to take account of any such weeks. Any SMP lost in this way is always at the weekly rate, not at the earnings related rate which is 90% of normal weekly earnings.

Case study: loss of SMP weeks

Kate is pregnant, and is finding work more and more difficult to cope with as the pregnancy progresses. She decides to commence her MPP, at the earliest opportunity, that is to say the 11th week before the EWC. She ceases work on Friday, 11 June 2004 and her MPP starts on Sunday, 13 June 2004. At the beginning of the second week of her MPP, Kate's boss rings to say that Kate is booked on a training course on the following Friday, the 25th June.

This date had been arranged for months but with everything else Kate had completely forgotten about it. Kate is keen to attend as the course is highly relevant to her job and she intends to return to work after giving birth. Kate tells her boss that she would still like to attend the course and her boss agrees.

Kate is paid a salary of £13,000 per annum, so an equivalent day's pay is calculated as per her contract of employment as £50 (£13,000 ÷ 260). She is paid calendar monthly and as there are two Saturdays in her MPP during June 2004, her employer pays her for one week's SMP at the earnings-related rate (ie 90% of her normal weekly earnings). However, no SMP is due for the week 20–26 June) as she worked on 25 June, but basic pay of £50 is paid in its place.

Her employer pays SMP again from 27 June and for the remaining weeks thereafter. As Kate does no further work during the MPP, she receives SMP for 25 weeks. However, Kate is still entitled to the earnings-related rate of SMP for the first six weeks for which SMP is payable in the MPP.

Working Elsewhere During the MPP [18.5]

Generally, SMP is not payable to a woman in respect of any week after she has been confined during which she works for any employer who is not liable to pay her SMP. Accordingly, an employer liable to pay SMP remains liable to pay SMP where the employee starts work for a new employer *before* confinement.

However, if the employee works *after* the confinement (and before the end of the MPP) for an employer who did not employ her during the QW, an employer liable to pay SMP is not liable to pay her SMP in any week in the MPP after she ceases work. In other words, an employer's liability to pay SMP in such circumstances ends completely at the beginning of the week in which she starts work.

Example

Vera has worked for her employer for a period of three years. She becomes pregnant and her EWC is the week running from 20 to 26 June 2004. Her QW is therefore the week beginning 7 March 2004.

Her MPP begins on Sunday, 30 May 2004 and her baby is born on 21 June 2004. Vera has average weekly earnings well in excess of the LEL for tax year 2003/04 and qualifies for SMP. On 19 July 2004, Vera ➡

gives her employer a month's notice and begins to work for a new employer on Monday, 23 August 2004.

Her former employer pays her SMP for the period running from Sunday, 30 May to Saturday, 21 August 2004, the Saturday before she starts work for her new employer. Vera loses entitlement to the remaining six weeks' SMP because she has returned to work after the birth of her baby but before the end of her MPP for an employer who did not employ her during her QW.

However, the above rule does not apply where a woman had two or more employers during the 15th week before the EWC and one or more of them was not liable to pay SMP. If she continues to work for the non-liable employer or employers after her confinement she will still be eligible for SMP.

A woman who after the date of confinement but within the MPP commences work with an employer who did not employ her in the QW is required to inform an employer liable to pay her SMP that she has commenced work (see **17.2**).

Employee Dies [18.6]

An employer is not liable to make payments of SMP in respect of a woman for any week within the MPP falling after the week in which she dies.

Questions and Answers [18.7]

Question

How does an employer know if one of their employees has been taken into legal custody during the MPP or starts working for another employer after the baby is born who did not employ her in the QW?

Answer

The employer in all probability does not know. However, under SMP legislation an employee is obliged to tell a former employer if she starts or returns to work for another employer after her baby is born. For the avoidance of doubt, such situations and the required employee action should be noted in the company's maternity policy, to avoid overpayments of SMP.

Question

Our annual bonus, which is payable in June, is not much but it is better than no payment at all. A few of the employees eligible to receive the bonus are in their MPP. Do we have to defer payment until the MPP is completed in order that the employee does not lose SMP entitlement?

Answer

Payments to employees during their MPP can be made, such as bonus, commission etc. It is not the payment that results in a loss of SMP weeks, it is work performed in the MPP. This is irrespective of whether the work is performed at the employee's normal place of work, at home or at a temporary workplace.

Question

One of our pregnant employees has decided to reduce her already part-time hours during her pregnancy. During the relevant period for calculating SMP, her earnings were above the Lower Earnings Limit (LEL). However, since the QW her earnings have dropped below the LEL. She is hoping to work until the week the baby is due to be born. Will she still qualify for SMP?

Answer

Once an employee qualifies for SMP, she will receive it even if her earnings drop below the LEL at a later date, for whatever reason.

19. How to Calculate Payments

Introduction [19.1]

Since April 2003, SMP is payable weekly during the MPP at:

- the earnings-related rate, in respect of the first six weeks of the MPP in respect of which it is payable; and
- the lesser of the earnings-related rate or the prescribed weekly rate (£100 in 2003/04), in respect of the remaining weeks of the MPP.

The employer is required to perform a calculation to arrive at average weekly earnings in order to verify whether the employee meets an eligibility criterion for entitlement to SMP (see **16.2**). In performing this calculation the employer will also derive the earnings-related rate.

Rate of Payment [19.2]

The SMP earnings-related rate is equivalent to 90% of the woman's normal weekly earnings for the period of eight weeks immediately preceding the 14th week before the EWC. A woman's normal weekly earnings are taken to be the average weekly earnings, which, in the relevant period, have been paid to her or paid for her benefit under the contract of service with her employer.

The earnings-related rate is paid for the first six weeks of the MPP even if it is less than the weekly rate in force at that time. However, where the employee works in the first six weeks of the MPP, she remains entitled to six weeks at the earnings-related rate.

For the remaining weeks of the MPP the amount paid is the lesser of:

- the earnings-related rate; and
- the prescribed weekly rate (£100 in 2003/04).

The weekly rate is usually announced annually in November in the Chancellor of the Exchequer's Pre-Budget Statement, and comes into force on or near the beginning of the following tax year. The weekly rate cannot be less than the weekly rate of SSP in force at the time (£64.35 in 2003/04) or, if there are two or more such rates, the higher or highest of those rates.

For the purpose of calculating the earnings-related rate, the employee's earnings in a prescribed period (the relevant period) are identified and then averaged. This is the same calculation performed to ascertain whether the employee's average earnings reach the LEL.

> ***Examples***
>
> 1. Jeni's QW is the week commencing Sunday, 21 December 2003. Her average weekly earnings in the relevant period are £80.00, which means that she is eligible for SMP as the weekly LEL in force immediately prior to the end of that week is £77 (for tax year 2003/04). The weekly earnings-related rate is 90% of Jeni's average earnings, ie £72.00 (£80 × 90%). Accordingly, for each of the 26 weeks of her MPP, Jeni will be paid £72.00.
>
> 2. Roxanne's QW also falls on the week commencing Sunday, 21 December 2003. However, her average weekly earnings in the relevant period are £120.00, which means that she is eligible for SMP as the weekly LEL in force immediately prior to the end of that week is £77 (for tax year 2003/04). The weekly earnings-related rate is 90% of Roxanne's average earnings, ie £108.00 (£120 × 90%). So, for each of the first six weeks of her MPP, Roxanne will be paid £108.00 and for each of the remaining 20 weeks she will be paid £100.00 as this is less than her weekly earnings-related rate.

Where a payment of SMP is made for any week at the earnings-related rate and the amount due for the week includes a fraction of a penny, the payment is rounded to the next whole number of pence

> ***Example***
>
> Hermione has average weekly earnings of £112.34. The earnings-related rate of SMP payable to her for the first six weeks of her MPP is therefore:
>
> £112.34 × 90% = £101.106, rounded up to £101.11 per week.

The weekly rate of SMP is usually revised at the start of each tax year. The rates payable for the past seven tax years are set out below. In the tax years prior to 2003/04 the weekly rate was known as the standard rate. The rate is advised each year in booklet E12, 'PAYE and NICs rates and limits'.

Tax year	Weekly SMP rate
1996/97	£54.55
1997/98	£55.70
1998/99	£57.70
1999/00	£59.55
2000/01	£60.20
2001/02	£62.20
2002/03	£75.00
2003/04	£100.00

Definition of Earnings [19.3]

For the purposes of determining the employee's normal weekly earnings, 'earnings' means gross earnings and includes any remuneration or profit derived from a woman's employment including payments of SMP, SSP, Statutory Paternity Pay (SPP) and Statutory Adoption Pay (SAP).

However, not included as earnings is any payment or amount which is:

- excluded from the computation of a person's earnings for the purposes of calculating Class 1 NICs; or
- subject to Class 1B NICs as included in a PAYE Settlement Agreement (but see **19.9**).

Payments or amounts excluded from being earnings for the purpose of Class 1 NICs include:

- reimbursement of business expenditure;
- money drawn by directors in anticipation of voting; and
- tax credits (eg Working Tax Credit).

This list is not exhaustive.

The following list shows payments which are included.

Checklist: Class 1 NIC Earnings

- wages or salary;
- overtime;
- holiday pay;
- commission, including any unusual payments, such as an annual bonus;
- round sum allowances; and
- gains from unapproved share options etc.

The above list is not exhaustive. It can also include, amongst other things, other payments liable to Class 1 NICs. This includes vouchers, which can be redeemed or exchanged for both goods and cash or cash alone and personal bills for goods and services supplied where the contract is between the employee and the provider and payment is made direct to the employee or provider.

All earnings paid in the relevant period must be included, even if they are for periods outside the relevant period. For example, a bonus which is paid on a pay date in the relevant period but relates to a period outside of it.

> *i* In practice, the earnings-related rate of SMP payable at 90% may often be well in excess of 100% of the employee's basic pay.

Calculating Average Earnings [19.4]

It is important to calculate a pregnant employee's average weekly earnings for two reasons:

- the employee must have average weekly earnings at or above the weekly LEL as at the end of her QW in order to be eligible to be considered for SMP (see **14.6**); and
- either the first six weeks or the entire 26 weeks of the MPP are payable at the earnings-related rate which is derived from the employee's average weekly earnings (see **19.2**).

The general rule is that earnings are added together over the relevant period up to and including the last normal pay date before the beginning of the fourteenth week before the EWC.

> **i** The relevant period is the period between: (a) the last normal pay day to fall before the appropriate date, and (b) the last normal pay day to fall at least eight weeks earlier than the normal pay day mentioned in (a). The appropriate date means the first day of the fourteenth week before the EWC or the first day in the week in which the woman is confined. The date in (a) is the end of the relevant period, and the day after the date in (b) is the start of the relevant period.

All earnings paid after the date in (b) up to and including those paid on the date at (a) must be included in the calculation.

The use of the term 'normal pay date' can sometimes complicate the calculation. The normal pay date for SMP purposes is defined as:

- a day on which the terms of a woman's contract of service require her to be paid; or
- the practice in her employment is for her to be paid, if any payment is due to her.

Example

Esther is paid weekly on a Friday and her QW is the period 15–21 August 2004. The last normal pay date before the end of the QW is Friday, 20 August. Esther is paid each week, so counting back from the 20 August, the previous eight pay dates are applicable:

week 8	week 7	week 6	week 5	week 4	week 3	week 2	week 1
25/06	02/07	09/07	16/07	23/07	30/08	06/08	13/08

The relevant period is 26 June 2004, the day after the pay date at 25 June 2004 (more than eight weeks before 20 August) to 20 August 2004.

There are a number of special rules, which apply when dealing with the subject of calculating average weekly earnings.

Checklist: Points to Consider with Average Earnings

(a) If a weekly paid employee receives a payment earlier or later than normal, (see **19.6**).

(b) If, on any pay date, the employee was not due any pay, for example, an employee on unpaid parental leave, the period over which the calculation is made remains the same, and blank weeks are included (see **19.5**).

(c) If a backdated pay rise is awarded which retrospectively increases the amount of earnings already paid in the relevant period, the employer will need to recalculate the average weekly earnings, (see **19.9**).

(d) An employee who fails to qualify because her average weekly earnings are below the LEL for NIC purposes, may be able to qualify if benefits and expenses, otherwise liable to Class 1 NICs, were paid to the employee in the relevant period (see **19.1**).

(e) If two or more employments are treated as continuous, and the eight week averaging period covers more than one employment, treat earnings from each employment as if they had all been paid by the last employer in the relevant period (see **16.8**).

Weekly Paid Employees [19.5]

Average weekly earnings for weekly paid employees (including those paid in multiples of a week) are calculated as follows.

Checklist: Average Weekly Earnings – Weekly Payees

(a) Establish the relevant period over which to calculate average earnings.

(b) Add together all the gross earnings during that period.

(c) Divide the result by the number of weeks in the period.

! Rounding should be done only when the total weekly payment at the SMP earnings-related rate is worked out ie the employer should not round the calculation of average weekly earnings.

Example

Rhoswen is paid each Friday. Her EWC is 19 September to 26 September 2004 and the QW starts on 6 June 2004. The last normal pay date before the end of the QW is 11 June 2004.

The last normal pay date at least eight weeks before that is 16 April 2004.

The relevant period is therefore 17 April to 11 June 2002, that is eight weeks.

Her earnings in that period were as follows:

23 April 2004	£134 including overtime
30 April 2004	£120
7 May 2004	£120
14 May 2004	£150 including bonus
21 May 2002	£0 unpaid leave
28 May 2004	£120
4 June 2004	£120
11 June 2002	£120

Grand total for the relevant period = £884

Average weekly earnings = £884 ÷ 8 (only seven weeks were actually paid but the blank week representing unpaid leave must be included) = £110.50.

If the average is at or above the LEL for Class 1 NICs purposes, which applied on the Saturday of the QW, the employee can qualify for SMP, irrespective of the fact that no Class 1 NIC liability has been paid.

Example

Jasmine has average weekly earnings of £77.00, which is the same as the weekly LEL in force at the end of her QW (28 March – 3 April 2004), but less than the earnings threshold for Class 1 NIC purposes (£89 per week). Consequently, Jasmine has no actual Class 1 NICs liability, but will still qualify for SMP as her average earnings are at the level of the LEL. The earnings-related rate of SMP payable is therefore:

£77.00 × 90%= £69.30 a week.

Monthly Paid Employees [19.6]

The average earnings calculation process for a monthly paid employee is as follows:

Checklist: Average Weekly Earnings – Monthly Payees

(a) Establish the relevant period.

(b) Aggregate all the earnings paid in the relevant period.

(c) Divide the total in (b) by the nearest number of calendar months covered by the payments, applying the rounded rules (see below). In most (but not necessarily all) cases this is two months.

(d) Multiply the total in (c) by 12 and divide by 52 to obtain the employees average weekly earnings.

> **!** Rounding should be done only when the total weekly payment at the SMP earnings-related rate is worked out ie the employer should not round the calculation of average weekly earnings.

If there is not a whole number of calendar months in the relevant period, the rounding rules are to be applied for monthly paid employees as follows:

- 30 and 31 day months: 15 days or less round down, 16 days or more round up.
- 28 and 29 day months: 14 days or less round down, 15 days or more round up.

Example

Niamh is expecting her baby during the week 28 March to 3 April 2004. The QW therefore begins on Sunday, 14 December 2003 and ends on Saturday, 20 December 2003.

It is the employer's practice to pay employees their December salary early but, apart from that, employees are paid on the last working day of each month.

Niamh's last normal pay date before the end of the QW is 18 December 2003. The last pay date at least eight weeks before that is 30 September 2003. The relevant period over which to average the employee's earnings is therefore 1 October to 18 December. ➡

In that period, the employer paid Niamh £647 on 31 October, £535 on 28 November and £645 on 18 December.

Total gross earnings in the period = £1,827

The payment covers three months (two months and 18 days is rounded up)

£1,827 ÷ 3 = £609

£609 × 12 = £7,308

£7,308 ÷ 52 = £140.53846 average weekly earnings

Employers must include all payments falling due to be made in the relevant period. If, in the above example, a bonus had become payable on 14 November 2003, and a supplementary pay run made, then the bonus payment would have been added to the other gross earnings in the relevant period.

Mistimed Payments [19.7]

A new interpretation of how the average earnings for weekly paid employees are to be calculated was introduced with effect from 6 April 1998.

This revised procedure applies where employees are paid weekly, or in multiples of weeks, and where a normal payment has been made early or late, so the relevant period (as in **19.4** above) contains more, or less, than eight weeks' pay, or is not an exact number of weeks. If this applies, then payments should be divided by the number of weeks covered by the payments rather than the number of weeks in the relevant period.

The change applies only to regular payments of earnings and does not affect other payments made within the relevant period, such as bonus payments or commission.

Examples

1. Morag works on an industrial estate and is pregnant. Her employer operates a holiday pay in advance scheme. She goes on holiday for two weeks and receives two weeks' holiday pay on the last pay date prior to the holiday starting. When her employer calculates her average weekly earnings, these two weeks were paid early on the last day before the start of the relevant period. Therefore, the first two weeks in the

relevant period are 'nil pay weeks' and there are only six weeks' earnings in the eight-week period. To calculate the average weekly earnings figure, Morag's earnings in the relevant period are divided by six and not eight.

2. Fiona was off sick and did not notify her employer within the required time. Two weeks' earnings were withheld until the matter was resolved two weeks after her return to work. Three weeks' earnings, including two weeks paid late, were paid together on the second pay date after the start of the relevant period for SMP calculations. There are ten weeks' earnings in the eight-week period. In this situation the ten weeks earnings are divisible by ten.

Employees Paid at Other Intervals [19.8]

If, unusually, an employee is paid at irregular intervals, the average earnings calculation is as follows:

- add together the gross payments in the relevant period;
- divide the total by the number of days the period covers;
- multiply by seven, but do not round the earnings figure.

Example

Catherine is part of the sales team and is paid on a commission-only basis at irregular intervals. Her EWC is 21 December 2003 to 27 December 2003 and the QW starts on 7 September 2002.

The last normal pay date before the end of the QW is 5 September 2003. The last normal pay date at least eight weeks before that, is 20 June 2003.

The relevant period is therefore 21 June 2003 to 5 September 2003.

Her earnings in that period were:

11 July 2003	£1200.54
15 August 2003	£1649.16
5 September 2003	£6494.46

Total earnings are therefore £9344.16

Number of days in the relevant period = 77

Average weekly earnings = £9344.16 ÷ 77 × 7 = £849.46904

Directors of Limited Companies [19.9]

The calculation of the average weekly earnings for SMP purposes of any director of a limited company who is paid contractually on a weekly or monthly basis should be carried out in exactly the same way as for employees in general depending on the earnings period.

In the case of directors who are paid only as a result of an annual voting of fees, it is important to note that any money drawn in advance of the voting is not classified as earnings for the purposes of calculating average weekly earnings. Only the amount actually voted annually can be included in the calculation and the date of the vote is the 'normal pay day' (see **19.4**) that must be used.

Where the director is paid contractually and by annual vote, if the annual vote falls within the relevant period, the amount voted is taken into account in the same way as any other payment. Otherwise, employers should calculate average weekly earnings in the normal way depending on the director's earnings period.

Example

Suzy is a director of a fashion company and her contract of employment stipulates that she is to be paid annually each year, at a date to be determined by the Board, at the company's Annual General Meeting. Her QW is the 15–21 August 2004. Her last pay date before the end of the QW, is the 30 January 2004. The last normal pay date falling at least eight weeks before this date is 29 November 2002, 14 months previous to the last pay date before the end of the QW.

The relevant period is 30 November 2002 (the day after the pay date at 19 November 2004) to 30 January 2002. Suzy is regarded as not being paid weekly or monthly and therefore is paid at irregular intervals. All earnings paid in this relevant period will be divided by the number of days in the relevant period (see **19.8**).

Earnings Covered by Backdated Pay Rises [19.10]

If a backdated pay rise is awarded, which retrospectively increases the amount of earnings payable during relevant period, the employee's average weekly earnings have to be recalculated by the relevant employer. As a result:

- an employee previously excluded could become entitled to SMP (see **14.6**); or
- the amount of SMP payable could increase (see **19.2**).

> ***Case law***
>
> *Facts*
>
> This follows a judgement given by the European Court of Justice in the case of *Gillespie v Northern Health and Social Services Board (C324/93) [1996] IRLR 214*. The employee argued that as she was in receipt of a backdated wage award, which included a sum that was payable for the relevant period used to calculate her average weekly earnings, the average weekly earnings must be recalculated.
>
> *Findings*
>
> The judgement given on 12 June 1996 ruled that employers must take into account those extra earnings even though they were actually paid and therefore received by the employee after the end of the relevant period. The employer therefore had to pay arrears of SMP to take account of the difference in pay between the amount actually received at the time, and the amount she would have received if the pay rise had been given on the date it was due.

The judgement and the consequential amending legislation is likely to affect payments of:

- normal wages and salary;
- overtime;
- commission payments, for example, where the commission is based on a percentage of goods or services sold and that percentage is increased as part of a backdated pay award.

Example

Veronica's certificate MATB1 gives her EWC as the week 6 to 12 June 2004. Her QW is the week beginning 22 February 2004. Her contract of employment specifies that she is paid on the last working day of each month. Veronica starts her MPP on 30 May 2004. The last normal pay date before the end of the QW fell on 30 January 2004.

The relevant period over which to average her earnings is 1 December 2003 to 30 January 2004.

In that period her earnings were:

30 December	£1,860
30 January	£1,860 + £250 special bonus.

Total earnings in the relevant period = £3,970.

Average weekly earnings: = £3,970 ÷ 2 × 12 ÷ 52 = £458.0769.

The earnings-related rate is £412.27 (ie £485.0769 × 90%) rounded up.

So, for the 26 weeks of the MPP Veronica is paid six weeks at the earnings-related rate of £412.27 and 20 weeks at the weekly rate, as this is less than the earnings-related rate.

However, on 25 September 2003, Veronica formally claimed she should be on a higher rate of pay. In March 2005, following a lengthy assessment of her grade and duties, her employer increases her salary retrospectively to 25 September 2003 and calculates the arrears of pay due. The increase equates to 3.1% on salary and overtime, but not the special bonus Veronica received in January 2004.

Because of the backdated pay award, Veronica's average earnings and therefore her earnings-related rate of SMP are to be recalculated, as follows.

30 December 2002	£1,860 × 1.031 = £1,917.66
30 January 2003	£1,860 × 1.031 = £1,917.66 + £250 special bonus

Total earnings in the relevant period = £4,085.32

Average weekly earnings: £ 4,085.32 ÷ 2 × 12 ÷ 52 = £471.3831, which gives a revised weekly earnings-related rate of £424.24 (ie £471.3831 × 90%).

The difference between the weekly earnings-related rate paid to Veronica in 2004 and the weekly earnings-related rate that she would have received had it reflected the increase in salary, is £11.97 (ie £424.24 – £412.27).

Veronica's employer calculates that she has been underpaid £71.82 (ie £11.97 × 6) in SMP, and pays this to her in April 2005.

Where a woman whose earnings were previously below the LEL becomes entitled to SMP only as a consequence of taking into account a backdated pay rise, the employer can:

- assume that she received MA (see **26.2**) payable directly by the Department for Work and Pensions; and
- only pay arrears of SMP, which exceed the standard rate of MA paid to her for each week.

The standard rate of MA is the same as the weekly rate of SMP: £100.00 a week for tax year 2003/04. If the woman has not received MA, or receives MA at less than the standard rate, she can get a letter from the Department for Work and Pensions stating either that she has not received MA or the rate she has received. The employer must then pay SMP in full or the difference between the MA she has received and the SMP the employer is due to pay following recalculation of average weekly earnings.

Example

Mona gives her employer notice that she intends to cease work on Friday, 14 November 2003 and to start her maternity leave then. Mona gives birth on 17 December 2003, which is within her EWC of week commencing Sunday, 14 December 2003.

As Mona's average weekly earnings in the relevant period are £70.40, which is less than the LEL in force at the end of the QW (£77 per week in 2003/04), she is not entitled to SMP. Accordingly, she claims MA from the Department for Work and Pensions and receives payment at the rate of £63.36 a week. However, during her maternity leave, Mona's employer awards her a pay increase of £8.00 a week, backdated to 1 April 2003. ➡

> Although her employer recalculates her average weekly earnings in the relevant period to be £78.40, this is less than the weekly rate of MA (£100 in 2003/04) and therefore he cannot at this time make a payment of SMP to Mona. Having had this explained to her, Mona provides her employer with a letter from the DWP showing that she has been paid £63.36 a week in MA. Her employer can now pay her SMP of £7.20 per week (£78.40 × 90% = £70.56 – £63.36) for 26 weeks.

The Gillespie judgement does not apply to:

- negative pay awards, eg wage reductions;
- late payment of earnings, eg where an error was originally made;
- any other amendments or payments made in the relevant period; or
- the calculation of average weekly earnings for SSP purposes (see **6.15**).

In the case of a woman who has given in her resignation and does not intend to return to work after the birth, the terms of the employment contract may state whether she benefits from any backdated pay rise. If she is entitled to the backdated pay rise, her average weekly earnings must be recalculated and any SMP arrears paid to her. Any additional payment of SMP should be included as part of gross pay as normal.

Case law

Facts

In *Alabaster v Woolwich PLC [2000] IRLR 754 EAT*, the Employment Appeal Tribunal (EAT) on 7 April 2000, again examined the issue of average weekly earnings calculations.

Mrs Alabaster's EWC was the 11 February 1996 and her relevant period was established as the eight weeks prior to 29 October 1995. Her annual salary during this period was £11,619, and the average weekly earnings calculation resulted in an SMP higher rate of £201.10 per week. However, from 1 December 1995 her basic annual salary was increased to £12,801 and her maternity leave period started on 8 January 1996. Her claim was based on the additional maternity pay that would have been payable had she enjoyed the benefit of the pay increase, which took effect after the end of the relevant period.

Findings

The EAT found that a woman was entitled to the benefit of a pay rise, whether backdated or not, which took effect at any time between the start of the relevant period and the end of her maternity leave period. The earlier Gillespie ruling did not confine itself to the relevant period the applicant was entitled to the benefit of the pay rise in the calculation of her SMP higher rate.

By June 2002, the *Alabaster* case had been referred to the European Court of Justice for a decision as to whether the current UK application of the *Gillespie* decision is contrary to European Law.

Earnings Covered by PAYE Settlement Agreements [19.11]

If an employee is excluded from SMP because her average weekly earnings were less than the LEL, the employer must check whether benefits or expenses were given which would otherwise have attracted a Class 1 NIC liability within the relevant period, but which were instead subject to a Class 1B NIC liability.

A Class 1B NIC liability arises where certain items are included in an employer's PAYE Settlement Agreement (PSA). A PSA is designed such that the employer and not the employee can meet the tax and associated NICs liability on expense payments and benefits in kind provided in the particular tax year.

If during the relevant period a benefit or expense was provided to the employee, its value for Class 1 NICs purposes is to be brought into the average earnings calculation. However, if the employee's average weekly earnings are such that there is entitlement to SMP without including the PSA item (or items) the value of the item is not to be included.

Examples

1. Sam has average weekly earnings of £75.00 in the relevant period and therefore at face value is excluded from receiving SMP in the tax year 2003/04. However, in addition for each of the pay weeks in the same period, the employer gives Sam a £5 Marks and Spencer gift voucher. This voucher is included as part of the employer's PSA and attracts an associated Class 1B NICs liability. In this instance the employee's average weekly earnings are £80.00 per week, as the earnings calculation must include the 'minor' benefit received by the

employee. (The majority of non-cash vouchers attract a Class 1 NICs liability with effect from 6 April 1999.)

Where a backdated pay award covers a relevant period and earnings included in a PSA have already been taken into account, average weekly earnings should be calculated by:

- using the original earnings excluding the Class 1B NIC earnings;
- adding on the backdated pay award; and
- including Class 1B NIC earnings at this point only if the woman's average weekly earnings are still below the LEL.

2. Cara's average weekly earnings in the relevant period are £68.00, which is less than £77 (the LEL in force in 2003/04). Although her employer includes a weekly voucher of £5 in a PSA, this only brings her average weekly earnings up to £73.00, still below the LEL. However, Cara receives a pay award backdated to before her relevant period, which means that her average weekly earnings are increased from £68.00 to £73.00. Adding the average weekly value of the vouchers means that her average weekly earnings exceed the LEL and she is therefore entitled to SMP. Of course, not being entitled in the first instance to SMP, Cara had claimed MA from the DWP. Her employer is only liable to pay her the difference between £70.20 (being £78 × 90%) and the weekly amount of MA Cara received.

Questions and Answers [19.12]

Question

What must an employer do about calculating average earnings if the baby is born before or during the QW?

Answer

If a baby is born early – before or during the employee's QW – then earnings should be averaged over the eight weeks ending with the last pay date before the week in which the baby was born.

Question

One of our employees has had a difficult pregnancy, such that she has been absent ill since the early stages. We do not operate an OSP ➡

scheme and therefore have only paid her SSP. When we come to calculate her average weekly earnings, we find that they are below the LEL. Can we pay her SMP as her average weekly wage when in work is well in excess of the LEL?

Answer

This is one of the ways in which the average earnings calculation can be most unfair for certain employees. If over the eight weeks in the relevant period, the employee had been ill and in receipt of SSP only, she will be ineligible to receive SMP (the weekly rate of SSP is currently less than the weekly LEL). The employer has no powers of discretion when applying the average earnings rules, the employee either meets the earnings condition or she does not. Particular circumstances, no matter how unfair they are perceived as, cannot be taken into account.

Question

We are due to pay our employees an annual bonus in December 2004. One of our senior managers has calculated that her average weekly earnings calculation is to be based on earnings falling due to be paid in the calendar months January and February 2005. Can we defer payment, so that this 'boosts' her SMP earnings-related rate?

Answer

A woman may gain if she receives more than her usual pay in the relevant period. She may be disadvantaged if she receives less. However, the relevant period is not a 'moving goalpost' that employers can adjust as they feel like it to best suit their employees. If such action was deliberately taken, the Inland Revenue would undoubtedly challenge this and would take into account the following two factors:

- what, if any, was the contractual date to receive the bonus payment; and
- if no contractual entitlement existed, when was the bonus payment made to other qualifying employees.

The Inland Revenue has previously stated that they are not aware that 'juggling' of earnings to boost SMP payment is a particular problem. However, it is one of the areas that they are continuing to monitor. ➡

Question

What happens if the employee receives a backdated pay award paid in the relevant period and she subsequently becomes pregnant again shortly after giving birth to the first child?

Answer

A woman may benefit twice from the same pay rise where it affects her earnings for the relevant period of a previous pregnancy. This will happen if the backdated pay award is paid in the eight-week period used for the second sequence of SMP payments, but covers the eight-week period used for the first sequence of SMP payments.

Question

We omitted to include an employee's overtime claim in a particular pay period, due to late receipt in the payroll office. This has adversely affected the employee's average earnings calculation and hence the earnings-related rate of SMP. Can we now adjust the earnings related calculation to take this payment of overtime into account?

Answer

There is no requirement within the SMP legislation to take into account any late payment of earnings where a mistake has originally been made. The only provision that applies is where a regular payment of earnings, such as a weekly wage has been 'mistimed', for instance where holiday pay has been paid in advance for a weekly paid employee. Other irregular payments like overtime, commission or bonuses are not to be adjusted in calculating the employee's average weekly earnings. It is earnings paid in the relevant period, irrespective of the fact that they may be for work performed outside the relevant period, that count.

20. Payment Process

Introduction [20.1]

Once the employer has established the employee's average weekly earnings and these are at or above the LEL (see **14.6**) which applies on the Saturday at the end of the employee's QW then the employer must prepare to pay SMP, if all other qualifying conditions have been met.

Timing of Payments [20.2]

Although there is no specific requirement regarding the timing of payment of SMP, other than where a decision has been made by an adjudication officer, it is intended that SMP should be paid in the same way and at the same time as normal wages are paid. If the employee is paid weekly, a week's SMP is usually paid for the same period, likewise for those paid in multiples of a week. If the employee is paid monthly, typically the amount of SMP the employer pays in any month depends upon the number of Saturdays in that month.

Example

Jayne's SMP period starts Sunday, 18 April 2004. She is contractually entitled to be paid her salary on the last working day of the month so SMP is paid as follows:

April: Sunday, 18 April to Saturday, 24 April (one week)

May: Sunday, 25 April to Saturday, 29 May (five weeks)

June: Sunday, 30 May to Saturday, 26 June (four weeks)

July: Sunday, 27 June to Saturday, 31 July (five weeks)

August: Sunday, 1 August to Saturday, 28 August (four weeks)

September: Sunday, 29 August to Saturday, 25 September (four weeks)

October: Sunday, 26 September to Saturday, 16 October (three weeks)

However, the employer may agree a different time with the employee or choose to make payment as a lump sum (see **20.4**) at the start of the MPP.

Pay Methods [20.3]

Payment of SMP may be made in a like manner to the employee's normal pay but an employer must *not* make payment:

- in kind; or
- by way of the provision of board or lodgings; or
- by way of services or other facilities

However, because the employee is not present at her employer's place of employment, BACS or posted cheques are likely to be the most convenient form of payment. SMP may lawfully be paid through an agent (eg a payroll service) but it remains the employer's responsibility to ensure that the SMP scheme is administered correctly, including operation of PAYE.

Lump Sum Payments [20.4]

Some employers choose to pay a woman her entire SMP entitlement in the form of a lump sum at the beginning of the MPP. This is usually the case where the woman will not be returning to work, perhaps due to redundancy (see **24.9**).

The employer should consider the following two points in connection with paying SMP as a lump sum:

- Class 1 NICs and PAYE income tax are payable on SMP and, where the SMP is paid in the form of a lump sum, it is included as earnings in the period in which it is paid. This could make a difference to the amount of Class 1 NIC paid both by the employer and the employee. The introduction of an additional one per cent on employee earnings above the Upper Earnings Limit (UEL) in tax year 2003/04 makes the use of lump sum payments less attractive for the 'higher paid' employee. For tax years prior to 6 April 2003, the fact that no employee NICs liability arose on earnings in excess of the UEL meant that a significant slice of any lump sum could legitimately avoid Class 1 NICs liability.
- The employee may do something, which would disqualify her from receiving SMP at some time during the MPP. In such an event, the employer would have made an overpayment of SMP (see **20.7**) and

would have to pay the appropriate sum previously recovered, back to the Inland Revenue Accounts Office.

Deductions from SMP [20.5]

SMP is treated like pay and so the employer must make deductions for PAYE income tax and Class 1 NICs in the normal way from any employee earnings that include an SMP element.

If an employee has an annual earnings period, for example a director, any SMP paid must be included as part of the total earnings for the whole tax year where assessing Class 1 NICs liability, even if the individual payment is below the weekly or monthly earnings thresholds.

Most deductions which can lawfully be made from pay, for example pension contributions and student loans, can also be made from SMP. However, unlike with SSP, attachment of earnings orders (in Scotland, arrestment of earnings orders) (AEOs), Council Tax AEOs and Deductions from Earnings Orders (DEOs) made by the Child Support Agency, do not apply to payments of SMP.

The legislation governing contributions to an occupational pension scheme stipulates that employee contributions during periods of 'paid maternity leave' (if required by the scheme rules) are to be calculated on the actual maternity pay (SMP and/or contractual pay) being paid to her. The employer must continue to pay contributions based on the employee's standard rate of pay, that is her normal remuneration as if she had still been working.

Offsetting SMP [20.6]

A number of employers operate Occupational Maternity Pay (OMP) schemes that are more generous than the SMP scheme (see **25.2**). In some cases, the OMP scheme lasts longer than the current statutory 26 weeks' MPP

A contractual obligation to pay maternity pay for the same week in which SMP is due is offset by any SMP received; ie SMP is not payable in addition to a contractual payment. Similarly, provided the contractual amount of maternity pay made is at least equal to the minimum amount of SMP due, the SMP liability is entirely satisfied by the payment of the OMP. If these contractual payments are less than the SMP due, the employer must pay the difference.

If OMP is paid from a jointly funded scheme (and it counts as earnings for Class 1 NICs purposes), only that proportion of the payment which has been funded by the employer can offset the employer's liability to pay SMP. Maternity pay derived from the employee's own contributions does not count as earnings for Class 1 NICs purposes and so cannot be used in any offsetting arrangement with a due payment of SMP.

> ***Example***
>
> Jennifer pays £1 a week to a maternity scheme arranged by her employer, which the employer matches with another £1. This scheme pays Jennifer £60 a week during the MPP. The employer can offset no more than £30 of this £60 against the SMP due to be paid each week.

People Unable to Act for Themselves [20.7]

If the employee is unable to act for herself (eg through serious illness) and the employer is in doubt as to whom SMP should be paid, the local Inland Revenue office will be able to appoint someone to handle the payments of SMP. In such cases, the appointee assumes all of the employee's SMP rights; this includes the right to:

- ask for information from the employer;
- ask for formal decisions from the Inland Revenue;
- lodge appeals, and
- receive any SMP due.

In the same way, the employer is able to ask the appointee to supply information relating to the employee's SMP and can expect them to advise of any changes in circumstances that may affect the employee's SMP entitlement.

Any Inland Revenue appointment will end if the employer is informed that:

- in England and Wales, the Court of Protection has appointed a receiver with power to deal with the employee's SMP;
- in Scotland, the employee's affairs are being handled by a tutor, curator bonis, or other guardian acting or appointed in terms of law, or
- in Northern Ireland, the High Court has appointed a controller with power to deal with the employee's SMP.

The receiver, tutor or controller will take over all the employee's rights and responsibilities.

Recovering Overpayments [20.8]

Overpayments of earnings can be recovered from SMP, even where this is the only payment being processed in the relevant earnings period. SMP legislation states that:

> 'For the avoidance of doubt, any agreement between an employer and an employee authorising any deductions from SMP, which the employer is liable to pay to the employee in respect of any period *shall not be* void ... if the employer:
>
> - is authorised by that or another agreement to make the same deductions from any contractual remuneration which he is liable to pay in respect of the same period, or
> - would be so authorised if he were liable to pay contractual remuneration in respect of that period'.

So, provided the contract of employment gives the employer the right to deduct any overpayment of earnings from later earnings, then the deduction can be made from the employee's SMP, even if that is the only earnings receivable by the employee for that later period.

A sample clause may read as follows:

> 'Deductions can be made from my wages or salary in respect of any previous overpayment of earnings including Statutory Maternity Pay'.

> *i* In practice, there is no statutory bar preventing an employer from enforcing a term of a contract of employment, whereby an overpayment of previous earnings is recovered from SMP.

Stopping SMP [20.9]

If an employee has worked into her QW, but is excluded from receiving SMP (see **Chapter 18**), then within seven days of deciding that SMP is not due the employer must:

- complete Form SMP1 (see **20.9**); and

- give the employee the Form SMP1, and any maternity certificate, usually Form MATB1(see **17.3**), previously given as evidence of the EWC by the employee; and
- retain a copy of MATB1, for record keeping purposes.

Form SMP1 must also be completed where the employee ceases to be entitled to SMP during the MPP. The employee can use Form SMP1 to assist her to make any claim for MA (see **26.2**).

Copies of Form SMP1 are available on the CD-ROM, contained in the employer's annual pack. The form can be printed off as an alternative to:

- ordering printed copies; or
- completing the form on-line or printing the form from the Department of Work and Pensions web pages at www.dwp.gov.uk/advisors/claimforms.htm

> ***Example***
>
> Eleanor works part-time and regularly receives £65.40 a week. Ellie's QW is the week beginning Sunday, 21 March 2004. During this week the weekly LEL was £77.00 a week (tax year 2003/04). Her employer calculates her average weekly earnings as £65.40 on receipt of maternity certificate MATB1. Ellie therefore fails to qualify for SMP. Her employer issues Form SMP1 the following day and returns the Form MATB1. Ellie claims MA from the Department for Work and Pensions.

Issuing Form SMP1 [20.10]

Form SMP1 (see below) explains why an employer is not paying SMP and tells the employee how to claim MA from the DWP. The employee will need the maternity certificate to claim MA (see **26.2**). The reasons why SMP is not payable are shown on the form as summaries only. The employer must ensure that all boxes, which apply are ticked accordingly.

In summary, the main situations where eligibility for SMP does not arise or ceases are as follows.

- The employee fails to satisfy the employment rule. The employee must have been continuously employed (or treated as being continuously employed) by an employer for at least 26 weeks into the 15th week before the EWC (see **16.3**).

Form SMP1

SMP1 SS
11/02

Statutory Maternity Pay (SMP)

Employee's surname

Other names

Address

Postcode

National Insurance (NI) number

Works or clock number

Why I cannot pay you SMP

I have ticked the box that applies to you.

☐ I cannot pay you SMP.
I have ticked one of the boxes on the next page of this letter to tell you why.

☐ I cannot pay you any more SMP after the week which ends on ☐ ☐ ☐ .
You are entitled to ☐ weeks SMP from me until then.
I have ticked one of the boxes on the next page of this letter to tell you why I cannot carry on paying you after this date.

■ What to do if you disagree

If you disagree with this decision, please get in touch with me. My name, address and phone number are at the bottom of this page. If you still disagree, you can ask Inland Revenue (NI Contributions) office for advice. You may be able to ask for an Inland Revenue officer's decision. You can contact them by phone, their phone number and address are in the phone book under **Inland Revenue**. You can get leaflet **NI17A** *A guide to Maternity Benefits* from your Jobcentre Plus or social security office for more information about SMP.

■ Maternity Allowance

You may be able to get Maternity Allowance if your earnings have been on average £30 a week or more. For more details contact your Jobcentre Plus or social security office. Ask your ante-natal clinic, Jobcentre Plus or social security office for a **MA1** *Maternity claim pack*.

■ How to claim Maternity Allowance

Fill in the claim form **MA1** which is in the pack and send it to your Jobcentre Plus or social security office with your *Maternity Certificate* **Mat B1** and this letter. If you gave me your **Mat B1**, I have sent it back to you with this letter. If you want to ask me anything about this letter, please get in touch with me.

Employer's signature

Employer' name and address

Postcode

Phone number

Date

(Substitute)(LexisNexis UK)

Form SMP1

Why I cannot pay you SMP – continued

I have ticked one of the boxes to tell you why I cannot pay you Statutory Maternity Pay (SMP).

☐	**You were not employed by me for long enough**	To get SMP you must be employed by me for at least 26 weeks in a row into the 15th week before the week your baby is due, even if your baby is born early. You would not have been employed by me for long enough even if your baby had not been born early. This is because you still would not have worked for me 26 weeks in a row into the 15th week.
☐	**Your earnings were too low**	To get SMP your average weekly earnings must be at least equal to the Lower Earnings Limit. Some employers have a special arrangement with the Inland Revenue to pay Class 1B NI contributions on some of your earnings. This may mean that your employer may not count all your earnings when working out your average earnings. Ask your employer if any of your earnings were included in such an arrangement and then ask them to recalculate your earnings as if you had been paying Class 1 NI contributions on them.
☐	**You did not tell me soon enough that you would be away from work**	To get SMP you must give me at least 4 weeks notice that you will be away from work because you are pregnant. You did not have a good reason for giving me less notice than this.
☐	**You did not give me medical evidence soon enough**	To get SMP you must give me your *Maternity Certificate* **Mat B1**, or other acceptable evidence, within 3 weeks of the start of your Maternity Pay Period. If you had a good reason for taking longer than this, I could only allow you up to 13 weeks to give me this evidence.
☐	**You did not tell me soon enough that your baby had been born**	To get SMP you must tell me about your baby within 4 weeks of the date your baby is born. If you had a good reason for taking longer than this, I could only allow you up to 13 weeks to tell me.
☐	**You were in legal custody**	You cannot get SMP if you are in legal custody at the beginning of your Maternity Pay Period. If you have been getting SMP, you stop getting it when you go into legal custody.

Employer

Please fill in the information on the next page. It helps your employee to claim Maternity Allowance.

Form SMP1

Why I cannot pay you SMP – continued

Some important dates that affect your claim for SMP

• **The week your baby is due**	The first day of that week is	☐ ☐ ☐
• **The week that is 15 weeks before the week your baby is due**	The first day of that week is	☐ ☐ ☐
• **Your Maternity Pay Period**	Your Maternity Pay Period is the period during which you could get SMP. Your Maternity Pay Period starts or would have started on	☐ ☐ ☐

If you work abroad

SMP can be paid anywhere in the world. If you are employed by a British employer but you work outside the United Kingdom, you may still get SMP in certain circumstances.
For further information check your local Inland Revenue office.

Social Security Office

Part of the Jobcentre Plus network,
Department for Work and Pensions

- The employee has average weekly earnings below the LEL in force at the end of the employee's QW; (see **19.4**).
- The employee gave late notification of the start of her MPP (see **17.2**).
- The employee fails to supply medical evidence. Form MATB1 (or other acceptable evidence), is normally required for SMP purposes (see **17.3**).

If an employee becomes pregnant but leaves her employment before the 15th week before her EWC, the employer need take no action and should not issue the former employee with Form SMP1.

Form SMP1 Issued in Error [20.11]

If an employer issues Form SMP1 and subsequently realises that it was a mistake to have done so, the employer should pay the SMP including any arrears of SMP. The employee should be informed and also the employee's local office of the DWP so that any State benefit paid can be stopped.

If the location of the employee's local DWP office is not known, the employer's local DWP office should be informed and they will pass the information on. The DWP will need details of the employee and the period concerned.

Questions and Answers [20.12]

Question

When should SMP be paid?

Answer

Normally SMP is paid at the same time as would the employee's normal wages or salary. However, the employer may agree a different time with the employee, for example, making the payment as a lump sum. If the employee is paid monthly, SMP is usually paid for four or five weeks (there is no daily rate of SMP), dependent on the number of Saturdays in the monthly pay period.

Question

One of our employees who is 15 and works as a 'Saturday casual' also works a few evenings after school. She has just informed us that she is pregnant. Her average earnings are slightly in excess of the LEL. Do we have to pay SMP?

Answer

A woman's age normally has no relevance to paying SMP. However, in this situation, age is relevant even though she may satisfy the other qualifying conditions, as she is not an 'employed earner'. Therefore neither the employee nor employer has a liability to pay Class 1 NICs.

The employer should complete Form SMP1, ticking the box relating to low earnings (not the correct technical reason but the nearest to it as form SMP1 does not specify an 'underage' disqualifying condition). This should be handed to the employee in order that she may claim a relevant social security benefit.

Question

Do we have to issue a P45 to an employee who is on maternity leave and still has a further eight weeks' SMP due? If we give her form P45 it will mean we must make all further payments to her as payments after leaving.

Answer

An employee has every right to request her P45 during her MPP if she is not intending to return to work. However, it would be prudent to enquire why she needs her P45, because if she is going to work for another employer after the baby is born, who did not employ her in the QW, your liability to pay SMP will cease.

21. How to Recover Payments from the State

Introduction [21.1]

Following on from the introduction of SSP in 1983, SMP liability for employers was introduced with effect from 6 April 1987. The stated intention was that employers would relieve the then Department of Health and Social Security of the role of administering the State's social security benefit for employees who stopped work to have a baby. The State, however, retained responsibility for meeting the cost of providing this social security benefit.

Originally all employers were able to reclaim 100% of the cost of providing SMP payments to employees and former employees. Employers recovered the amount of SMP they had paid from the total NICs due for payment to the Inland Revenue Collector of Taxes each month or quarter.

Since SMP payments are liable to Class 1 NICs, additional help was given to employers to compensate them for the cost of paying the NIC liability. Employers were originally also able to recover an additional 7% of the SMP paid, but this rate of compensation has gradually been reduced over the years.

Furthermore, as a result of paying for the improvements to SMP coming into effect in respect of women with an EWC on or after 16 October 1994, the following provisions were made:

- The rate by which many employers were reimbursed for the SMP payments they make was reduced from 100% to 92% with effect for payments from 4 September 1994 and the additional compensation, by then set at 4%, was abolished. (Effectively, the amount of SMP recovery fell from 104% to 92%.)
- Small employers, that is employers who pay £40,000 (£20,000 for tax years prior to 6 April 2002) or less annually in gross Class 1 NICs, continue to receive reimbursement at the 100% rate and retain entitlement to the additional compensation.

The additional compensation rate payable to small employers has varied since 6 April 1995 (see Appendix 2) and the rate set for the tax year 2003/04, is now 4.5% of the employer's SMP liability.

Standard Reimbursement [21.2]

Employers who do not qualify for small employer's relief who make a payment of SMP are entitled to recover an amount equal to 92% of their SMP payments from the payment to the Inland Revenue Collector of Taxes each month or quarter.

The employer can recover SMP from PAYE tax, NICs, student loan deductions and Construction Industry Scheme deductions. These monies are also used by the employer for recovery of payments of tax credits, Statutory Adoption Pay and Statutory Paternity Pay. However, if there is, or is likely to be, insufficient money the employer can apply to the Inland Revenue for advance funding (see **21.5**).

If SMP was paid in a previous tax year but was not recovered by the employer, for whatever reason, the employer must complete Form SP32 (available from the employer's order line 0845 7 646 646) to obtain reimbursement and send to their nearest Inland Revenue office. Recovery of SMP paid in a previous tax year cannot be claimed directly from the Accounts Office.

Checklist: SMP Recovery

(a) Calculate for the month (or quarter) the aggregate of:

- deductions of PAYE income tax;
- NICs payable;
- deductions made in respect of student loan recoveries;
- deductions made on account of tax from payments to sub-contractors;
- SAP; and
- SPP.

(b) Calculate the total SMP liability for the month (or quarter).

(c) Calculate 92% of the amount in (b).

(d) Subtract the amount calculated at (c) from the amount calculated at (a) to arrive at the amount payable to the Collector of Taxes for the month or quarter (see **8.2**).

Case study: SMP reimbursement

Sparta Luxury Goods Ltd is a medium-sized employer specialising in designer goods. During the 2003/04 tax year it has calculated the SMP due to Mary during her MPP as being payable at the earnings-related rate of £312 per week for the first six weeks followed by the weekly rate of £100.00 for 20 weeks. Mary is the only employee on SMP during this period.

The SMP payments to Mary fall as follows:

Tax Month 3	£936.00
Tax Month 4	£1036.00
Tax Month 5	£500.00
Tax Month 6	£400.00
Tax Month 7	£400.00
Tax Month 8	£500.00
Tax Month 9	£100.00

Since Sparta Luxury Goods Ltd is not able to claim small employers' relief, it is only able to claim reimbursement for 92% of the SMP it pays out by making an equivalent deduction from the payments it makes to the Inland Revenue Accounts Office each tax month. The total remittance is reduced on account of Mary's SMP as follows:

Tax Month 3	£861.12
Tax Month 4	£953.12
Tax Month 5	£460.00
Tax Month 6	£368.00
Tax Month 7	£368.00
Tax Month 8	£460.00
Tax Month 9	£92.00

Small Employer's Relief [21.3]

The small employer's relief scheme allows certain small employers to claim reimbursement from the State for 100% of the cost of providing SMP to an employee or former employee. In addition, small employers may, in respect of any payment of SMP made on or after 6 April 2002, claim an additional amount equal to 4.5% of the SMP payment.

The Inland Revenue calculates this additional percentage from the total amount of employer Class 1 NICs estimated to be paid on SMP during the relevant tax year. This is expressed as a percentage of the total amount of SMP estimated to have been paid by all employers during that same tax year.

An employer is treated as a small employer for the purposes of small employers' relief if it paid, or was liable to pay, a set amount or less in gross Class 1 NICs in the qualifying tax year. The qualifying tax year is the tax year preceding the tax year in which the qualifying day falls. The qualifying day is the first day in the employee's qualifying week (ie the 15th week before the EWC).

For qualifying weeks, beginning:

- Sunday, 6 April 2003 to Sunday, 4 April 2004 inclusive, the qualifying tax year is 2002/03;
- Sunday, 11 April 2004 to Sunday, 3 April 2005 inclusive, the qualifying tax year is 2003/04.

The set amount of gross Class 1 NICs made in the qualifying tax year is £40,000. Thus, for SMP paid in the 2003/04 tax year in respect of an employee with a QW of week commencing 11 April 2003 or later, the gross Class 1 NICs in 2002/03 must not have exceeded £40,000.

The set amount of gross NICs is the aggregate of both primary (employee) contributions and secondary (employer) contributions net of employee and employer rebates due in respect of contracted-out pension schemes (salary related or money purchase). The amount of the contribution payments is determined without regard to any other statutory deductions that may be made from them and Class 1A (paid on company cars and other benefits) and Class 1B (payable on PAYE Settlement Agreements) contributions are ignored.

Once an employer qualifies for small employer's relief for a particular employee, the employer can claim it for the whole period for which her SMP is paid.

> **!** The employer must look at the gross Class 1 NIC liability in the last completed tax year before each pregnant worker's qualifying week. Just because an employer qualifies for one employee or in one tax year, this does not mean that the employer automatically qualifies for all employees or all future tax years. If the total amount of gross Class 1 NICs exceeds the set amount in a qualifying tax year, the employer ceases to be eligible for small employer's relief.

The Inland Revenue estimates that in doubling the qualifying threshold for small employer's relief in tax year 2002/03, 60% of all firms can now claim back their SMP costs in full.

Transitional rules applied when the small employer's relief threshold was increased to £40,000 at the start of tax year 2002/03. If the employer newly qualified from 6 April 2002 (that is their gross Class 1 NIC liability was previously between £20,001 and £40,000), they could recover 100% plus NIC compensation on SMP paid from that date. Payments made before 6 April 2002 to the same employee were only recoverable at the normal rate of 92%.

Example

A small company, Just Growing Ltd, has total Class 1 NIC liabilities in recent years as follows:

1998/99	£17,498.34
1999/00	£35,567.23
2000/01	£45,979.88
2001/02	£48,127.43
2002/03	Expected to be in excess of £50,000

Georgia began her MPP on 4 July 2000. Her QW was the week beginning 19 March 2000 and so falls in the 1999/00 tax year. The last complete tax year before Georgia's qualifying week is, therefore, the 1998/99 tax year. Just Growing Ltd qualifies for small employer's relief and can reclaim 100% of the SMP paid to Georgia, plus NIC compensation at the appropriate rate (See Appendix 2).

Jadzia began her MPP on 28 July 2002. Her QW was the week beginning 14 April 2002 and so falls in the 2002/03 tax year. The last complete tax year before Jadzia's QW is, therefore, the 2001/02 tax ➡

year. Just Growing Ltd does not qualify for small employer's relief and can reclaim just 92% of the SMP expenditure it incurred for Jadzia.

New Employers [21.4]

Special arrangements exist for new employers in the qualifying tax year. In the case of a new employer who has paid Class 1 NICs in some, but in less than 12, of the tax months in the previous tax year, for the purposes of testing whether the employer qualifies for small employer's relief, the threshold amount is estimated by:

- adding together all the gross Class 1 NICs made;
- dividing the total amount by the number of months in which they were paid; and
- multiplying the result by 12.

Where in the previous tax year the employer made no NIC payments, but has made contributions in the current tax year, then the same calculation is performed as outlined above as if the contributions had been made in the previous tax year.

Advance Funding [21.5]

The employer can recover the amount of SMP (and any additional amount in respect of small employer's relief) from the monthly or quarterly remittances to the Inland Revenue Accounts Office. The deduction is made as shown in **21.2** above except where and insofar as:

- those amounts either relate to earnings paid before the beginning of the income tax month (or income tax quarter) in which the SMP was paid, or are paid later than six years after the tax year in which the SMP was paid;
- the employer has either received advance funding from the Inland Revenue, or has made a request in writing that the amount of SMP which he is entitled to recover be paid directly to him and he has not received notification from the Inland Revenue that the request has been refused.

If the amount of SMP that an employer is entitled to recover is more than the sum of the Class 1 NICs and income tax due, the employer can deduct the excess from the following month's payment. However, employers can never deduct the excess due for month 12 from month 1 as it is in a different tax year (see **21.2**).

> **!** Current SMP legislation prohibits the employer from recovering SMP in a month earlier than the one in which it is paid.

Where there is, or is likely to be, insufficient money available in the monthly (or quarterly) remittance to recover the amount of SMP, the employer should apply in writing to the Inland Revenue for advance funding. This may be necessary where for example there is nil PAYE or NIC liability or the amount paid in tax credits is high. When making written application for advance funding, the employershould include the following points.

Checklist: Direct SMP Recovery

(a) The amount of SMP that has been paid (will be paid) to the relevant employees.

(b) The amount to be recovered, that is set out the calculation method used in arriving at the recoverable amount.

(c) Direct reimbursement is required because you as the employer will not be able to recover SMP from the payments of NICs and PAYE.

On receipt of the written request, the Inland Revenue Accounts Office can arrange to send payment to the employer.

> *i* In practice, all amounts of SMP received in this way must be entered on the P35 employer annual summary return, in order to reconcile the payment totals.

Questions and Answers [21.6]

Question

We have mistakenly recovered SMP at the wrong percentage rate for this tax year. What should we do?

Answer

If an employer does not recover SMP at the correct rate on a month by month basis then he or she may make an adjustment prior to the ➡

end-of-year returns, Forms P14 and P35 being submitted to the Inland Revenue. For example, if an employer starts to recover SMP under the small employers' relief method when not eligible or recovers at a rate of say 90% instead of 92% it will be necessary to amend the next PAYE remittance due to the Inland Revenue Accounts Office. If too little SMP has been recovered and the sum is more than the next total payment due to the Collector of Taxes then the adjustment can be spread over a period of time, within the same tax year.

Question

Our Accounts Manager makes the monthly PAYE remittance payment but in error he has not recovered any SMP from the remittances made to date. We have only just discovered this error when reconciling our P35 return in preparation for the end of the tax year. Can we recover these sums, back-dated to the start of the tax year?

Answer

Yes, you can recover the SMP. You should contact the Inland Revenue Collector of Taxes to discuss how to effect recovery. This might be from any final remittance due for the tax year in question or by advance funding.

22. Correcting Mistakes and Keeping Records

Introduction [22.1]

The Inland Revenue can supply employers with an SMP record sheet, Form SMP2 (see below), free of charge. This optional form was designed to meet the needs of smaller employers. Many employers will keep these records in computerised form. To obtain copies, contact the employer's order line on 0845 7 646 646 or visit www.inlandrevenue.gov.uk. Many commercial record-keeping systems are also available.

Mandatory SMP Records [22.2]

Employers are required to maintain certain SMP records for a period of at least three years after the end of the tax year in which the maternity pay period ended. The records, which must be kept, are:

Checklist: SMP Records that must be Kept

(a) The date of the first day of absence from work wholly or partly because of pregnancy or confinement as notified by the employee and, if different, the actual date when such an absence first occurred.

(b) Any medical evidence (see **17.3**), for example, the maternity certificate, Form MATB1, as provided by the employee.

(c) A copy of any medical evidence, if the original has been returned to the employee, for example, if for some reason Form SMP1 has been issued (see **20.9**) as the employer's liability to pay SMP has ended.

(d) The weeks in that tax year in which SMP was paid and the amount paid in each week.

(e) Any week in that tax year which was within the employee's MPP period but for which no payment of SMP was made to her and the reasons why no payment was made.

Form SMP2

Inland Revenue

Statutory Maternity Pay (SMP)

Statutory Maternity Pay record sheet

1 About this form

This form is for you, the employer, to use to record details of your employee's SMP where the baby is due on or after 6 April 2003. You must keep these details, but you may keep more if you wish.

Keeping an accurate record will help make sure you pay the correct amount of SMP.

You do not have to use this form, but you may find it helpful.

However, you must keep SMP records for at least 3 years after the end of the tax year to which they relate.

2 What to do now

Please

- read the guidance notes at Part 4, and
- fill in Parts 5 and 6, making any additional notes in Part 7, if appropriate.

3 Further information

For further information on how and when you must pay SMP and what records you must keep, see Employer's Help Book *Pay and time off work for parents, E15.* (Use Employer's Help Book *E15(SD)* if you operate a simplified deduction scheme for National Insurance contributions.)

You can get more copies of this form and the above help books from either

- our website - go to www.inlandrevenue.gov.uk/employers, or
- the Employers Orderline on **0845 7 646 646**.

If you need help with this form or with the SMP scheme, please get in touch with your nearest Inland Revenue office. Alternatively, you can contact the Employer's Helpline on **0845 7 143 143**, or arrange a one-to-one visit with our Business Support Team. You can contact them online at www.inlandrevenue.gov.uk/bst/index.htm, or by phoning your nearest Inland Revenue office.

4 How to use this Statutory Maternity Pay record sheet

This record sheet is in two parts. Use

- Part 5 *Record of notification of maternity absence* when your employee tells you the date she wants to start her maternity absence and as her maternity absence begins, and
- Part 6 *Record of SMP pay period* when her pay period is about to start. You must keep a record of this period even if your employee cannot get SMP for any week or does not come back to work afterwards. If she does not qualify for SMP from the start you only need to fill in the first week of the record.

Recycled Paper

please turn over

Form SMP2

5 Record of notification of maternity absence

Employee's details

Surname

First forename

Other forename(s)

National Insurance number

Tax year(s) / /

Please ✓ the appropriate box(es) and fill in the necessary details.

1. What date does she intend to start her maternity absence? / /
   Enter the date as soon as you know it.

2. What date did she tell you about her maternity absence? / /
   You will find it useful to have a record of this date if you decide not to pay SMP because your employee has told you less than 28 days before she wants to start her maternity absence.

3. What date did she start her maternity absence? / /
   Fill in this date if it is different from the date at question 1.

4. Was this because the baby was born early, or because she suffered from a pregnancy related illness? No ☐ Yes ☐

5. When is the baby due? / /
   *Her doctor or midwife will give her medical evidence of the date her baby is due, up to 20 weeks before her baby is due. The evidence will be the Maternity Certificate, form **MAT B1** or other acceptable medical evidence. You must keep the MAT B1, or other medical evidence, or a copy if you have to give it back to your employee, for 3 years after the end of the tax year you paid SMP in.*

6. What date was the baby born? / /
   Fill in this date if her baby was born early and this changed the date you could start to pay her SMP.

7. Is she entitled to SMP? No ☐ Yes ☐ *from what date?* / /
   If she is not remember to show why in the 'Notes' column when filling in Part 6.

8. Did you give her *Why I cannot pay you SMP*, form *SMP1*, to tell her that she is not entitled to SMP? No ☐ Yes ☐ / /
   You can get these forms from Jobcentre plus/social security offices - see the phone book, or go to www.dwp.gov.uk/advisers/claimforms.htm
   You may find it useful to keep a copy of this form if your employee disagrees with your decision.

2

please see opposite page ▶

Form SMP2

6 Record of SMP pay period

	Note the date of each week until SMP ends	Show number of the tax week the end of SMP week is in	✓ one box for each week **W** = Worked **P** = Paid **E** = Excluded from SMP *Put reasons in 'Notes' column*			Show how much SMP paid in each week.	This will help you to calculate how much SMP you can get back. *See Employer's Help Book, Pay and time off work for parents, E15, or E15(SD) for further information.*	Note here any reasons why she cannot get SMP *Continue on page 4, Part 7 if necessary*
	Start date of SMP week	**Week No**	**W**	**P**	**E**	**Amount of SMP paid**	**Running total of SMP**	**Notes**
1	/ /					£	£	
2	/ /					£	£	
3	/ /					£	£	
4	/ /					£	£	
5	/ /					£	£	
6	/ /					£	£	
7	/ /					£	£	
8	/ /					£	£	
9	/ /					£	£	
10	/ /					£	£	
11	/ /					£	£	
12	/ /					£	£	
13	/ /					£	£	
14	/ /					£	£	
15	/ /					£	£	
16	/ /					£	£	
17	/ /					£	£	
18	/ /					£	£	
19	/ /					£	£	
20	/ /					£	£	
21	/ /					£	£	
22	/ /					£	£	
23	/ /					£	£	
24	/ /					£	£	
25	/ /					£	£	
26	/ /					£	£	

3

please turn over

The employer may keep these records in any way he finds convenient (for example, in computerised form). However, the records must be accessible to Inland Revenue Inspectors on request within a reasonable time.

In relation to computerised records, the Inland Revenue accepts that employers can format and produce data in the cheapest and easiest way possible on the proviso that the employer also provides the means to read the data, this includes printing and viewing records.

Employers must also keep a record of any additional payment of SMP made as a result of the backdating of a pay increase following Gillespie's case (see **19.9**). The records required are:

- the SMP records, eg Form SMP2, for the relevant tax year;
- the Deductions Working Sheet, Form P11 or computerised equivalent at the time the additional payment is made; and
- the employee's end-of-year summary, Form P14, for the tax year when the additional payment is made.

In such cases, if the employee left the employment in an earlier tax year, the payroll department will need to create Forms P11 and P14 to record the payment.

When completing the Form P11, the gross amount of SMP paid each payday must be included in column 1g. Customised payroll records must give the same data.

Any additional reimbursement received from the Inland Revenue Accounts Office (see **21.5**) will need to be recorded on Form P35 (Annual Statement, Declaration and Certificate) for the tax year in which the additional payment was made.

All the above records should be kept for a minimum of three years after the end of the tax year to which they relate.

Optional SMP records [22.3]

Employers may wish to consider keeping the following optional records for three years after the end of the tax year to which they refer.

Checklist: Recommended SMP Records

(a) Details of in-house rules about notification of absence, together with the dates on which employees actually gave notice of their absence, for use if there is any dispute over non-payment of SMP because of late notification.

(b) Copies of any applications for decisions from, or appeals to the Inland Revenue, (an adjudication officer, social security appeal tribunal, social security commissioner or the Secretary of State for decisions prior to 1 April 1999) and a copy of each decision and a record of the date it was received.

(c) A copy of the relevant application or appeal to explain why the employer has not yet paid SMP if the formal decision or the result of an appeal is still due.

(d) A record of the average earnings calculation in the relevant period (see **19.4**) and of the higher initial rate of SMP (see **19.2**).

(e) A record of the date of commencement of employment.

(f) A record of how much SMP or SMP compensation was recovered during the year on Form P32.

Tax-year-end Records [22.4]

The employer must also maintain certain records for tax-year-end purposes. At the end of the tax year, when giving details on the annual summary return, Form P35, the employer must show:

- the amount of SMP recovered; and
- the additional amount recovered, if appropriate, under the small employer's relief scheme (see **21.3**).

In addition the SMP amounts paid are recorded for each employee on each pay date on the Deductions Working Sheet, Form P11. At the end of the income tax year, the total SMP paid for the year (from Form P11) is entered on the end-of-year summary Form P14. The Form P14 must be submitted no later than 19 May for the tax year ending 5 April, eg for tax year 2003/04 by 19 May 2004.

When completing the P11 and the P14 or any computerised record, the employer must record for each employee the full amount of NICs due and the gross amount of SMP paid. This includes recording additional SMP as a result of a backdated pay award (see **19.9**).

A reduction in the amount of SMP information required on Form P35 applied from the start of the 1996/97 tax year onwards. Employers are no longer required to include details of SMP actually paid during the tax year on Form P35, the employer's annual summary return.

The tax-year-end records should be kept for at least three years after the end of the tax year to which they relate.

> ***Example***
>
> Records relating to SMP payments made to relevant employees in February 2004 should be retained until at least the 5 April 2007.

SMP Mistakes [22.5]

From time to time an employer may make an error in calculating and recording SMP payments. Indeed, mistakes are uncomfortably common. The Inland Revenue employs Inspectors to make visits to check employers' administration of SMP. Compliance Inspectors have consistently found monetary errors in 25% to 30% of SMP cases examined.

If the employer makes a mistake in the current year they must:

Checklist: Action to Take if a Mistake is Discovered

(a) Rectify the error.

(b) Correct the employee's SMP records.

(c) Correct the PAYE remittance due to the Inland Revenue Accounts Office.

(d) Inform the local office of the Department for Work and Pensions office if the employer has issued Form SMP1 (see **20.9**), as it may affect the employee's right to claim Social Security benefit (see **Chapter 26**).

If there is any doubt as to what action to take to remedy the mistake, the local Inland Revenue office should be contacted.

If the Inland Revenue itself discovers an error in relation to SMP, it will advise the employer how to proceed. An employer who disagrees with the Inland Revenue's decision on an overpayment or underpayment of SMP need not do anything until they receive formal notification. It is for the

Inland Revenue officer who disagrees to ask for a formal decision (see **23.4**). If the employer is formally notified of a positive decision, the payment must be corrected unless the employer wishes to appeal. If the employer agrees that there has been an error, it should be corrected immediately.

SMP Overpaid [22.6]

Any employer who has discovered an error after paying an employee SMP in the form of a lump sum payment (see **20.4**) should contact the employee's local DWP office for advice. If this is not known, the employer should contact their local DWP office which will pass the information on. It is more difficult for an employer to recoup any overpayment of SMP paid to an employee who is no longer in employment eg where the lump sum payment was made at the start of the maternity pay period due to the employee being made redundant (see **24.9**).

Checklist: Issues to Consider with SMP Overpayments

(a) For the income tax month in which the overpayment of SMP occurred, the amount recoverable from the Collector of Taxes must be recalculated. Any adjustment must be included in the next available monthly or quarterly remittance to the Inland Revenue Accounts Office, provided this falls within the same tax year.

(b) Records must be amended, even if recovery is not made from the employee. This should be done for records in the current year by drawing a line through the relevant figure on the Form P11 or alternative pay records, so that the figure can still be read or extracted, and then inserting the correct figure, or by keeping appropriate computer records.

(c) If the overpayment of SMP means that the employee has been overpaid wages, then the procedures and law pertaining to deductions from wages and restitution apply (see **20.8**).

(d) If the employee has been paid SMP for a period in which she had no entitlement to it then the employee's local DWP office should be informed as the employee may be entitled to State benefit instead (which may be MA (see **26.2**)). The DWP will need details of the employee and the period concerned, but there is no requirement to complete and send Form SMP1, in these circumstances.

If the employee was entitled to SMP but the employer simply paid too much SMP, eg miscalculating the SMP earnings-related rate or paying SMP for too long, the DWP need not be informed.

SMP Underpaid [22.7]

If an employee has been paid too little SMP, any additional amount due should be paid to that employee as soon as the mistake is discovered. The employer merely has to pay the employee the correct amount of arrears owing. These arrears must be recorded in the normal way (see **22.2**). It will be necessary to recalculate the amount recovered from the Inland Revenue Collector of Taxes.

However, if the employer has also issued incorrectly Form SMP1, the employee's local DWP office must be informed to check whether there has been a resulting overpayment of State benefit. If the employer is not sure which DWP office deals with the employee's home address, advise the nearest DWP office which will pass on the information. The DWP will need details of the employee and the period concerned.

If the employee was entitled to SMP but the employer simply paid too little SMP, eg miscalculating the SMP earnings-related rate or paying SMP for 16 instead of 26 weeks, the DWP need not be informed.

SMP Mistakes in Previous Tax Years [22.8]

If a mistake is discovered after the end-of-year tax returns have been sent, the employer should contact the Inland Revenue Accounts Office to find out if the returns have been sent on to the National Insurance Contributions Office (NICO) in Newcastle. If they have not, an adjustment may still be possible to the returns. If they have, the employer should seek advice from the local Inland Revenue office. Under no circumstances should the error be corrected in the payments or records for the current tax year.

> *i* In practice, there is a six-year time limit for making any adjustments in cases where the employer believes that it is entitled to any unclaimed reimbursement in an earlier tax year.

If SMP was paid in a previous tax year but was not recovered by the employer, for whatever reason, the employer must complete Form SP32 (available from the employer's orderline, and see **8.4**) to obtain reimbursement and send to the nearest Inland Revenue office. Recovery of SMP paid in a previous tax year cannot be claimed directly from the Accounts Office.

Questions and Answers [22.9]

Question

Can we as an employer recover an overpayment from future SMP payments, if this is the only payment due?

Answer

Provided the recovery of the overpayment is lawful, eg there is relevant provision in the contract of employment, the deduction can be made from the employee's SMP, even if that is the only earnings receivable by the employee for that later period.

However, the Inland Revenue has pointed out that the MPP can be a time of hardship for some families and this is especially so if an employee does not enjoy the protection offered by an OMP scheme. In such circumstances, an Inland Revenue Inspector might urge an employer to recover any earlier overpayment from the earnings due for the first full pay period falling after the employee has returned to work. Such a policy would avoid an employee on maternity leave possibly receiving no pay at all during part of their MPP.

Question

We have been advised by our local PAYE Tax Office that they intend to carry out a compliance visit. However, in preparing for this visit, we have discovered that we no longer have certain records, which we are statutorily required to keep in respect of SMP. What should an employer do?

Answer

In the event of being asked to produce records by the Inland Revenue, which have been lost or destroyed, the best approach is one of open admission explaining the circumstances as to why these are unavailable. It will also be helpful if the employer can prove that a record keeping system is now in place to prevent such a reoccurrence. The Inland Revenue does have statutory powers to fine employers in relation to a failure to keep the required records in connection with SMP but in practice it is unlikely these will be imposed unless fraud or wilful neglect can be proved against the employer. ➡

Question

How long does an employer have to keep SMP records for?

Answer

Appropriate records must be kept for three years under SMP legislation, but it is advisable to keep them for at least six years plus the current year for inspection by company auditors or Inland Revenue Compliance Officers.

23. Dealing with Disputes, Offences and Penalties

Introduction [23.1]

The regime governing disputes, appeals and reviews changed extensively as a result of the merger of the Contributions Agency and Inland Revenue in April 1999. Notably, responsibility for answering questions relating to SMP passed from the Department of Social Security to the Inland Revenue, and responsibility for hearing appeals against such decisions passed from the Social Security appeal tribunal and Social Security Commissioners to the Tax Commissioners.

Disputes [23.2]

If an employee disputes an employer's decision not to pay SMP, or disputes the amount that is due, it is usually best for the dispute to be processed through the employer's own grievance procedures in case it can be resolved at this stage. An airing of the issues in this way may be useful to both parties in any event. However, an employee has a right to ask the Inland Revenue for a formal decision. The Board of the Inland Revenue is the first of the authorities that decide questions about entitlement for an employer to pay SMP.

> *i* In practice, such decisions are given judicially by authorised officers acting on behalf of the Board of the Inland Revenue. They work from local Inland Revenue offices and their decisions are given strictly in accordance with the facts and the law.

Prior to asking for a formal decision from the Inland Revenue, the employee will be expected to have requested a written statement (see **23.3**) about her SMP position.

Checklist: SMP Disputes Procedure

(a) Before the employee can approach the Inland Revenue she must ask her employer for a written statement about her SMP situation.

(b) If the employee does not agree with the decision made by the employer she can ask the Inland Revenue for a formal decision. The employer cannot approach the Inland Revenue.

(c) The Inland Revenue will then ask both parties to state their observations on the case in writing but neither will have to appear in person before the officer making the decision.

(d) From this information the Inland Revenue will make a decision and written notification will be sent to both the employer and the employee.

(e) If the decision is made in favour of the employee, the employer must pay the SMP due within the time scale fixed unless he or she appeals against the decision.

(f) If the decision is made in favour of the employer, the employee may appeal against it.

(g) Both the employer and the employee have the right to appeal against the decision to the Tax Appeal Commissioners.

Employee Right to a Written Statement [23.3]

If the employer decides not to pay SMP for whatever reason, the employer should explain the decision to the employee. The employee has a right to ask for a written statement at any time and the employer is required to comply 'to the extent to which the request was reasonable'. If the request was reasonable, the statement must be supplied within reasonable time, for example, within seven days of the request.

In the case of SMP the specific information to be given in the written statement may be one or more of the following:

- which weeks (if any) within the MPP the employer regards as weeks for which SMP is payable;
- the employer's opinion as to the amount of SMP to which the employee is entitled in respect of each of those weeks; and
- the reasons the employer does not consider SMP to be payable for the other weeks in the MPP.

Form SMP1 can be treated as the written statement.

> ! The Inland Revenue will wish to see anything that the employer has issued in writing in connection with the employee's SMP.

Formal Decisions on SMP [23.4]

If an employer refuses to pay an employee SMP, or the employee feels the appropriate amount has not been paid, the employee may apply to the Inland Revenue, which has the power to overrule the employer's decision. Only the employee can apply, as the employer has no such right, although the employer will be able to appeal against the Inland Revenue's decision. Inland Revenue officers may also request a formal decision.

An employee who disputes her employer's decision must, in order for questions to be considered, apply to the Inland Revenue within six months of the earliest day for which SMP liability is in dispute. The application must be in writing and state the grounds (if any) on which the employer has refused to make payments and specify the period to which that refusal relates.

The Inland Revenue officer will ask both the employer and the employee for their observations in writing before reaching a decision. Each party can also provide written evidence in support of its position. If there is a subsequent appeal, each party's evidence will be sent to the other. Neither party will be called to give evidence in person. When the Inland Revenue has reached its decision it will notify both parties, using Form DAA1, giving a fixed time limit by which any SMP due must be paid and also explaining how to appeal against the decision, using Form DAA3.

In some cases, decisions are required under law to be made by the Board of Inland Revenue. These decisions are:

- whether a person is or was an employer or employee of another and the period of that employment (see **15.2**);
- whether the employment is to be treated as continuous (see **16.3**);
- the employer's entitlement to recover SMP and whether they qualify for small employer's relief (see **21.3**);
- whether two or more employers are treated as one for SMP purposes (see **16.7**);
- whether earnings under separate contracts with the same employer should be aggregated together for Class 1 NIC purposes.

Checklist: Formal Inland Revenue Decisions

(a) Formal decisions in respect of SMP are made by officers of the Board of Inland Revenue.

(b) A formal decision is merely a mechanism for granting a right of appeal and settling a dispute.

(c) The issue of a decision does not alter the date from which payment was due or the amount of any interest charge.

(d) A notice of decision involving SMP will be made when the employee or an officer of the Inland Revenue has requested one.

(e) Copies of formal decisions will be issued to professional advisers and agents and appeals accepted from them.

(f) The Tax Appeal Commissioners will hear appeals against decisions, which cannot be settled by agreement.

(g) Appeals will be listed for hearing in the same way as tax appeals and taken to the General Commissioners by the local Tax Office.

SMP Appeals [23.5]

Either party can appeal against the formal decision of an Inland Revenue officer. Information about the procedure will be contained in the written notification of the formal decision, which will be sent to each party.

There is a time limit for making an appeal. This is 30 days from the date when the notice of the formal decision was issued, on Form DAA1. The time limit may be extended if the applicant can establish that there were good reasons for the delay and that he or she has taken action as soon as is reasonably possible.

On receipt of a notice to appeal, the Inland Revenue officer who made the formal decision will first contact the parties to see if the subject of the appeal can be resolved by agreement. However, before reaching an agreement with the appellant the Inland Revenue will try to take into account the interests of any non-appellant. The Inland Revenue will not normally enter into an agreement to vary the decision where it is believed that it will not be acceptable to a person who has not appealed without making that person aware of their view of the correct position first.

If agreement is not possible, the appeal will go to the Tax Commissioners. Both parties have the right to appear in person and/or be represented at the hearing. The Tax Appeal Commissioners are an independent tribunal.

The hearing will normally be informal. Applicants present the facts of their case and their arguments and may call witnesses. After hearing the parties' representations, the Commissioners may come to a decision immediately or they may issue a written decision at a later date.

If there is a point of law of general importance to be decided, a claimant or the Inland Revenue may appeal, with leave, to the Court of Appeal, or in Scotland, to the Court of Session. Appeals to the higher Courts must be made within 56 days of a Special Commissioner's decision or 30 days of a General Commissioner's decision. For further more detailed information concerning appeals – see Inland Revenue Booklet IR37, 'Appeals against tax, NICs, SSP and SMP' – download from www.inlandrevenue.gov.uk/pdfs/ir37.htm or telephone 0845 9000 404.

Instead of appealing against an Inland Revenue formal decision or if new facts come to light, a party affected by the decision may ask to have the decision reviewed. If the party affected by the decision is dissatisfied, he or she may appeal against it, as if it were the initial decision.

> ! It is in all parties' interests to put all the facts before the officer making the decision as soon as they are requested.

Enforcement [23.6]

If the Inland Revenue or Tax Commissioners issue a formal decision that the employee is entitled to an amount of SMP, the employer must pay it by a certain date. The SMP must be paid not later than the first normal pay day following:

- where an appeal has been brought, the day on which the employer receives notification of the decision;
- where leave to appeal has been refused (and there remains no further opportunity to apply for leave), the day on which the employer receives notification of the refusal; or
- in any other case, the day on which the time for bringing an appeal expires (see **23.5**).

If payment on the first normal pay date is not practicable, due to the employer's method of accounting and paying wages, then the SMP is to be paid on the next pay date. Where the pay is not yet due, it need not be paid until the date it is due, eg where wages are paid a 'week in hand'.

If an appeal to the Courts is in progress an employer does not have to pay the disputed SMP until the case is settled.

> ! If the employer fails to pay the SMP by the required date following the issue of a formal decision, then liability to make the payment may be assumed by the Inland Revenue who will in turn prosecute the employer.

SMP Offences [23.7]

There are a number of offences within Social Security law which arise in connection with the operation of SMP. These are broadly as follows:

Checklist: SMP Offences

(a) Failure to pay SMP within the time allowed, when the Board of Inland Revenue has given a formal decision that it is payable.

(b) Failure to keep the required records in connection with SMP.

(c) Failure by an employer to provide information as required by the Inland Revenue (in writing, if requested) in connection with the determination of questions arising in respect of SMP.

(d) Failure by an employer to provide information, eg Form SMP1, to their employees in relation to a claim for MA (see **26.2**) or Incapacity Benefit (see **13.2**).

Any person who, without reasonable excuse, contravenes or fails to comply with any of the above provisions shall be guilty of an offence.

SMP Penalties [23.8]

There are various criminal offences in relation to SMP and provision is made for the recovery of penalties on summary conviction of any such offence. In some cases, a prison sentence may also be imposed.

Checklist: SMP Penalties

(a) A maximum fine up to £1,000 for a failure to pay SMP within the time allowed.

(b) £1,000 for a failure to maintain the statutory records. Where there is continued failure to keep records after conviction, a fine of up to £40 for each day of such failure.

(c) A maximum fine up to £1,000 for a failure to provide information required by the Inland Revenue. Where there is continued failure to provide such information after conviction, a fine of up to £40 for each day of failure.

(d) A maximum fine up to £1,000 for a failure by an employer to provide an employee with Form SMP1. Where there is continued failure to provide such information after conviction, a fine of up to £40 for each day of such failure.

A more serious penalty is exacted for producing, furnishing or causing or knowingly allowing to be produced or furnished, any document or information which is known to be false in a material particular when purporting to recover amounts by way of SMP. A penalty can be imposed of a maximum fine not exceeding £5,000 or a term of imprisonment not exceeding three months, or both.

Employer Insolvency [23.9]

If an employer is formally declared insolvent, any SMP outstanding from the week of the insolvency to the end of the MPP automatically becomes the liability of the Inland Revenue. Any SMP due for the period before the week of insolvency remains the liability of the employer.

Questions and Answers [23.10]

Question

One of our employees disagrees with the amount of SMP that has been calculated and paid to her. What is the best procedure to adopt in a situation like this?

Answer

A good procedure to be adopted in the event of an employee–employer dispute regarding SMP is:

- to re-check the original calculation of SMP to establish if there has been a simple miscalculation or misunderstanding of the facts; and
- if satisfied that the calculations and dates used are correct, draft a letter outlining the relevant points of dispute together with an explanation of the rational behind the initial decision; and

- if this does not clarify the situation to the employee's satisfaction, to arrange a meeting to discuss the matter with the employee; and
- have the events of any such meeting recorded by a representative of the company; the employee should be allowed to have a witness present, such as a trade union official.

If the payment is discovered in the first instance to be wrong the correction should be made on the next available pay date or, alternatively, an interim manual payment prepared. If the employee still disagrees she should follow the appropriate employer internal appeal procedure, prior to asking for a formal decision from the Inland Revenue.

Question

Several of our employees are claiming that we owe them SMP, as a result of a back-dated pay award from over ten years ago. Surely we don't have to go back that far in our records?

Answer

Employers must consider past cases where a woman has been on maternity leave and the maternity pay she received was based on earnings that had been increased by a back-dated pay award and the award itself was made on or after 12 June 1996.

However, the European Court of Justice judgement in the *Gillespie* case (see **19.9**) has no retrospective time limit and the only limits are the circumstances of the individual employees. The guidance issued by the Department of Social Security at the time the judgement was pronounced was for employers to review all cases in the two years prior to the ruling. However, where requested, the employer must review any case where a back-dated pay award affected the woman's earnings in the relevant period as the European Court of Justice is legally binding.

24. Special Employment Situations

Introduction [24.1]

This section deals with a number of special employment situations which affect SMP entitlement.

Contract of Employment [24.2]

Generally, a contract of employment is a 'contract *of* service', as opposed to a 'contract *for* services' (i e self-employment). Any arrangement providing for the terms of appointment of an employee may amount to a contract, which need not be in writing but may be verbal or implied. Workers employed under a contract of service, with earnings attracting a liability for employer's Class 1 NICs, or would if they were high enough are employees for SMP purposes. Whoever is liable to pay the employer's share of Class 1 NICs is the employer.

An employee with a contract of employment with two or more separate and distinct employers can qualify for SMP from both of them.

If the employee satisfies both the continuous employment rule (see **16.3**) and the earnings rule (see **19.4**), the employer must pay SMP even if the contract of employment ends at some time during the MPP.

Death [24.3]

An employer's liability to pay SMP ends of the Saturday of the week, in which the employee's death occurs. Therefore, if an employee dies on Monday, 7 June 2004 and this is in her MPP, then the SMP payments end on Saturday, 12 June 2004. SMP cannot be paid to any other member of the family.

Dismissal [24.4]

If an employer is found to have unfairly dismissed a pregnant employee and she is subsequently reinstated through an agreement brokered:

- by the Advisory Conciliation and Arbitration Service (ACAS); or
- under a 'compromise agreement' under employment protection legislation; or
- by order of an employment tribunal;

all the weeks that fall between the date when the employee's dismissal took effect and the date of the resumption of employment count towards the 26-week continuous employment test. The same applies if under the same circumstances the employee is reinstated or re-engaged by the employer's successor or an associated employer.

Women have statutory protection against dismissal on the grounds of pregnancy or childbirth. Such a dismissal is unlawful, and women may make a complaint of unfair dismissal to an employment tribunal. The protection against dismissal applies only to dismissals on maternity-related grounds. Dismissal on other grounds may still be found by an employment tribunal to have been a fair dismissal. In such a case, if an employee has been fairly dismissed and so is no longer employed during the 15th week before the EWC, SMP is not payable.

Conversely, if, in such a case, the employee is fairly dismissed after the 15th week before the EWC, SMP is payable to the dismissed employee. Dismissal for SMP purposes has the same meaning as in the *Employment Rights Act 1996, Part X*. This includes redundancy, expiry of a fixed-term contract and constructive dismissal, where an employee is entitled to terminate the contract without notice because of their employer's conduct.

The MPP starts on the Sunday after the week in which her employment ends or the Sunday of the 11th week before the EWC, whichever is the later.

Employment of Spouse [24.5]

A woman who is employed by her husband in a family business may similarly be entitled to SMP if the normal requirements are satisfied.

Holiday Accrual [24.6]

An employee on ordinary maternity leave (OML) (see **27.2**) remains entitled to accrue holidays under the *Working Time Regulations 1998* (*SI 1998 No 1833*). The Regulations currently provide an employee with a minimum entitlement of four weeks' annual leave.

They also expressly prohibit payment in lieu of any of the four weeks' annual leave except on termination of employment. However, annual leave in excess of the four weeks is subject to the terms and conditions of the contract of employment, which may provide for payment in lieu.

Although SMP is payable for the MPP which correlates to the employee's OML period, there is no statutory obstruction to the employee taking her annual leave during with either the ordinary or the additional maternity leave period. There is also no statutory restriction on untaken leave being taken before or at the end of the leave periods, or indeed to being carried forward from holiday year to another. Whether leave can be taken or carried forward is determined by the contract of employment.

Part-time Employees [24.7]

SMP is payable to part-time employees on the same basis as they are paid to full-time employees. There is no requirement to have worked a minimum number of hours. Some part-time employees may, in practice, not be eligible because their average earnings are less than the weekly LEL (see **14.6**). With the introduction of the National Minimum Wage, which was increased to £4.50 per hour for pay reference periods starting on or after 1 October 2003, an employee working on average just over 17 hours a week during the relevant period will satisfy the earnings test for SMP.

Pension Membership [24.8]

The *Social Security Act 1989, Schedule* 5 deals with the treatment of women who are on maternity leave.

The level of any employee contributions made by the member while on paid maternity leave (ordinary or additional leave) is dependent on the pay she actually receives (including SMP, occupational maternity pay (OMP) or a combination of both) during the period of paid absence. However, any employer contributions for the same period must be based on the pay she would have received had she continued to work normally.

Whether or not a woman receives SMP or OMP or neither, her service for pension purposes must continue to accrue during the OML period, as if working normally. Whether pension rights continue to accrue during a period of unpaid additional maternity leave (AML) (see **27.3**) is determined by the rules of the pension scheme.

Redundancy [24.9]

Making a woman who is pregnant or on maternity leave redundant because of reasons related to maternity will automatically be found to be an unfair dismissal by an employment tribunal. It is possible to make a woman who is pregnant or on maternity leave redundant for other reasons but it must be justifiable as a fair dismissal. All employees are protected against unfair selection for redundancy during pregnancy.

An employee will invariably be treated as unfairly dismissed if she has been made redundant while pregnant and the principal reason for her selection for redundancy was because of her pregnancy. Cases may arise where a pregnant employee is made redundant and it is found that the selection for redundancy was both fair and equitable. In such a case, if as a result of the redundancy she is no longer employed during the 15th week before the EWC, SMP is not payable. Conversely, if, the employee is selected for redundancy after the start of the 15th week before the EWC, then SMP is payable. Once entitlement to SMP is established it cannot subsequently be lost due to the employee being made redundant.

Second and Subsequent Pregnancies [24.10]

If an employee exercises her right to take ordinary or additional maternity leave and then subsequently returns to work, all the weeks between the dates she was first absent and the date she returned to work count towards her period of continuous employment.

Share Incentive Plans [24.11]

Buying partnership shares under a Share Incentive Plan may affect an employee's entitlement to SMP (or SSP (see **Chapter 3**)). This is because the payment is made as a pre-tax and NIC deduction, such that the employee's earnings may fall below the LEL for Class 1 NIC purposes. The employer should advise employees likely to be affected in advance of making any purchase of partnership shares.

The *Employee Share Ownership Plans (Partnership Shares – Notice of Effects on Benefits, Statutory Sick Pay and Statutory Maternity Pay) Regulations 2000 (SI 2000 No 2090)* set out the form that this notice must take. The wording is as follows:

> 'Deductions from your pay to buy partnership shares under this agreement may affect your entitlement to or the level of, some contributory social security benefits, SMP and SSP.

'They may also have a similar effect in respect of some contributory social security benefits paid to your wife or husband.

'With this agreement you should have been given information on the effect of deductions from your pay to buy partnership shares on entitlement to social security benefits, SSP and SMP. The effect is particularly significant if your earnings are brought below the LEL for National Insurance purposes, and is explained in the information: it is therefore important that you read it. If you have not been given a copy, ask your employer for it. Otherwise a copy may be obtained from any office of the Inland Revenue, the Department for Work and Pensions, or, in Northern Ireland, the Department for Social Development. You should take the information you have been given into account in deciding whether to buy partnership shares.'

SSP and SMP Interaction [24.12]

No employee may receive SSP and SMP simultaneously. A woman can receive SSP if she is sick while pregnant up until the time the baby is born, provided the illness is not directly related to her pregnancy and her MPP has not started. If an employee is already sick with a pregnancy-related illness in the fifth week before the baby is due and her pregnancy-related illness continues into the fourth week before the EWC, the MPP must start on the Sunday of the fourth week (see **17.6**).

> ! The *Employment Act 2002* reduced the pregnancy-related sickness trigger for the start of the MPP from six weeks to four weeks before the EWC, for all women with an EWC on or after 6 April 2003. Where the MPP is triggered by an absence from work because of pregnancy-related illness, the MPP will start immediately. The definition of a week in relation to the MPP in these cases means a period of seven consecutive days.

Since SSP counts as earnings for Class 1 NI purposes, it counts towards earnings for SMP calculations and vice versa.

Timing of Leave and Returning to Work [24.13]

The following is an outline of the procedure from the onset of pregnancy to the return to work.

Case study: the maternity cycle

Clara joins Carp Products as a part-time employee, working 9 am to 5 pm Thursdays and Fridays, with an hour for lunch (ie 14 hours per week). She is paid a salary of £475 per month. Carp Products is a mean-spirited employer and does not offer any occupational maternity benefits, or any other benefits for that matter.

Thursday, 17 April 2003 — Clara starts work at Carp Products, all bright and breezy ready to throw herself into the challenges of a new job.

Monday, 19 June — Unfortunately Carp Products are unlikely to win any employer of the year awards and Clara has begun to feel the strain of working for her new employer. After a weekend feeling unwell, she visits her GP who suggests, much to Clara's surprise, that she may be pregnant. The GP carries out a blood test.

Monday, 16 June — On her return visit, Clara's GP confirms to her that she is pregnant. Having discussed the possibility with her partner, Clara knows that she wants to proceed with the pregnancy.

Thursday, 10 July — Having waited during the early stages of pregnancy, Clara informs Carp Products that she is pregnant. Mr Carp, the proprietor, is not pleased, muttering that she has only been with the company five minutes (nearly three months in fact, although it felt to Clara more like three years). She reports that her GP had indicated the baby would be due in the week beginning 11 January 2004. Mr Carp asks to see the medical evidence, but Clara informs him that this cannot be issued until the 20th week before the baby is expected. Mr Carp scowls in annoyance.

Tuesday, 5 August to Wednesday 20 August — Clara is ill with slightly high blood pressure, perhaps caused by the pregnancy but equally likely to have been caused by having to see Mr Carp's scowling face every day. Her GP prescribes bed rest. The 7, 8, and 14 August are waiting days in Clara's PIW and Carp Products pays Clara SSP for 15 August. She recovers and returns to work on Thursday 21 August, not looking forward to it.

Thursday, 11 September — Clara informs Mr Carp that antenatal appointments are now being provided on a shared-care system between her GP and the hospital and are held on a Thursday. Mr Carp's face changes from a scowl to a grimace. He reluctantly agrees that Clara can have paid time off to attend and whilst he would dearly love her to have to make up for the lost time, at another time during the week, he realises that this would be unlawful.

Thursday, 18 September — Following an antenatal appointment, Clara is given maternity certificate MATB1. This states that Clara can expect her baby in the week that includes 25 January 2004.

Clara passes Form MATB1 to Carp Products personnel officer, Mrs Haddock. She consults the SMP tables in Booklet E15 (also reproduced in **Chapter 15**), and identifies the EWC as the week running from 25 January 2004 to 31 January 2004. The tables also give:

- the week commencing 12 October 2003 as the QW (the 15th before the EWC);
- the date of 26 April 2003 as the latest start date for employment for the 26-week employment test;
- the week running from 9 November 2003 as the start of the eleventh week before the EWC; and
- the week running from 28 December 2003 as the start of the fourth week before the EWC.

From these dates Mrs Haddock knows that as Clara began work eight days before 26 April 2003, i e on Thursday, 17 April 2003, and was also employed during the week 12–18 October 2003, she has satisfied the 26-week employment test and must be paid SMP. She visits Mr Carp's office, and informs him that Clara is entitled to receive SMP. On hearing from Mrs Haddock that Clara is entitled to be absent from work for 52 weeks, comprising of 26 weeks' ordinary leave and 26 weeks' additional leave, Mr Carp mumbles something about being had 'hook, line and sinker'.

Mrs Haddock explains to Clara that she must give notice no later than 18 October (i e the end of the qualifying week) of the date she wants to start her maternity leave. Mrs Haddock also explains that Clara is eligible for SMP and that Mr Carp wants the notice in writing.

Although Clara feels like stopping work immediately and telling Mr Carp what he can do with his job, she knows that she cannot afford to do so. She is also comforted by the thought that she can be away from work for 52 weeks.

Clara looks at the calendar and decides that she will give written notice that she will start her maternity leave on 17 January 2004 (after her last working day of Friday, 16 January). In the letter she states she is pregnant and that her EWC is week commencing 25 January 2004. She also states that she wants her SMP to be paid from this date.

On receipt of the letter Mr Carp promptly replies in writing to Clara confirming that:

- she is eligible for 26 weeks' OML and 26 weeks' AML;
- as her maternity leave starts on 17 January 2004, it will end on 16 January 2005;
- if she wants to change the date she starts her leave she must, if at all possible, let him know at least 28 days before the earlier of her proposed new start date or her original start date; and
- if she wants to return to work before 16 January 2005 she must give him at least 28 days' notice.

In the same letter Mr Carp confirms that Clara is eligible for SMP which will be paid to her at the earnings-related rate of £98.66 a week from week commencing Sunday, 18 January 2004 to week ending Saturday, 17 July 2004. Clara's average weekly earnings are £109.62, which gives a SMP earnings-related rate of £98.66 (ie £109.62 × 90%). As the earnings-related rate is less than the weekly rate of £100 she will be paid the earnings-related rate throughout the MPP.

Mr Carp also lets Clara know that if she decides not return to work she must still give him proper notice, but this will not affect her entitlement to SMP.

Friday, 16 January 2004 – Clara begins her maternity leave, and her MPP starts on Sunday, 18 January 2004.

Monday, 14 June 2004 — Clara visits Carp Products, with baby Alice, and talks to Mrs Haddock as pre-arranged. (Mr Carp is away at a seminar.) It is agreed that Clara will return to work on Thursday, 22 July 2004, as Clara needs her normal weekly wage.

Monday, 21 June 2004 – Clara writes to Mr Carp informing him that she intends to return to work on Thursday, 22 July 2004, thereby giving the requisite 28 days' notice.

Tuesday, 22 June – Mr Carp telephones Clara and says he is delighted she will be returning as he has a long list of things for her to do. After the call Clara updates her CV and contacts a local recruitment agency.

Trade Disputes [24.14]

Industrial or trade disputes have no effect on the start of the MPP. If the employee is involved in such a dispute, the employee can still give the employer notice of the date her maternity leave will start. This date can be within the period of the dispute. Any notice that the employee has already given to their employer is not affected by a subsequent trade dispute.

Questions and Answers [24.15]

Question

One of our employees has undergone a sex change operation and she is inquiring as to whether she would be eligible for SMP. Are we liable to pay SMP?

Answer

SMP is only payable to female employees. In Social Security law reference is made to the sex of an individual at birth, as determined by the birth certificate. An individual claiming to have undergone an operation to change their sex, who claims to be able to bear a child, surrogate or otherwise will not have any eligibility to SMP.

Question

We are about to make one of our female members of staff redundant and she is pregnant. We have established that she qualifies for SMP. What should we do about paying SMP and Form P45?

Answer

SMP payable to an employee after the contract of employment has ended can be paid as a lump sum or at the same interval as regular earnings. If payment is made as a lump sum, then this is taxable under PAYE and the SMP should be included in the figures issued on Form P45. If payments are to continue using the same pay interval before the employee left, then in strictness Form P45 should be issued when the employee is made redundant and any further payments should be taxed at the basic rate. However, provided the woman does not request Form P45, PAYE can be deducted from payments of SMP using the normal code number and preparation of Form P45 delayed until the final ➡

payment is made. The date of leaving on Form P45 should then be the date on which the final payment of SMP is made.

Question

One of our employees is undergoing a course of IVF fertility treatment, in an attempt to conceive a baby. Are we obliged to grant her time off to attend the necessary hospital appointments?

Answer

There is no legal entitlement for an employee to receive time off with or without pay during normal working hours where she undertakes a course of fertility treatment. The SMP legislation relates solely to the employee being pregnant and not to the causes of pregnancy. The employer may allow discretionary 'compassionate leave' where the employee undergoes a lengthy course of treatment.

Question

Do we make additional SMP payments to women who have multiple births?

Answer

The rate of SMP paid is the same for a single birth as it would be for a mother having twins, triplets or quads.

25. Occupational Maternity Pay

Introduction [25.1]

An employer may offer occupational maternity pay (OMP), which is above the minimum levels of SMP afforded under the State scheme. However, there is no legal requirement to pay anything other than SMP to a pregnant employee. An OMP scheme cannot offer payment terms which are less beneficial than SMP.

The employer has a number of options, in considering whether to enhance SMP. These are broadly as follows:

Checklist: OMP Options

(a) Reducing or abolishing the 26-week service qualification applicable to SMP before OMP becomes due (see **16.3**).

(b) Lengthening the period of paid maternity leave beyond the statutory minimum.

(c) Increasing the level of maternity pay above the level of SMP.

(d) Paying a bonus to employees who return to work (see **25.5**).

The rules of the scheme should be included in the employee's contract of employment or by reference to a separate company maternity pay handbook. Employees should be fully informed of their entitlement to OMP in order that later disputes over eligibility and entitlement are avoided.

OMP Eligibility Conditions [25.2]

The following is a summary of the key features of an employer OMP scheme with regard to eligibility.

Checklist: Eligibility for OMP

(a) Any qualifying period of service before entitlement to OMP begins and how this is calculated, eg rules on breaks in service.

(b) Consequences of failing to comply with the rules of the OMP scheme, eg notice and evidence requirements if unusually these are different to SMP.

(c) Circumstances when the employee will not be covered by the OMP scheme rules.

> *i* In practice, few female employees will be excluded from the right to receive SMP because of the 26-week service qualification.

Employers need to ensure their scheme is applied equally across their workforce as any special conditions and especially exclusions for certain classes of employee, part-time staff for instance, could well result in claims of indirect sex discrimination (see **24.7**). *The Part-time Workers (Prevention of Less Favourable Treatment) Regulations 2000 (SI 2000 No 1551)* provide that a part-time worker has the right not to be treated less favourably than comparable full-time workers as regards, for example, pay and conditions of employment.

The Regulations apply directly to contractual maternity pay. The benefits that a full-timer receives must also apply to part-timers pro rata. The only exception will be if the different treatment is justified on objective grounds.

OMP Payment Schemes [25.3]

The length and rates used in an OMP scheme will vary from employer to employer. A common formula is to grant the employee six weeks at full pay. Other examples of OMP pay patterns are:

Checklist: OMP Pay Patterns

(a) The SMP earnings-related rate of 90% of average weekly earnings paid for a greater proportion of the MPP.

(b) Normal basic wages or salary for longer than six weeks.

(c) 12 weeks at full pay, followed by fourteen weeks at half pay.

(d) Full pay for the whole of the MPP.

The terms used with OMP do not necessarily have to have the same meaning as in SMP. It is possible that if an employee receives a substantial bonus during the relevant period used to calculate SMP then 90% of average earnings may be greater than 100% of the employee's basic pay.

The rules of an OMP scheme, which offers, say, 100% of basic pay for the first six weeks of the MPP must therefore specify that the employee will receive 90% of her average earnings, ie SMP higher rate, if this proves to be greater than 100% of basic pay.

No special rule is necessary if 100% of pay is calculated using the same rules for calculating SMP higher rate payments.

> *i* The amount of SMP payable is never affected by the amount of OMP, though the amount of OMP is often affected by the amount of SMP.

It is good practice to show OMP as a separate pay element from SMP on the employee's pay statement. The employer must also keep records of OMP and SMP separate as only SMP is reclaimable in part or in full (see **21.2**) from the State. OMP is always subject to tax and National Insurance even if payment is made exceptionally on a discretionary (*ex gratia*) basis.

Offsetting SMP [25.4]

Where OMP is granted in respect of the same week(s), during which SMP is also payable in the MPP, then offsetting rules are applied.

If the employer provides OMP to employees, the amount of contractual maternity pay paid counts towards the amount of SMP that is due. Similarly, if there is a contractual undertaking to pay OMP to an employee, the payment of SMP goes towards satisfying the contractual obligation. This mutual discharge of SMP and contractual remuneration to prevent double payment is commonly referred to as 'offsetting'.

The weekly amount of SMP calculated is the minimum due for a maternity pay week. If the OMP for a week is less than the SMP due for that same week, then the minimum amount due for that week is the amount of SMP.

> ***Example***
>
> Laura receives OMP equivalent to £200 per week for weeks 7–26 of the MPP. SMP is payable at £100.00 per week for the same period. Laura would be paid £200 each week, split as £100.00 SMP and £100.00 OMP.

Therefore, some schemes may require the employee to repay all or part of her OMP if she does not return to work for a minimum length of time, say three months. If this is a requirement, it must be stated within the contract of employment or the occupational maternity policy, which the employee should sign to state that she agrees to abide by the terms and conditions of the policy in advance of her starting her MPP. This is to prevent the employee claiming a subsequent illegal deduction from wages, under the *Employment Rights Act 1996, s 13.*

Where recovery of OMP is made because the employee does not return to work, Social Security regulations permits the employer to recover NICs, both the primary (employee) and secondary (employers) Class 1 contributions. If the employee repays the OMP to the employer in the same tax year of payment, any tax and NIC deducted from it must be corrected on the employer's PAYE returns. Usually, the employee will refund a net amount leaving the employer to reclaim the tax and NI from the Inland Revenue (see **12.9**).

Class 1 NICs refunds can only be given where the employee has repaid the OMP or the employer has, in the view of the Inland Revenue, made every conceivable effort to make that recovery. This is subject to an overriding time limit of six years, from the year in which payment was made.

Return-to-work Bonus [25.5]

A return-to-work bonus is sometimes paid by employers to induce a woman to return to work following a period of maternity leave. Sometimes bonuses are paid to persuade a key employee to return to work earlier than the normal end of the AML period (see **27.3**). In the majority of cases the bonus represents a far smaller cost to the employer than the training and investment required in hiring a new employee for the same position.

A return-to-work bonus is usually paid only if the employee returns to work for a minimum specified period. Some employers will, rather than pay the bonus as one lump sum, pay the bonus incrementally as an addition to basic pay over a period of time, say three months.

If the employee decides not to return to work she may lose her right to that bonus depending on the OMP scheme rules. For example, some employers have been caught out by employees returning to work for only one day in order to qualify for the bonus, only to hand in their resignation the very next day.

Questions and Answers [25.6]

Question

What is a good OMP scheme?

Answer

Whatever scheme works for the employer and employee. The rules of an OMP scheme can be as complex or as simple as both parties agree. Obviously, the more nuances included, the more time spent on administration, but where the scheme is not properly thought out, employees have been known to explore loopholes, such as qualifying for a return to work bonus and then immediately resigning.

The rules should be fair, easy to understand and apply and meet the needs of both employee and employer.

Question

We do not wish to operate an OMP scheme, due to the extra administration, but on the other hand do not wish the employee to suffer financial hardship during her maternity leave period. Any ideas?

Answer

An employer could consider offering a personal loan. Provided this sum does not exceed £5,000 throughout the tax year and the employee repays the sum in full, then there are no tax or NIC consequences. Any agreement would need to be in writing and provide for repayment in the event of the employee not returning to work and also the rate of repayment, when she does resume work. A loan equivalent to a maximum of three months' net salary would seem reasonable, repayable over a period of up to 12 months upon the employee resuming work.

Question

We are considering providing childcare vouchers as part of our OMP policy. What are the perceived benefits?

Answer

The employer provision of childcare vouchers to employees for children under the age of 16 is specifically exempt from any Class 1 NICs liability, although there is still an income tax liability on the employee. The employee can use the voucher as payment in part or in full to the person or business providing the childcare. Childcare can include looking after pre-school children in a registered nursery. There are a number of commercial enterprises offering voucher schemes to employers, some offering a discount on the face value of the voucher, say up to 10%.

Some employers have used vouchers to operate a 'salary sacrifice' scheme, whereby the employee commutes part of their salary in exchange for receiving childcare vouchers of an equivalent value, with the primary aim of reducing both the employee and employer Class 1 NICs liability.

26. State Benefits

Introduction [26.1]

SMP takes priority over all other forms of benefit. Receipt of, or entitlement to, SMP disqualifies an employee from SSP, MA and short-term lower rate Incapacity Benefit (see **13.2**).

However, it is possible for an employee to go on receiving Severe Disablement Allowance (SDA) and an adjusted rate of short-term (higher rate) or long-term Incapacity Benefit (IB) if they were receiving this when the MPP started.

Maternity Allowance [26.2]

Maternity Allowance (MA) is a State benefit which may be payable to a pregnant woman who does not satisfy the eligibility criteria for SMP, eg she had not worked for long enough (see **16.3**) or has low average earnings (see **14.6**). It is a weekly benefit paid for up to 26 weeks. MA is not liable to income tax and the payment does not attract a Class 1 NIC liability. Maternity Allowance is payable at the lesser of the weekly rate of £100 or 90% of average weekly earnings.

The earliest MA can be paid is the start of the eleventh week before the EWC, unless the baby is born prematurely, in which case MA starts on the day following the day of confinement. Payment of MA starts at this date if, at the start of the eleventh week before the EWC, the woman:

- has stopped working; or
- is claiming contribution-based Jobseeker's Allowance; or
- is no longer employed or self-employed but is claiming Incapacity Benefit (IB) or Severe Disablement Allowance (SDA).

However, payment of MA will begin later if at the start of the eleventh week before the EWC if the woman:

- is still working as an employed or a self-employed person; or
- is receiving SSP from her employer; or
- has not yet given up work but is claiming IB or SDA.

If the baby is born before the date when the employee was going to stop work, payment of MA starts from the day following confinement. Where the employee is absent from work, wholly or partly because of pregnancy on or after the start of the fourth week before the EWC, payment of MA starts from the day following the first complete day of absent from work for a pregnancy-related illness.

MA Eligibility [26.3]

An individual can only receive MA if she is not eligible for SMP, and has been employed or self-employed and earned on average at least £30 a week in a 13-week period within the 'test period'. The 'test period' is the period of 66 weeks up to and including the week before the employee's EWC. Unlike with SMP, earnings with more than one employment can be aggregated together for this purpose.

The employee must also have been employed or self-employed for at least 26 weeks in the 66-week test period. The 26 weeks do not have to be consecutive weeks and it does not matter how much the employee has earned during those weeks. Weeks when the employee has not worked a full week can count towards meeting the 26 weeks' service test.

The employee may not be able to get MA (or will stop getting receiving MA) in the following circumstances.

Checklist: Reasons for Being Excluded from MA

(a) The employee is receiving SMP from an employer.

(b) The baby is stillborn earlier than the 25th week of the pregnancy (see **18.2**).

(c) The employee is imprisoned or detained in legal custody (see **18.3**), but the employee may be able to get MA on release.

(d) The employee is in a country outside the EEA or one with whom the UK has no bilateral treaty agreement (see **16.9**).

If the employee cannot receive MA, she may be able to receive Incapacity Benefit for part of the pregnancy (see **13.2**).

How to Claim MA [26.4]

A woman can claim MA when she reaches the 14th week before the week in which the baby is due (the 27th week of pregnancy). A claim pack should be available at the person's local social security office or the maternity clinic or child health clinic. A claim for MA is made on Form MA1.

Once claim Form MA1 has been completed in full, the person must take it or send it to her local office of the Department for Work and Pensions, together with medical evidence (see **17.3**) of when the baby is due and any relevant payslips as evidence of earnings in the 13 week 'test period'. Claims can be made without the supporting documentation but this must be submitted at a later date.

Form SMP1 (see **20.9**) must be sent with Form MA1, if the person was employed at any time in the 15th week before the EWC. If a claim is made more than three months after the end of the MA pay period the person may not be able to receive MA.

MA is payable direct into a bank or building society account or at a Post Office by order book, giro cheque or Payment Card. If an employee returns to work during the MA pay period, the local Social Security office must be advised of the return to work.

Ineligible to Claim MA [26.5]

If a woman is not entitled to receive either SMP or MA, she may be able to qualify for IB, if she satisfies the NIC qualifying conditions (see **13.2**). If the woman or her partner is in receipt of Income Support, income-based Jobseeker's Allowance or Working Tax Credit, she may be able to get a Sure Start Maternity Grant from the Social Fund. Details of these are available in leaflet BC1 *Babies and children*, available from a social security office.

If a person makes a claim for MA, the claim will automatically be considered for IB if the individual does not qualify for MA. There is no need to make a separate claim and Form MATB1 is accepted as evidence of incapacity for work.

An individual may be able to claim Income Support (an income-related benefit) from the period beginning 11 weeks before the EWC and ending seven weeks after the date the pregnancy ends. The person may also be able to claim at any time during the pregnancy if she is unable to work because of the pregnancy. However, income support is not normally available if the woman (or her partner) has savings amounting to £8,000 or more or works 16 hours a week or more (24 hours for partners). Families in which one parent is working 16 hours a week or more may alternatively be entitled to Working Tax Credit.

If a woman is ill when her MA ends and she cannot receive SSP from her employer, or is no longer employed, she may claim IB. The employer should complete change-over form SSP1, stating the reason the employee is excluded, perhaps because of low average weekly earnings.

Questions and Answers [26.6]

Question

We know one of our employees has been in receipt of MA, but have so far not received details of the MA paid. She has now resumed work and we need this information to calculate her PAYE tax, as she is on a cumulative tax coding. Where can we find out the pay received?

Answer

The DWP will not issue a Form P45, in cases where MA is payable, as the payment itself is not taxable nor for that matter subject to a Class 1 NIC liability. The employee may receive tax rebates from her employer during the statutory maternity leave period where a cumulative tax code is operated and no gross pay is received. Such tax rebates should not be withheld pending the return of the employee, as the employee's contract of employment continues throughout the leave period and PAYE should be operated as normal.

Question

An employee has failed to notify us of a change in her circumstances, which affects her SMP entitlement. We have therefore overpaid her six weeks SMP. What should we do?

Answer

The employee is responsible for notifying the employer of a change in her circumstances, where this impacts on her employer's liability to make payments of SMP, such as going into legal custody. If she does not, the employer will not be responsible for any overpaid SMP.

If SMP has been paid and the employee is no longer entitled to it the employer should notify the employee's local DWP office. The employer may need to provide details of the period of overpayment in order that the employee may claim MA instead.

27. Pay and Employment Rights

Introduction [27.1]

There are three terms that are fundamental to an understanding of the maternity leave provisions. These three terms are described immediately below.

Ordinary Maternity Leave [27.2]

Women have a basic entitlement of 26 weeks' ordinary maternity leave (OML). The entitlement applies regardless of an employee's length of service.

> ! From April 2003 the length of the ordinary paid maternity leave period was extended from 18 to 26 weeks.

An employee may take a period of maternity leave but this does not automatically give her the right to SMP payments.

Additional Maternity Leave [27.3]

A woman may qualify for additional maternity leave (AML) of 26 weeks if she has at least 26 weeks' continuous service with her employer by the start of the fourteenth week before the EWC. The AML follows on immediately from the 26 weeks of OML.

Compulsory Maternity Leave [27.4]

There is a period during an employee's OML when her employer must not allow her to work This compulsory leave period encompasses the confinement, and is usually either:

- two weeks; or
- four weeks, if the employee works in a factory.

The employer commits an offence if he allows the employee to work during this period.

The compulsory leave period may be longer where the employee is suspended on health grounds (see **27.8**).

Notification of Maternity Leave [27.5]

The notification procedure is the same whether the woman is entitled to just OML or whether she also qualifies for AML (see **27.3**). In both cases, the maternity leave period may begin at any time from the beginning of the 11th week before the EWC provided the employee gives a minimum of 28 days' notice before starting her maternity leave. The employee must notify her employer before the end of the QW, unless this is not reasonably practicable:

- that she is pregnant;
- of the date of her EWC; and
- of the date she wants to start her maternity leave.

These notifications can be given at different times, if the employee wishes. The start date of maternity leave should be notified in writing if the employer so requires. However, a woman no longer has to state in the notification that she is 'exercising her right to return to work' (see **24.10**).

A woman that fails to give the required notification may lose the right to start maternity leave on her intended start date. The time limit can only be extended where it was not reasonably practicable for notification to be given any earlier.

In the following circumstances an employee is required to notify her employer of the date she started her maternity leave.

- Where she is absent for a pregnancy-related reason in the four weeks before the EWC.
- Where she gives birth before her maternity leave starts.

The notice, which is to be in writing if the employer requests it, must be given as soon as is reasonably practicable.

The employee can vary the start date of her maternity leave by giving 28 days' notice to her employer. This notice must also be in writing if the employer requests it.

In addition to giving notice about the start of her maternity leave, the employee is required to inform her employer of the date she wants payment of SMP to begin. This notice is usually given at the same time as the notice of the date on which the woman wants her maternity leave to start.

The employer is required to respond to the employee's notice (or notices) and reply in writing. The response is to state the period of the maternity leave and its start and end dates. It is essential that the employer responds in this way, as otherwise the employee may:

- return from maternity leave sooner without giving notice; or
- not return on the expected date (e g at the end of the 26 weeks' OML) but be protected in law from being subjected to the employer's disciplinary rules.

Benefits During Maternity Leave [27.6]

During her maternity leave, the employee continues to enjoy rights under the contract of employment and also under employment law. However, there is a fundamental difference between the rights available during OML as compared to those during additional maternity leave.

During maternity leave (ordinary and additional) the contract of employment continues. This means that the period of leave counts as qualifying service for statutory rights, e g continuity of service.

During OML, the employee has a statutory right to continue to benefit from the terms and conditions of employment which would have applied to her had she been at work and not on leave, with the exception of those providing for her wages or salary. Examples of terms and conditions include:

- accrual of holiday entitlement whether under the contract of employment or the *Working Time Regulations 1998* (*SI 1998 No 1833*);
- participation in share schemes;
- reimbursement of professional subscriptions;
- use of a company car (unless provided for business use only);
- medical insurance;
- pension rights.

Whether a bonus is payable to an employee on maternity leave depends on the type of bonus and the terms of the particular bonus scheme.

A woman's employment contract continues during additional maternity leave, unless either party expressly ends it or it expires. However, there is no statutory right to receive remuneration from her employer during this AML period. The following are the terms and conditions which continue during AML:

Checklist: Terms and Conditions During AML

- contractual redundancy rights;
- contractual disciplinary or grievance procedures;
- contractual notice period requirements;
- trust and confidence from the employer and the employee in turn to act in good faith towards their employer;
- other contractual terms, such as disclosure of confidential information, acceptance of gifts and participation in any other business.

The continuation of any other terms and conditions during AML are a matter for negotiation and agreement between the employer and employee (or their representatives).

Antenatal Care [27.7]

All pregnant employees, regardless of service, have the right not to be unreasonably refused paid time off during working hours in order to attend antenatal care classes. However, the following employees are specifically excluded from the right to time off for antenatal care:

- members of the police force;
- masters or crew members engaged in share fishing paid solely by a share of the catch.

The legislation does not precisely define the term 'antenatal' care but the courts have established that the term is not restricted to medical examinations and it includes relaxation classes and parentcraft classes.

If time off is unreasonably refused, or if an employer refuses to pay the employee her normal rate of pay, she can make a complaint to an Employment Tribunal. The employee should provide medical evidence of her pregnancy and an appointment card, or similar document, if asked for it by her employer, unless it is her first appointment.

The employer is responsible for ensuring that an employee is paid the correct amount for the time taken off to attend for antenatal care. Where the employee's pay is based on the number of hours worked during the week various formulae are to be used to calculate the amount due. Payment is only required for time taken off during normal working hours.

> ### *Example*
>
> Ruth normally works from 9.00 am to 5.30 pm. She makes an appointment to attend an antenatal class at 4.30 pm, for which she leaves work at 3.30 pm and returns home at 6.30 pm, she is only entitled to be paid her normal rate of pay from 3.30 pm up to 5.30 pm.

If the number of hours worked per week is regular, the hourly rate is calculated by dividing the amount of a week's pay by the number of normal working hours in a week for that employee under the contract of employment in force on the date the time is taken. If the number of hours worked per week is irregular, the average rate over the previous twelve complete working weeks is used. Overtime is counted only if it is compulsory under the terms of the employment contract.

Maternity Suspension [27.8]

Where an employee who is pregnant, or has recently given birth (within the last six months), or is breast-feeding, stops doing her normal job on health and safety grounds, she has the right to be offered suitable alternative work if this is available, prior to being suspended. The terms and conditions applying to the alternative work must not be substantially less favourable than her normal terms and conditions.

If there is no suitable work and the employee is therefore suspended from work, the employee must be paid her full normal rate by her employer during the period of suspension. The employee loses this right if she unreasonably refuses alternative work. The employee continues to be employed during the maternity suspension period and contractual benefits are likely to continue, unless both parties have mutually agreed to vary them.

The amount of pay during the period of suspension is based on the contractual remuneration for working the normal working hours in one week. Where there are no normal working hours, it is the average contractual remuneration calculated over a 12-week period. All these rights apply regardless of the employee's length of service or hours of work.

Return to Work **[27.9]**

The *Employment Act 2002* altered the procedures to be observed by the employee and the employer as regards notification and return to work. The employee does not have to give any notice to the employer about her return to work as she is expected to return at the end of the ordinary or additional leave period, depending on her entitlement. The employer is required to notify the employee of the end of the leave period (see **27.5**). Failure to give the requisite notice may mean that the employee:

- can return from maternity leave sooner without giving notice; or
- not return on the expected date (eg at the end of the 26 weeks' OML) but be protected in law from being subjected to the employer's disciplinary rules.

If the employee wishes to return sooner than the end of her maternity leave, whether ordinary or additional leave, she must give her employer 28 days' notice of the date when she wants to return. If she gives less than 28 days' notice, the employer can allow her to return or insist on her returning not before the 28 days are served unless this would go beyond the end of the maternity leave. A woman returning from OML is entitled to return to the same job under the same terms and conditions, as if she had not been absent. Such terms include pay, seniority and pension rights. This is unless a redundancy situation arises; in which case she is to be offered a suitable alternative vacancy.

Woman who do not return to work after ordinary or additional maternity leave due to sickness must submit medical evidence and follow the usual notification rules in order to qualify for SSP and/or OSP. If no medical evidence is produced the employer may treat the absence as unauthorised and the employer must apply the normal contractual arrangements for sickness absence.

A dismissal for non-return in these circumstances may be unfair, wrongful and discriminatory. This point has been clarified by the maternity leave rules, which make it clear that a woman's contract of employment remains in existence during additional maternity leave.

If disciplinary action (including ultimately dismissal) is taken against the employee, such a dismissal will not automatically be regarded as unfair, although an employee may still present a complaint to an employment tribunal.

An employee entitled to additional maternity leave, has a right to return to the same job as she was employed in before her absence or, where not reasonably practicable, to a job with at least the same terms and conditions as her old position, and of an equivalent or better status. This right varies where an employee works for a company employing five people or less (including the employee herself) at the point when her additional maternity leave ends.

Flexible Working [27.10]

Although there is no specific statutory right for women to change their working conditions e g hours of work, the *Employment Rights Act 1996*, as amended by the *Employment Act 2002*, provides that, since April 2003, women have a statutory right to request a change in their contract. However, they must meet certain conditions, including that they have worked continuously for their employer for at least 26 weeks at the time of making the application to vary the contract.

The purpose of the request must be to enable them to care for their child. The change requested must relate to:

- the hours the employee is required to work;
- the times when the employee is required to work; and
- where the employee is required to work.

Working patterns such as annualised hours, compressed hours, flexitime, homeworking, job-sharing, self-rostering, shift working, staggered hours and term-time working are covered.

An application must:

- state that it is an application to vary the contract;
- specify the change and the date on which it is proposed it will become effective; and
- explain what effect if any the employee thinks the change will have on the employer and how the effect can be dealt with.

The application must be made before the fourteenth day before the day on which the child reaches age six or, if disabled, age 18. Once an application has been made a further application cannot be made within twelve months of the date of the previous application.

Members of the armed forces are excluded from this right, and agency workers are not able to make such an application. For this purpose an agency worker is a person supplied by an agent to do work for another person under a contract or other arrangement made between the agent and that other person.

Where an employee makes such an application the employer is required give it serious consideration. Within 28 days of receiving the application the employer is to arrange a meeting with the employee to explore the proposed work pattern. Within fourteen days of the date of the meeting the employer must write to the employee either to agree to the proposed work pattern with a start date, or to provide clear business grounds as to why the application cannot be accepted and set out the appeal procedure. These time periods can be extended where agreed by the employee and employer.

The business grounds for rejecting the proposed work patterns will usually comprise of one or more of the following:

- the burden of additional costs;
- detrimental effect on ability to meet customer demand;
- inability to reorganize work among existing staff;
- inability to recruit additional staff;
- detrimental impact on quality or performance;
- insufficiency of work during periods the employee proposes to work; and
- planned structural changes.

There may be circumstances where a refusal to permit a woman to return to work part-time amounts to unlawful indirect sex discrimination. An employer would have to show that there were objective reasons, which had nothing to do with her sex, for requiring her to work full-time.

Questions and Answers **[27.11]**

Question

What is the procedure if an employee wishes to return to part-time work after April 2003?

Answer

Where a request for flexible working is made, the employee should submit a written request to her employer, which should then be ➡

followed up with a meeting to discuss the issues. The employer should either accept the request, setting a date for when the new arrangements are to apply from (eg on return from maternity leave) or reject the request, setting out the business reasons for doing so. The employee will have a right of appeal, with ultimate redress through an employment tribunal. The tribunal will examine whether the employer has a justifiable business case for the decision.

Question

We employ a number of female workers of childbearing age and wish to provide help and information in relation to their maternity pay and employment rights. Where can this be obtained?

Answer

In respect of pay, leaflet NI17A 'A guide to Maternity Benefits' is available from www.dwp.gov.uk or from Department for Work and Pensions offices. Guidance on maternity employment rights is available by going to www.dti.gov.uk/er/maternity.htm or telephoning the DTI order line on 0870 150 2500. For interactive information, employees should visit www.tiger.gov.uk

Question

One of our employees has completed her additional maternity leave period but has not returned to work. Do we have to pay her contractual sick pay, even though she has not physically returned to work?

Answer

It depends on the terms and conditions applicable to the employee. Sickness at the end of maternity leave is the same as sickness at any other time. Some employers insert a clause in their OSP schemes, requiring the employee to serve a qualifying period, say three months, after any period of 'unpaid' leave before qualifying for contractual sick pay. Unpaid leave could include maternity leave, sabbaticals and compassionate leave, the latter two being available to both sexes, to avoid any charge of indirect sex discrimination being levelled against the employer.

In the case of additional maternity leave, it is quite likely the employee will not be eligible for SSP, as her average weekly earnings may be below the LEL at the start of the PIW, if no payments have been made since the completion of the MPP.

Question

What happens to payments of SMP if the employee decides not to return to work after the baby is born?

Answer

Statutory Maternity Pay still remains payable for the duration of the MPP. The exercise or otherwise of the employee's maternity employment rights is irrelevant. A woman who does not wish to return to work after either ordinary or additional maternity leave must give her employer notice of the termination as required by her contract of employment.

Question

We have had to suspend one of our pregnant employees in order to protect her health and that of her unborn child, as we were unable to offer her suitable alternative work in the circumstances. Can we insist that she starts her maternity leave eleven weeks before the baby is due as we are having to pay the full normal rate of pay while she is on maternity suspension?

Answer

Unfortunately not, as the employee can choose to start her maternity leave whenever she wants after the 11th week before the EWC, with the exception of where she is absent from work for a pregnancy-related reason before her intended start date. There is probably not much incentive for her to start her maternity leave early, whilst she is receiving full pay during suspension but she must nevertheless comply with the usual notification rules regarding her maternity leave start date.

28. Paternity Pay

Introduction [28.1]

The *Employment Act 2002* amended the *Employment Rights Act 1996* and the *Social Security Contributions Act 1992*, and introduced a statutory right to paternity leave and to paternity pay for parents of children born on or after 6 April 2003. The right to paternity leave and pay can be exercised by employees, whether men or women, who meet the eligibility criteria.

Paternity leave is available where either a child is born or adopted. The actual start date can be chosen by the employee, but it cannot be started until the birth or placement of the child with the adopter. The statutory paternity leave period is two weeks. Statutory Paternity Pay (SPP) is payable for up to two weeks.

The employee can choose to take one or two weeks of paternity leave, but if two weeks are taken the second must run consecutive to the first. The leave cannot be taken in odd days. In the case of adoption the leave must be taken within 56 days of the date on which the child is placed with the adopter.

Entitlement to Leave and SPP [28.2]

To qualify for paternity leave, the employee must:

- have or expect to have responsibility for the child's upbringing;
- in the case of childbirth, be the biological father of the child and/or the mother's husband or partner or, in the case of adoption, be the partner or husband of the adopter;
- have worked continuously for his or her employer for 26 weeks ending with the fifteenth week before the EWC in the case of childbirth, or the week in which he or she has been notified of being matched with the child for adoption in the case of adoption;
- remain in continuous employment with the employer until the birth of the child or to the date of placement of the child in the case of adoption; and
- be taking the time off work either to care for the child or to support the child's mother or the adopter.

To qualify for SPP the employee must meet the above criteria but also:

- have average weekly earnings at or above the LEL in force at the end of the QW in the case of childbirth, or on the first day of the matching week in the case of adoption; and
- must give 28 days' notice of the date on which SPP is to be begin.

The employee is required to provide a self-certificate of entitlement to paternity leave. The employee must give this by a certain date and also supply certain information.

In the case of adoption the self-certificate must be given within seven days of the date when the adopter was notified of being matched with a child or soon as is reasonably practicable. It must state the date when:

- the adopter was notified of being matched with a child;
- the child is expected to be placed with the adopter;
- the leave is to start and whether the employee wants to take one or two weeks leave.

In the case of childbirth it must be given by the end of the fifteenth week before the EWC or as soon as is reasonably practicable. It must state:

- the EWC; and
- the date leave is to start and whether the employee wants to take one or two weeks' leave.

The actual start date of the paternity leave can be on any day of the week. The employee can change the start date by giving 28 days' notice, or as soon as is reasonably practicable.

Following the birth, as soon as is reasonably practicable, the employee is required to inform the employer of the date of birth.

The rules on continuous employment and calculation of average weekly earnings mirror those for SMP (see **16.3** and **19.4**). The rules where the employee has more than one job (see **16.7**), works abroad (see **16.9**), gives birth early (see **17.5**), dies (see **18.6**) or is taken into legal custody (see **18.3**) are also consistent with the current maternity provisions.

Unlike SMP, however, entitlement to SPP cannot be established until the baby has been born or the child adopted. Once entitlement has been established it cannot be lost, for example if the employee was made redundant after the date of birth but before he or she had planned to start the Paternity Pay Period (see **28.3**).

Even if more than one child is born as the result of the same pregnancy, only one period of SPP is available. If the baby is stillborn before the 25th week of pregnancy (treated as the 16th week before the EWC) there is no entitlement to SPP, in the same way that there is none for SMP (see **18.2**). Entitlement to SPP will not end if either the mother or baby die.

Statutory Paternity Pay [28.3]

Statutory Paternity Pay (SPP) is payable to those employees who meet the qualifying criteria (see **28.2**) for the paternity pay period (PPP), which coincides with the employee's paternity leave period. During the PPP the employee may be entitled to SPP from his or her employer, for either one or two consecutive weeks as he or she chooses. The weekly rate of SPP in 2003/04 is the lesser of £100 a week or 90% of average weekly earnings.

Any occupational paternity pay can be offset against the employee's statutory entitlement. For example, an employee entitled under his employment contract to a week of paternity leave on full pay will only be entitled to a further one week of SPP.

An employer cannot pay SPP to an employee for any week during which the employee does some work for that employer. Since payments under the new SPP scheme will be replacement earnings they will be subject to tax under PAYE.

An employee will not be able to receive SSP and SPP for the same period. If the employee is sick before having started the PPP, it must be delayed until he or she is no longer incapacitated. There is no extension to the 56-day period in which SPP can be paid in these circumstances. If the employee notifies the employer that he or she is sick during the PPP then there is no entitlement to SPP during any week in the PPP in which the employee is entitled to be paid SSP. An employee can receive SPP while sick and serving waiting days for SSP. An employee who is, exceptionally, entitled to SPP but not SSP can continue to receive SPP while sick.

Reimbursement of SPP [28.4]

Employers administer SPP in the same way as SMP. Employer reimbursement is at the rate of 92% of the SPP paid by most employers, with small employers who are entitled to small employer's relief able to claim 100% plus an additional amount. The qualification for small employer's relief and the amount of compensation is to be the same as for SMP (see **21.3**).

Employers will be able to request advance funding from the Inland Revenue where the amount of SPP they have to pay their employees exceeds the tax and NICs etc that they are due to pay to the Inland Revenue.

SPP in Adoption Cases [28.5]

Both men and women can be entitled to SPP. Where a married couple are adopting jointly one can elect to receive Statutory Adoption Pay (SAP) and the other to receive SPP. Where only one member of a couple is adopting, only that person is entitled to SAP, but the other member of the couple may be entitled to SPP, as long as they meet the qualifying conditions (see **28.2**).

The employee is required to confirm to his or her employer in writing that he or she has elected to receive SAP rather than SPP.

Record Keeping and Compliance for SPP [28.6]

The employers will be required to notify the employee if he or she is not entitled to receive SPP. The Inland Revenue supply form SPP1: 'Why I cannot pay SPP' for this purpose'.

Employers will also need to keep the same kinds of records that they need to keep for SMP. Details of the SPP paid and recovered will need to be recorded on the required legislative returns (P14/P35 or equivalent) as they are now for SMP.

To ensure compliance with the new system of SPP, the *Employment Act 2002* provides that:

Checklist: Employer Compliance in SPP Cases

(a) Employers must keep appropriate records and make periodic returns to the Inland Revenue.

(b) Employers must produce those records for inspection by the Inland Revenue.

(c) Employers must provide information about entitlement to their employees.

(d) The Inland Revenue can obtain relevant information from both employers and applicants for SPP.

(e) The Inland Revenue can impose penalties where there is refusal or repeated failure to comply.

(f) The Inland Revenue can make decisions on entitlement in the event of dispute.

(e) The Independent Tax Commissioners will hear appeals against decisions made and penalties awarded.

Questions and Answers [28.7]

Question

When did the statutory rules relating to paternity pay come into force?

Answer

The rules started impacting on employers from as early as November/ December 2002. Paternity leave and pay were available to parents whose children were due on or after 6 April 2003. However, if the baby was born before that date, SPP became payable if all the qualifying conditions were met.

Question

Can an employee transfer SPP and associated leave between employers?

Answer

The period of leave and pay must be taken within eight weeks. Payment of leave is for one or two weeks and it cannot be split into individual days. These rules overcome any potential difficulties of employers having to transfer periods of unused paternity leave.

Question

Who is liable to pay SPP and who is liable to receive SPP?

Answer

Employees and employers; an employee is defined as a person whose earnings attract a Class 1 NIC liability, or would do so if they were ➡

high enough, and an employer is the person liable to pay the employer's share of Class 1 NICs. People normally falling to be treated as self-employed, such as agency workers can be treated as an employee by regulations.

29. Adoption Pay

Introduction [29.1]

The *Employment Act 2002* amended the *Employment Rights Act 1996* and the *Social Security Contributions Act 1992*, and introduced a statutory right to adoption leave and to adoption pay for persons adopting children. Employees who meet the eligibility criteria can exercise the right to adoption leave and pay. Employees who qualify are entitled to take up to 52 weeks' adoption leave in respect of the placement of a child for adoption. The 52 weeks is made up of 26 weeks' ordinary adoption leave and 26 weeks' additional adoption leave. The additional adoption leave follows on from the end of ordinary adoption leave.

Statutory Adoption Pay (SAP) is payable for up to 26 weeks during the adoption pay period (APP) which coincides with the ordinary adoption leave period. The additional adoption leave is unpaid.

Where couples adopt a child, they may decide who will take adoption leave and who will take paternity leave.

Entitlement to Leave and SAP [29.2]

To qualify for adoption leave, the employee must have:

- been matched with a child;
- agreed with the adoption agency the date of placement of the child; and
- worked continuously for the same employer for 26 weeks ending with the week in which he or she has been notified of having been matched with the child.

To qualify for SAP, the employee must meet the above criteria but also:

- have average weekly earnings at or above the LEL in force on the first day of the matching week; and
- must give 28 days' notice of the date on which SAP is to be begin.

The employee is required to provide notification and evidence to his or her employer as soon as is reasonably practicable. Within seven days of the date of being notified of being matched with a child, the employee is required to inform his or her employer (in writing if requested) of:

- the date when he or she expects the child to be placed with him or her; and
- the start date of the adoption leave.

The employer can request to see evidence of the adoption. This is contained in documents, such as the Matching Certificate, supplied by the adoption agency. The evidence comprises of:

- the notification date of the child's placement;
- the date when the child is expected to be placed with the adopter; and
- the name and address of the adoption agency.

The adoption leave can begin on the day the child is placed with the adopter or any other day but not more than fourteen days before and not later than the expected date of placement. Leave can only be taken in whole weeks.

The employee can change the start date of the leave by giving the employer 28 days' notice. This may be necessary where, for example, the child's placement is delayed.

The adoption leave period may end earlier than the full 52 weeks where, for example, the employee decides to return to work or the employment terminates. The adoption leave automatically ends eight weeks after the week in which:

- the employee is informed that the placement of the child will not occur; or
- the child dies; or
- the child is returned to the adoption agency.

> *i* In practice, the Matching Week is the week in which the person adopting the child is notified that they have been matched with a child.

A matching certificate will confirm entitlement to SAP. This will be given to the employee by the adoption agency. Only approved adoption agencies are able to issue matching certificates, which will ensure that only those adopting a child through the approved process will be entitled to SAP. An employer cannot pay SAP without a matching certificate. The matching certificate must be passed to the employer within seven days of issue. It is considered 'best practice' for the adoptive parent to let their employer know informally that he or she will be taking adoption leave when he or she is approved for adoption, prior to any match being made.

Leave and pay are available when a child up to the age of 18 is newly placed for adoption. Adoption leave and pay will end when the child reaches 18, if their 18th birthday occurs during the leave period.

Entitlement to SAP can be established when the adopter is notified that they have been matched with the child. Once entitlement has been established it cannot be lost, for example, if the employee was made redundant after the start of the MW. This is similar to the rules for SMP (see **24.9**). Even if more than one child is placed as part of the same arrangement, only one period of SAP is available.

Entitlement to SAP will remain if the placement is disrupted after it has started, or if the child dies after placement.

There are special rules for people adopting a child from overseas. Arrangements for overseas adoptions can vary considerably from those in the UK and from country to country. In particular, the concept of a placement for adoption may not apply to overseas adoptions. Those adopting from overseas will need a certificate of approval from the Secretary of State for Health.

Adoption leave and correspondingly pay will not apply to step family adoptions (eg where a husband adopts the children of his wife's previous marriage) or adoptions by a child's existing foster carers, where there is already an established relationship.

Statutory Adoption Pay [29.3]

Statutory Adoption Pay (SPP) is payable to those employees who meet the qualifying criteria (see **29.2**) for the 26 weeks of ordinary adoption leave. During the 26 weeks of the adoption pay period (APP) the employee is paid SAP either at the earnings-related rate or the weekly rate, whichever is the lesser. In 2003/04 the earnings-related rate is 90% of average weekly earnings, and the weekly rate is £100.

An employer cannot pay SAP to an employee for any week during which the employee does some work for that employer. SAP will also end if the employee dies or is taken into legal custody (mirroring SMP).

Any contractual adoption pay can be offset against the employee's statutory entitlement. An employee will not be able to receive SSP and SAP for the same period. If the employee is sick before starting the adoption pay period, this period must be delayed until he or she is no longer incapacitated. There is no extension to the 26 weeks' entitlement to SAP in these circumstances. If the employee notifies the employer that he or she is sick during the adoption pay period then there is no entitlement to SAP during any week in the adoption pay period in which the employee is entitled to be paid SSP. An employee can receive SAP while sick and serving waiting days for SSP. An employee who is exceptionally entitled to SAP but not SSP can continue to receive SAP while sick.

Reimbursement of SAP [29.4]

Employers administer SAP in the same way as SMP. Employer reimbursement is at the rate of 92% of the SAP paid by most employers, with small employers who are entitled to small employer's relief able to claim 100% plus an additional amount. The qualification for small employer's relief and the amount of compensation is to be the same as for SMP (see **21.3**).

Employers are able to request advance funding from the Inland Revenue where the amount of SAP they have to pay their employees exceeds the tax and NICs etc that they are due to pay to the Inland Revenue.

Record Keeping and Compliance for SAP [29.5]

The employer is required to notify the employee if he or she is not entitled to receive SAP. The Inland Revenue supply Form SAP1: 'Why I cannot pay SAP' for this purpose.

Employers will also need to keep the same kinds of records that they need to keep for SMP. Details of the SAP paid and recovered will need to be recorded on the required legislative returns (Forms P14 and P35 or equivalent) as they are now for SMP.

To ensure compliance with the new system of SAP, the *Employment Act 2002* provides that:

Checklist: Employer Compliance in SAP Cases

(a) Employers must keep appropriate records and make periodic returns to the Inland Revenue.

(b) Employers must produce those records for inspection by the Inland Revenue.

(c) Employers must provide information about entitlement to their employees.

(d) The Inland Revenue can obtain relevant information from both employers and applicants for SAP.

(e) The Inland Revenue can impose penalties where there is refusal or repeated failure to comply.

(f) The Inland Revenue can make decisions on entitlement in the event of dispute.

(g) The Independent Tax Commissioners will hear appeals against decisions made and penalties awarded.

Return to Work [29.6]

Where the qualifying parent taking adoption leave wishes to return to work before the end of the period, he or she must give 28 days' notice to the employer of the date of return. Employees have the right to return to the same job following ordinary adoption leave, and have protection from suffering detriment and unfair dismissal in connection with taking adoption leave. This protection begins when the parent is approved for adoption.

Questions and Answers [29.7]

Question

How likely is it that an employer will have to consider paying SAP?

Answer

Current Government figures as contained in its Regulatory Impact Assessment document on adoption pay indicate that there are around 2,000 adoptions taking place each year in the UK. So SAP is not that likely a scenario, relative to the total employment strength of the UK workforce.

Question

What is a Matching Certificate?

Answer

This is the certificate given by the approved adoption agency to the person adopting the child, when he or she is notified of having been matched with a child. This is similar to the Form MATB1 issued to expectant mothers and will be used as evidence that the employee will be having a child placed with them.

Appendix 1 – SSP Payment Rates

Statutory Sick Pay weekly rates

	From 6/4/98	*From 6/4/99*	*From 6/4/00*	*From 6/4/01*	*From 6/4/02*	*From 6/4/03*
	£	£	£	£	£	£
Average earnings threshold	64.00	66.00	67.00	72.00	75.00	77.00
Rate	57.70	59.55	60.20	62.20	63.25	64.35

Statutory Sick Pay daily rates tables

From 6 April 2003

Unrounded daily rates	No of QDs in week	1	2	3	4	5	6	7
(£)		(£)	(£)	(£)	(£)	(£)	(£)	(£)
9.1929	7	9.20	18.39	27.58	36.78	45.97	55.16	64.35
10.7250	6	10.73	21.45	32.18	42.90	53.63	64.35	
12.8700	5	12.87	25.74	39.61	51.48	64.35		
16.0875	4	16.09	32.18	48.27	64.35			
21.4500	3	21.45	42.90	64.35				
32.1750	2	32.18	64.35					
64.3500	1	64.35						

From 6 April 2002

Unrounded daily rates	No of QDs in week	1	2	3	4	5	6	7
(£)		(£)	(£)	(£)	(£)	(£)	(£)	(£)
9.0357	7	9.04	18.08	27.11	36.15	45.18	54.22	63.25
10.5417	6	10.55	21.09	31.63	42.17	52.71	63.25	
12.6500	5	12.65	25.30	37.95	50.60	63.25		
15.8125	4	15.82	31.63	47.44	63.25			
21.0833	3	21.09	42.17	63.25				
31.6250	2	31.63	63.25					
63.2500	1	63.25						

From 6 April 2001

Unrounded daily rates	No of QDs in week	1	2	3	4	5	6	7
(£)		(£)	(£)	(£)	(£)	(£)	(£)	(£)
8.8857	7	8.89	17.78	26.66	35.55	44.43	53.32	62.20
10.3667	6	10.37	20.74	31.10	41.47	51.84	62.20	
12.4400	5	12.44	24.88	37.32	49.76	62.20		
15.5500	4	15.55	31.10	46.65	62.20			
20.7333	3	20.74	41.47	62.20				
30.1000	2	31.10	62.20					
62.2000	1	62.20						

From 6 April 2000

Unrounded daily rates (£)	No of QDs in week	1 (£)	2 (£)	3 (£)	4 (£)	5 (£)	6 (£)	7 (£)
8.6000	7	8.60	17.20	25.80	34.40	43.00	51.60	60.20
10.0333	6	10.04	20.07	30.10	40.14	50.17	60.20	
12.0400	5	12.04	24.08	36.12	48.16	60.20		
15.0500	4	15.05	30.10	45.15	60.20			
20.0667	3	20.07	40.14	60.20				
30.1000	2	30.10	60.20					
60.2000	1	60.20						

From 6 April 1999

Unrounded daily rates (£)	No of QDs in week	1 (£)	2 (£)	3 (£)	4 (£)	5 (£)	6 (£)	7 (£)
8.5071	7	8.51	17.02	25.53	34.03	42.54	51.05	59.55
9.9250	6	9.93	19.85	29.78	39.70	49.63	59.55	
11.9100	5	11.91	23.82	35.73	47.64	59.55		
14.8875	4	14.89	29.78	44.67	59.55			
19.8500	3	19.85	39.70	59.55				
29.7750	2	29.78	59.55					
59.5500	1	59.55						

From 6 April 1998

Unrounded daily rates	No of QDs in week	1	2	3	4	5	6	7
(£)		(£)	(£)	(£)	(£)	(£)	(£)	(£)
8.2428	7	8.25	16.49	24.73	32.98	41.22	49.46	57.70
9.6166	6	9.62	19.24	28.85	38.47	48.09	57.70	
11.5400	5	11.54	23.08	34.62	46.16	57.70		
14.4250	4	14.43	28.85	43.28	57.70			
19.2333	3	19.24	38.47	57.70				
28.8500	2	28.85	57.70					
57.7000	1	57.70						

Appendix 2 – SMP Payment Rates

Rates of SMP

2003/04

For weeks of SMP from Sunday 6 April 2003 to Saturday 3 April 2004.

Earnings-related rate	90% of the employee's average weekly earnings
Weekly rate	£100.00 (or the earnings-related rate if less than £100.00)

Employers can recover only 92% of SMP from the State except where the employer qualifies under the small employer's relief scheme. A small employer can recover 100% of SMP plus 4.5% as compensation.

2002/03

For weeks of SMP from Sunday 7 April 2002 to Saturday 5 April 2003.

Lower rate	£75.00
Higher rate	90% of the employee's average weekly earnings

Employers can recover only 92% of SMP from the State, except where the employer qualifies under the small employer's relief scheme. A small employer can recover 100% of SMP plus 4.5% as compensation.

2001/02

For weeks of SMP from Sunday 1 April 2001.

Lower rate	£62.20
Higher rate	90% of the employee's average weekly earnings

Employers could recover only 92% of SMP from the State, except where the employer qualified under the small employer's relief scheme. A small employer could recover 100% of SMP plus 5% as compensation.

2000/01

For weeks of SMP from Sunday 2 April 2000.

Lower rate	£60.20
Higher rate	90% of the employee's average weekly earnings

Employers could recover only 92% of SMP from the State, except where the employer qualified under the small employer's relief scheme. A small employer could recover 100% of SMP plus 5% as compensation.

1999/00

For weeks of SMP from Sunday 4 April 1999.

Lower rate	£59.55
Higher rate	90% of the employee's average weekly earnings

Employers could recover only 92% of SMP from the State, except where the employer qualified under the small employer's relief scheme. A small employer could recover 100% of SMP plus 5% as compensation.

1998/99

For weeks of SMP from Sunday 5 April 1998.

Lower rate	£57.70
Higher rate	90% of the employee's average weekly earnings

Employers could recover only 92% of SMP from the State, except where the employer qualified under the small employer's relief scheme. A small employer could recover 100% of SMP plus 7% as compensation.

1997/98

For weeks of SMP from Sunday 6 April 1997.

Lower rate	£55.70
Higher rate	90% of the employee's average weekly earnings

Employers could recover only 92% of SMP from the State, except where the employer qualified under the small employer's relief scheme. A 'small employer' could recover 100% of SMP plus 6.5% as compensation.

Appendix 3 – SSP Control Lists for Common Illnesses

The following is a list of the diagnoses commonly given by doctors as the cause of incapacity on medical certificates issued by them. Rather than specify every illness or disease, the list:

(a) groups similar illnesses under one heading;

(b) suggests a period of absence from work (in months) after which the employer might wish to consider seeking advice.

If the employee is absent for a reason stated below, the employer might wish to consult Medical Services if the absence exceeds the periods stated, which are given in months. If the employer wishes to obtain advice, they should write to their nearest Inland Revenue Office.

Illness	**Months absent**
Addiction (drugs or alcohol)	6
Anaemia (other than in pregnancy)	4
Arthritis (unspecified)	6
Back and spinal disorders (PID, sciatica, spondylitis)	6
Concussion	1
Fractures of lower limbs	6
Fractures of upper limbs	2
Gastroenteritis, gastritis, D&V	1
Haemorrhage	3
Headache, migraine	1
Hernia (strangulated)	6
Inflammation and swelling	1
Joint disorders other than arthritis and rheumatism	3
Kidney and bladder disorders, cystitis, UTI	3
Menstrual disorders, menorrhagia, D&C	3

Miscellaneous symptoms and diagnosis, anorexia, debility, fainting, giddiness, insomnia, investigation, NYD, obesity, observation, tachycardia	1
Mouth and throat disorders	1
NAD	immediate
Nervous illnesses	3
Post-natal conditions	6
Respiratory illness:	
asthma	6
cold, coryza, URTI, influenza	1
bronchitis	2
Skin conditions, dermatitis, eczema	2
Sprains, strains, bruises	1
Ulcers:	
perforated	9
peptic, gastric, duodenal	2
varicose	6
corneal	2
Wounds, cuts, lacerations, abrasions, burns, blisters, splinters, FB	1

The following is a list of common abbreviations used on medical certificates issued by GPs.

CAT	coronary artery thrombosis
CHD	coronary heart disease
COAD	chronic obstructive airways disease
CVA	cerebrovascular accident
D&C	dilation and curettage
DS	disseminated (multiple) sclerosis
DU	duodenal ulcer
D&V	diarrhoea and vomiting

FB	foreign body
GU	gastric ulcer
IDK(J)	internal derangement of the knee (joint)
IHD	ischaemic heart disease
LIH	left inguinal hernia
MI	myocardial infarction
MS	multiple sclerosis
NAD	no abnormality detected
NYD	not yet diagnosed
OA	osteoarthritis
PID	prolapsed intervertebral disc
PUO	pyrexia of unknown origin
RIH	right inguinal hernia
URTI	upper respiratory tract infection
UTI	urinary tract infection
VVs	varicose veins

Appendix 4 – SSP Eligibility Flowchart

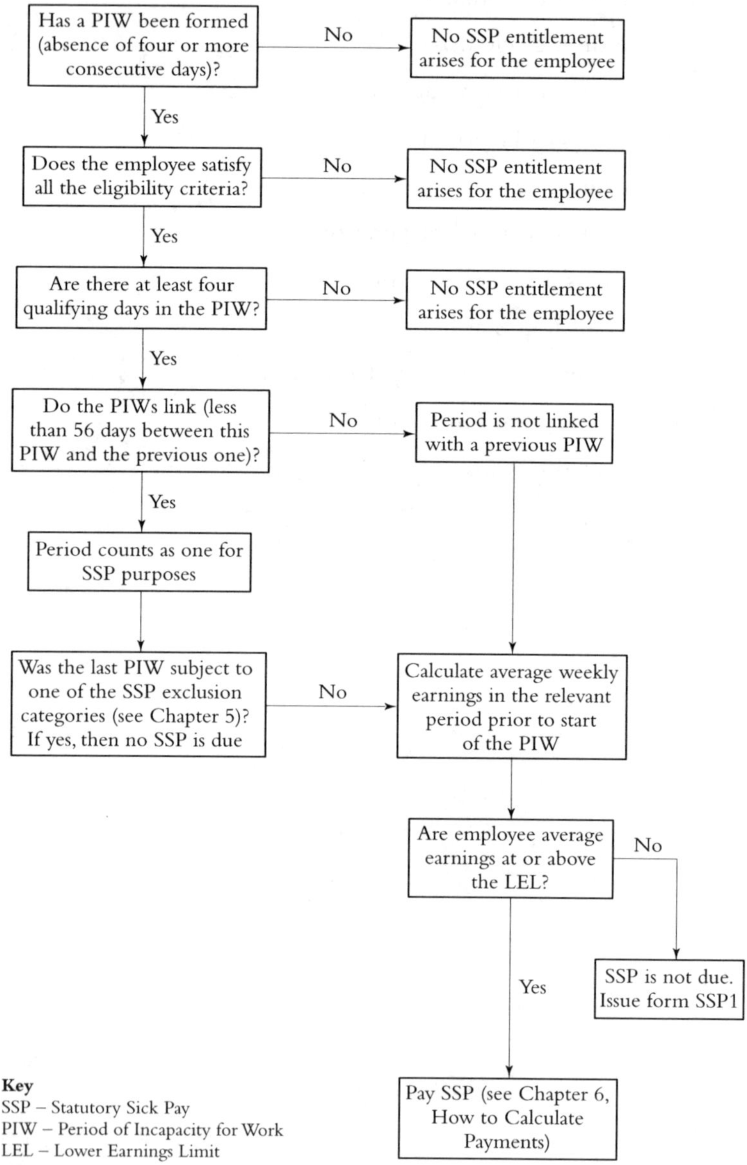

Key
SSP – Statutory Sick Pay
PIW – Period of Incapacity for Work
LEL – Lower Earnings Limit

Appendix 5 – SMP Eligibility Flowchart

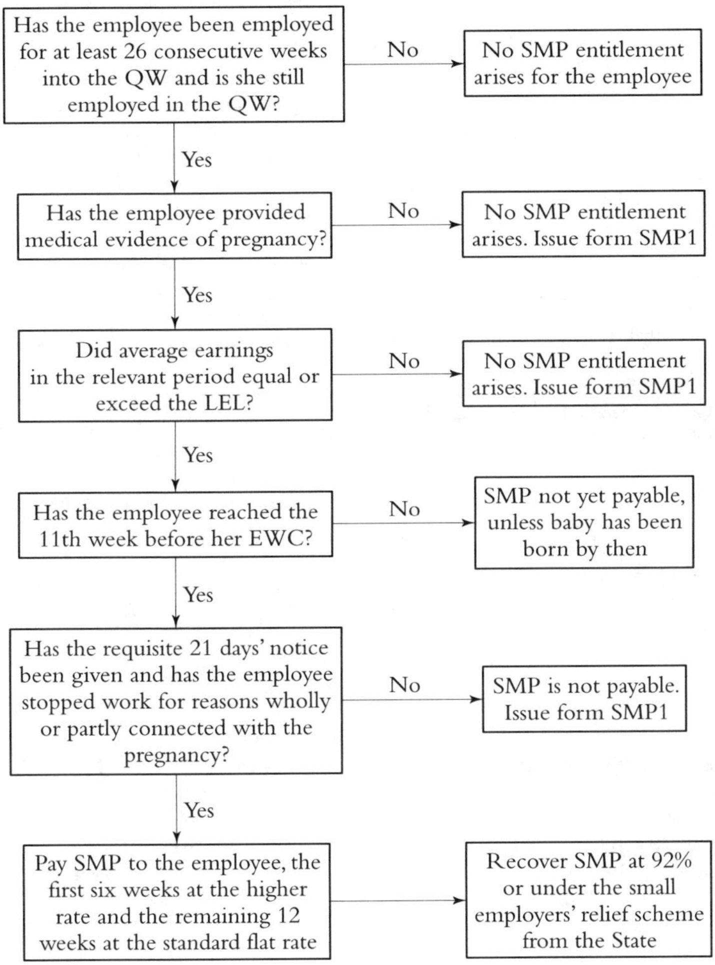

Key
SMP – Statutory Maternity Pay
QW – Qualifying Week
EWC – Expected Week of Confinement
LEL – Lower Earnings Limit

Index

References are to paragraph numbers.

L

M

N

O

P

T

W